MW01126692

Nekkid In Austin

Nekkid In Austin

Drop Your Inner Child Down A Well

Fred Reed

Writers Club Press
San Jose New York Lincoln Shanghai

Nekkid In Austin
Drop Your Inner Child Down A Well

All Rights Reserved © 2002 by Frederick Venable Reed, Jr.

No part of this book may be reproduced or transmitted in any form or by any means, graphic, electronic, or mechanical, including photocopying, recording, taping, or by any information storage retrieval system, without the permission in writing from the publisher.

Writers Club Press
an imprint of iUniverse, Inc.

For information address:
iUniverse, Inc.
5220 S. 16th St., Suite 200
Lincoln, NE 68512
www.iuniverse.com

ISBN: 0-595-23713-4

Printed in the United States of America

To Blonde Poof and the Lounge Singer, daughters extraordinary. May you always find an empty boxcar, never get bent on the deep walls, and travel the weird parts of the earth. I'll be there.

Contents

Foreword

Two and a half years and one book ago, when I began writing these essays, I planned to plug my favorite country—this one. The job should have been easy. Hadn't America produced Harley-Davidson, Elvis, and the Space Shuttle? Howlin' Wolf and Austin, Texas? The mini-skirt? The Internet? Silly Putty? It didn't occur to me that writing about the country would feel more like reading a biopsy.

The America I grew up in was just...fun. I wanted to talk about it. I wasn't a virulent patriot. I happily conceded that a Brit or Frenchman or Russian might feel affection for his patch of the world, and write a book about it, which I might read with admiration and enjoyment. Nor did I think that the Great Squirrel Cage North of Mexico was perfect, or worked as well as it thought it did. Yet the place appealed to me. It was *my* country, *my* patch of wherever we are. Its warts and blemishes suited me.

The problem was that the America I knew had left for other parts, leaving me in another country that had crept into the same place.

I knew the old America. My footprints were all over it. I'd hitch-hiked thousands upon thousands of miles through the land as a kid, met all sorts of people, slept in ditches and weedful lots, shaken scorpions out of my shoes in the cotton fields come morning, lain during the heat of day in a Nevadan arroyo with a bottle of Apple Jack wine. I knew the country's diners and gas stations, its highways and back roads. I'd hopped freight trains and rattled down the Eastern seaboard on top of a box car under a huge moon; done a hitch in the Marines; wandered drunkenly through bad parts of Manhattan. The America I knew was wholesome, vigorous, self-confident, strong.

It was a hopeful place, sure of itself, and endlessly flavorful. I remembered two-step halls in Texas with the girls twirling in cowgirl dresses and the guys boot-scoot strutting; the optimism and energy of its music, the rural passion for muscle cars and hot bikes, the Spanish accents in the smoky evening of the border towns and the upholstered drawls of the Mississippi Delta, sweet as Karo syrup; the somber valleys and raw deserts, the sassy friendliness of its women and the self-reliance of its men. It was wonderful.

All of that is gone, or going. The knell rings for the America I knew. I do not know why.

Something terrible had happened in a few short years. It was as if someone had put a minus sign before the national parentheses. Somehow all we once believed in had fallen into contempt—not by everyone, but by too many. The moral climate had become unrecognizable. Industry and studiousness had been discovered to be elitist, and replaced by the prideful ignorance of the ghetto. The Catholic church became a Caligulan gay bath devoted not to God but to the buggering of acolytes. The military, once where boys went to become men, was a place where bottom-feeding women went to become mothers.

The notion of character had changed. Once it was thought manly, and womanly, to bear up without complaint under adversity; today, whimpering is believed to be a manifestation of moral authenticity. The national slogan might be, "Dare to Snivel." Weakness is become strength and strength, weakness.

And my God, the psychobabble. I listened to endless therapeutic chatter and thought, These people need to get out of touch with their feelings.

On and on it went. Schools routinely ejected boy children for any display of independence, masculine competitiveness, or taste for adventure. We now ban tag as violent. Instead we must be sensitive, soft, and remorselessly good. We no longer even know what sex we are. Male models are shaven-chested and oiled, male radio voices an octave higher than in the last generation. Women wear shoulder pads.

We celebrate shiftlessless. People rut like barnyard animals and calve incontinently. Literature vanishes from the book stores, replaced by self-help, twelve-step programs, books with titles like, "The Agony of Split Ends: A Guide to Coping," and other books on the care and feeding of the Inner Child, that embodiment of infantile gooberishness. Life is therapy, and public discourse, a tapestry of lies. The fiber is rotting.

Always America has changed, of course, from the flappers of the Twenties to the Depression, the war, the duck-tailed muscularity of the Fifties, but there was always in it a rude strength. No longer. The music also changed: Tin Pan Alley, big band, blues, rock, country, but it was always the music of people who, if sometimes down, were never quite out. It fit what the country was and had been. Now music runs from self-pity and whining to grotesque obscenity and the jungle grunting of rap. This isn't change. It is degradation.

The ash drifts deeper over Pompeii, the inner savages grow bolder in the thickening murk, and the best yield to epicene forcelessness and drab androgyny. Culturally, though not yet commercially, America is, I think, on the way out.

As empires die, the barbarians usually gather at the gates, preparing a final rush. Unfortunately our savages are already inside. They are in the public schools, the universities, and downtown in the cities. They make our movies, set social policy from afar, instill appropriate values in our children. They do not know that they are savages. They now rule us, and there is nothing we can do about it.

Except watch. Vast disasters make splendid theater. This one is going to be a doozy.

Some of the essays that follow document the accelerating decline, some the fading world that came before, and a few I just wrote for the hell of it. I added a couple, such as the one on going to sea in a missile submarine, because I thought they might be interesting. Many are light-hearted, or pretend to be, as it is more satisfying to laugh and smack the bejesus out of the pygmies as the night deepens and poisoned darts fly.

The curtain falls, as eventually it must on everything. Meanwhile, here is a circus worthy of the admission, a fabulous suicide, more astonishing than the implosion of the Soviet Union. We see a new kink in the historical rope: a dominant culture, the inventor of the modern world, once supreme militarily, in the sciences, commercially, boisterously confident even thirty-five years ago, suddenly and piously drinking hemlock.

Eating Each Other At Harvard

At first no one took it seriously. Harvard was quick to point out that it was not really a Department of Cannibalism, but rather the Department of Non-Western Nutrition. Once the media got hold of the story, though, there was no stopping them. In the public mind, it would forever be the Cannibalism Department.

It all began when the conservative students of Harvard held a mass meeting on a Saturday night in November. Both decided that since, in their words, "every other damn-fool idea finds flowering expression here, we'll take lunacy a step further. You know. We'll be progressives."

They were joking. They thought everyone would understand. They should have known better.

They put together the Ivy League's first magazine of cannibalism and called it *Long Pig*, subtitled *Serving Your Fellow Man*. Actually it wasn't so much a magazine as a stapled mass spit out on a laser printer. There were only ten copies, left strategically around campus.

It wasn't high art. *Long Pig* was pretty much the *Mad Magazine* of liberated eating. Articles meant to be tongue-in-cheek dealt with urban hunting, fattening prisoners, soy substitutes in time of peace, and various recipes involving Mexicans and hot sauce. There was a piece on making jerky using traditional nature-respecting Inuit techniques, involving a song to the walrus god. The lead editorial argued that cannibalism was merely an advanced form of recycling. It would, said the authors, cut down on the methane emitted by beef cattle, and thus prevent global warming. The slogan was "Eat Each Other: Save the Ice Caps."

An ad showed Eeyore and Pooh comforting a sad-eyed Piglet who was, by implication, pondering a future association with fried eggs.

Cannibalism would save him. Green Peace, PETA, and the Sierra Club immediately came on board. The local Four O'clock News picked up the story.

The conservative students were astonished. "It was a joke for God's sake," said the bemused publishers to a reporter for *Time*. "It wasn't real. We were trying to be funny. Why did this happen?"

It happened because it was the sort of thing that only sociologists could take seriously, and did. Dr. Lara Johnstone-Lingamfelter, chairwoman of the Department of Lesbian Chicana and Transsexual Micronesian Studies, found a copy and, seeing the word "progressive," assumed that she had discovered a new oppressed group. Wanting to get in on the ground floor, she immediately penned an article for the *Journal of Appropriate Thought*, the de facto trade publication of the Ivy League professoriate, demolishing patriarchal linear-thinking hierarchical discrimination against traditional cuisine.

"Who people eat behind closed doors is their own business," she said.

Misunderstandings continued, amplifying what amounted to a collegiate prank. A reporter for the *Washington Post* telephoned Leona Mikoyan-Gurevich, the chief attorney for NOW, to get her opinion. Unfortunately she had called at a bad moment. Mikoyan-Gurevich was defending a woman in California who had poisoned 173 children in a kindergarten, her defense being that she was in a bad mood, which was caused by the stress of living in a society dominated by oppressive white males. The attorney, "frazzled" as she later put it, was hurriedly skimming papers on cyanide toxicology.

Barely looking up, she said, "What? They eat men? It's a good idea."

This put militant feminism behind the new movement. Patricia Ireland was later reported to have said, "This is a little wacky, even for us, but if Mikky likes it, we'll run with it. Though *I'd* never eat one of the disgusting creatures." Disgusting creatures everywhere doubtless felt safer.

Attention from the media grew like kudzu on a Georgia road-cut. Journalists began treating Cannibal Studies as if it actually existed. A tee-shirt emporium near Harvard peddled shirts to college boys that said, "Can-Stud, Will Travel," and "Eat Me, I'm A Protein Source." The shirts created outrage in progressive circles, as they suggested that adolescent males at Harvard might be having sexual thoughts about women. The boys denied it. They said they were merely protesting their demeaning status as a marginalized link in the food chain. They would never, ever think dirty thoughts about girls.

This didn't mollify feminists among the studentry. The Gay, Lesbian, Transgendered, Bisexual, Pan-gendered and Still-Considering Women's Coalition Against Hegemonic Colonialism swung into action. They held three Take Back The Night marches, installed blue anti-rape lights all over campus, and told each other comforting stories about how seven out of every three women had been raped at least twice in the last ten minutes. What this had to do with cannibalism wasn't clear.

Things were getting out of hand.

A riot nearly erupted shortly afterward. The Harvard Union for Liberation of Oppressed Sexual Minorities was holding a support meeting, the topic being, "Snuff: The Difficulty of Finding a Lasting Relationship." (Their slogan was, "Not Just A Tobacco Product.") Anyway, several boys in Can-Stud shirts had shown up arguing that the two groups were complementary. They were pursued for six blocks before hiding in a Dempster Dumpster.

Later one of the instigating conservatives, seeking to make as much trouble as possible (adolescent conservatives are nonetheless adolescents) tried to call the US Supreme Court. He wanted to ask about the constitutionality of human sacrifice. He planned to argue that it was a folkway of Native Peoples, such as Aztecs, and therefore heartwarming, which made it constitutional.

Knowing that Sandra Day O'Connor favored partial-birth abortion, he figured she was his best shot. He didn't reach her. Nonetheless the

Justice replied, through a clerk, that she had no objection to human sacrifice, but was worried about the possible religious associations.

The adventure might have gone on forever. Then a mob of students showed up at the home of Harvard's President, Lawrence Summers, to demand a Department. Many of them were not sure what the rally was for, but a rally was a rally. They held hands in a circle and sang Kum Bah Yah with verses interspersed from One-Eyed One-Horned Flying Purple People Eater—adding that "Purple People" did not indicate disrespect for oppressed people of that color.

Summers was perhaps in a departmental mood. That week he had approved a Department of Left-handed Parsees with Three Thumbs Studies. Possibly he thought cannibalism was a minor stretch. He said, "Of course you can have a department...Of what? Not that it matters."

The Department began hiring. The conservative students went back to their chemistry homework. They had been humbled. When it came to lunacy, they weren't ready for the Ivy League.

Space Aliens At Roswell: Hant Did It

T'other day I walked up the holler to ask Uncle Hant about space aliens. It's because Hant knows everything—most nearly.

It was spring and birds were hooting and hollering in the rail cut through the woods to Hant's place and bugs were shrieking. The he-bugs, anyway. They rub their legs together like fiddle bows and screech so maybe the she-bugs will get smitten and the he-bugs will get laid. Then she goes away and leaves his kids in a pile under a leaf, all twelve million of them, and he never sees them. I don't see how evolution's made much difference.

We get lots of space aliens in West Virginia, like May flies around a porch light. Nobody knows why. Maybe they like trailer parks. Some folks reckon the aliens believe the satellite dishes are little cute saucers and come to visit.

Anyway, last week Miss Brody Lou Callister, that nice old-maid librarian, was down by the rusty tipple by the tracks. Sure enough, this strange *light* came from up in the air, the way it always does, and sucked her up like a Hoover-matic. She met Elvis and Hitler and got the weird sexual examination.

She pitched a tent by that tipple and lives there, hoping.

Hant was out back at his still, cutting wood to fire the cooker. He's a real moonshiner, and sells to yuppies out of DC. Actually he gets authentic bulk-lot alcohol from Buffalo, Moonshine Flavor from an outfit in Taiwan that does coal-tar chemistry, and real antique stone-ware jugs from a toilet factory in Newark. He adds a little rust-dissolver to give it a kick. He says they got lots of yuppies in Washington, so a few here and there don't matter.

"Hant, you have to tell me about space aliens, and Extra Terrestrial Intelligence."

He's a long tall sucker, kind of stiff with age now, and looks like nine miles of bad road. He wears a floppy hat that you just know used to be something else before the flatbed ran over it.

He leaned on his ax so he'd be picturesque and said, "Son, if it's terrestrial intelligence, it damn sure ain't extra."

Sometimes Hant's hard to talk to. I tried again.

"Hant, the lady on the satellite said this flatland scientist named Serge done gone and hooked together about a million computers to find space aliens. I reckon he's one of them Russians. Probably a comminest."

He sat on a stump and reached for a jug. He's got a jaw like a backhoe that needs a shave and doesn't look natural unless he's leaning on something. Of course, he usually is.

"Want a swig?" he asked.

"That death dew got rust-cutter in it?"

"Not hardly. I like the enamel on *my* teeth. This here's Beam. Who's this Serge rascal?"

"Serge for Extra Terrestrial Intelligence. That CNN lady said the Air Force has a whole barn full of space aliens in New Mexico. And they think space is just crawling with them."

"Can't be," he said. He had that smug look he gets, like a man that's got a date with somebody else's wife and just drew five aces too.

"Why?"

"Can't be anything in space, or it wouldn't be space. Ain't nothing there. That's how you can tell it's space. *Any* fool knows that."

I hadn't thought about it that way. Hant's pretty smart, considering he don't exist. He's just a filament of the imagination.

"Maybe they ain't in space, but the CNN lady said a flying saucer crashed out in Roswell. It's a town in New Mexico. They got 'em stacked up like cord wood and the Feddle Gummint wants to find more."

Hant got that funny embarrassed look like he wanted to change the subject.

"The Feddle Gummint couldn't find next week with a month to hunt." He was quiet for a moment. Then he took a big three-gurgle hit on the jug and looked thoughtful. I could tell he was about to show off.

"I remember that night. I guess it was my fault." You could see he was proud of himself.

"What was?"

"The crash."

I figured he must have got a running start on that jug before I got there.

"Ol' Joe Float come up that night and bought two gallons of shine. Yep, it was my fault."

Joe Float was the local drunk when I was just a kid. His name wasn't really Float, but he drank so much people thought he ought to, so that's what they called him.

"Next morning we found him in a field that was scorched in a circle. The jugs was next to him, empty, but he was stone cold sober. We were afraid the shock might kill him."

From all I heard about old Joe, being sober would at least have confused him considerable. He hadn't tried it since he was about nine years old.

"I guess them old space aliens must of sampled that panther sweat. Joe said that saucer was flying upside down and sideways before it spit him out. Everybody just rattled around, Hitler and Judge Crater and the Lost Tribe. 'Course they didn't have Elvis yet."

"Hant, you aren't making this up, are you?"

He didn't say anything for a minute, just looked at me all sorrowful like he'd just noticed that I'd poisoned him.

"It's getting so don't nobody trust a literary apparition these days. Seems like it ain't worth getting out of bed in the morning."

He was just trying to be pitiful. You couldn't get him out of bed before noon with a bird dog and a buzz saw.

Still, he could have been telling the truth. They made this movie once in Bluefield about space monsters that crashed in the mountains and starting turning folks into cocoons. People would go out at night and you'd find them hanging in trees, all wrapped up. They looked like big tent-caterpillar nests.

It must have been a pretty good movie because it played in drive-ins all over the country and everybody said the teenagers would have liked it if they'd seen it. The reviewer in Wheeling gave it three thumbs up, which you can only get in West Virginia. Ever since then Hollywood's tried to get movies reviewed here.

So maybe that's what happened. Seems like space aliens don't drive too good anyway, and with that brain paralyzer Hant makes, they wouldn't have a chance.

I told you Hant knows everything.

Because We Say So

Perhaps society's answer to some things should simply be, "No. Because we say so." A culture should at times assert its collective will, impose the communal understanding of right and wrong, and not apologize. "Some things," a people should say to the moral undercurrents welling from below, "you will not inflict on us."

But we have forgotten, irreversibly I suspect, the virtues of "Because we say so."

A question: Do you want young children, or yourself, to be exposed to grotesque scatology on television, to explicit copulation ("Daddy, what are they *doing*?"), romanticized use of drugs, garish homosexuality, and bloody godawful violence?

Why not?

It can be harder than one might think to give a satisfactory answer. Your opponent will marshal meretricious arguments: We should not teach our children that sex is wrong, as doing so might lead to repression. Sex and homosexuality after all are natural. (So are cholera and sun-ripened peaches. So what?) Sordid movies are merely being realistic, showing the world as it is. To allow censorship would be to transgress the First Amendment, leading shortly to repression of the classics of literature and, eventually, to control of all forms of expression (presumably making pornography the rock sustaining our way of life). And so on.

The answer should be simply, "No. You will not put these things on television, *because we say so.*"

Much of the unpleasantness of modern life occurs because we will say "No" to almost nothing. For example, there exists, most unfortunately, a puerile nonentity, purporting to be a singer, who with gut-wrenching cuteness calls himself Eminem. His lyrics are sufficiently repellent that countries debate whether to give him a visa. He is simply a societal brat, and should be treated as such. Yet in the United States, committees of high import debate solemnly the merits of his spewings, worrying greatly about Art and freedom of expression.

In 1950, when the society had a backbone, any radio station to which he had carried his records would have said, "No," and called the police. We don't. We lack the conviction. We cannot utter the aggregate "No." And so the bilge washes over us.

Why does this happen?

It happens because, instead of deriving law from morality, we now derive morality from law. In a healthy society, laws enforce morality; they do not dictate it. In America today, the opposite is true.

If the courts say we must listen to tedious obscenity—why, then we must. If the courts say that we must offer condoms to children in school, eschew prayer, tolerate any and all vileness, permit our daughters to get abortions without so much as notifying their parents, we obediently do so. Is there *anything* the courts cannot make us do?

I doubt it.

Recently a boy in Washington was expelled from high school. Yes. It seems the school issued him a condom, and caught him praying for a chance to use it.

(All right. It probably didn't happen. But it's true anyway.)

The problem with being too much a nation of laws is that whoever controls the laws then controls the nation. Laws by their nature are endlessly arguable. A case, more or less plausible, can be made for anything, and for its opposite. This means that a judiciary, having an agenda, yet accountable to no one, can come to any conclusion it chooses. By untying law from the anchor of morality, we give up control over our lives.

The objection will be made that that imposing the morality of the many will result in the oppression of the few. But we now have the oppression of the many by the morality of the few. And perhaps the depravity of the few is such as to need repressing. When all has been said, the question remains: Somebody's morals are going to be imposed. Ours, or theirs?

A healthy society need not be intolerant by virtue of imposing the collective morality. A culture can, and should, admit of positions between "yes" and "no." Consider homosexuality. A society may agree that if homosexuals choose to be discreet, then society in return will leave them alone—that they will suffer no persecution or penalties, that gay bars discreetly run will be discreetly ignored. The compromise is a useful one. It permits homosexuals to live largely as they wish, yet heterosexuals will not have thrust on them practices that they find repugnant.

The compromise can be maintained by the public will, just as (so far) the tacit injunction against riding naked on the subway has been maintained. Some things you don't do. Logical argument fails against either. Why not ride naked?

Once society cedes its moral authority to a court of law, then all things become possible. Consider the logical progression:

In any large city, there are clubs of hobbyist sadomasochists who gather in curious costumes to tie each other up and paddle each other. It is done discreetly and harms no one. Nothing needs to be done about it.

But note that exactly the same arguments that justify homosexuality in the schools apply to sadomasochism. It's natural, prominent people do it, it's a way of life. If children in grade school are to be taught that the one is merely a stylistic preference, why not the other? We now have books in schools with titles like, "*Bobby Has Two Daddies.*" Why not, "*Sally's Daddy Wears A Leash*"? Why not S&M clubs in school, as there are now gay and lesbian clubs?

Because we say so.

Why not pedophilia? There exists (with a website) an outfit called NAMBLA, the North American Man Boy Love Association, whose members believe they are entitled to engage in anal intercourse with your ten-year-old son. They aren't kidding, and they begin to get support from advanced minds in academia.

Here too a society that cannot simply say "No" finds itself at the mercy of logic-choppers. Proponents of pedophilia might (and do) argue that it is natural, that our repugnance for it is merely a cultural artifact, a product of repressive patriarchal Christianity. The ancient Greeks engaged in it. Our designation of 15 or 18 as the age of consent is purely arbitrary; a boy of nine is human, has civil rights, and can choose. Anyway, pedophilia is harmful only because we teach our children that it is shameful, instead of teaching them that it is a natural celebration of life and love. Those who have tried it know it to be a warm and loving, etc.

The answer is "No. Because we say so." Some things you don't do. This is one of them.

We just can't say it.

Fred Says Reparations Owed For Slavery

I see by the papers in the Yankee Capital that Johnny Cochran, and of course Jesse and Al, are wheezing and blowing like a county-fair calliope with a leaky boiler. They always are. This time it was about the need to pay reparations for the ravages of slavery. It got me to thinking.

I hate it when that happens.

Now, I know I'm hard-hearted, and mean-spirited, and no damn good. It's probably my only virtue. But on consideration, I realized that they might be right. The ravages of slavery do run deep, and cause motingator trouble, with no end in sight. I decided that compensation was only reasonable. Sometimes you don't like a conclusion, but you have to reach it. All right. I'll be a man about it.

You can pay me reparations, Johnny.

To start with, I figure you owe me for three bicycles. Maybe it's a small thing, but I'm tired of losing bicycles. Are we talking market value or replacement? What I really want to be paid for is having to keep my latest two-wheeler in my living room. Do you know how many times I've knocked the fool thing over? And, oh, the scratch in my granddad's antique desk that the brake lever made. What's that worth?

Call it three grand. OK? Direct deposit would be nice.

But…how do we dollarize cultural retrogression? God knows I appreciate your offer of reparations, but I'm having trouble with the arithmetic. Help me.

A few years back, my middle-school daughter brought home a horrendously misspelled science hand-out. Now, Johnny: You and I both know that it's easy to make a typo, and write "phenylkeetone" instead of "phenylketone." But "feemelkeebome" is stretching it. The errors were of this sort. An understanding of chemistry clearly had never rippled the serene surface of the woman's mind.

Without thinking, I asked, "What color is your teacher?" (If I had thought carefully, I would have asked, "What color is your teacher?") My daughter responded with an anguished, "*Da-d-d-d-y!*" She had made the connection, but knew she wasn't supposed to.

I've got no problem with black teachers, if they are competent. No problem at all. But a teacher who is too ignorant to spell her subject, and too lazy to use a dictionary, ought to be flipping burgers. Simple burgers, with no moving parts. Thing is, we can't fire ignorant teachers, Johnny, because of the lingering effects of slavery. I can yell at an ignorant white teacher, but not at a black one. To expect blacks to meet standards is racist. You can send me the price of four years of tuition in a private school outside the country.

What's the cost of permanent welfare? Subsidized everything? Enormous police departments? What do you figure? Just add it to your tab. Have you thought about setting up an endowment?

But here's a large ravage of slavery, Johnny: Fear.

What price do we put on looking over our shoulders? On watching to be sure we don't go one subway stop too far? Warning our girlfriends not to drive on certain streets? Checking the clientele of Seven-Eleven before going in at night?

People in, say, Switzerland can walk their streets after dark. We can't. Why? What have we got that they don't, that might cause fear? What have we got lots of?

Elvis impersonators, Johnny. Yep. Switzerland doesn't have any Elvis impersonators. Check for yourself.

What's fear worth? Is it a minimum-wage job? Forty-hour week or twenty-four hours a day? Benefits? Seniority pay as people grow older, weaker, and less able to defend themselves? You see the actuarial difficulty. Accounting is a more difficult trade than you might think.

The white guy beaten to death 100 yards from my door last year—they never caught the killers, but—what you reckon, Johnny? Do you figure it was white Presbyterian women from the old-ladies' home? That's my guess. That's who usually does it. Anyway, you can send me $540 for the Sig 9mm pistol I bought after blacks started moving into the neighborhood and crime went up. And ammo, carry permit, Hydra-Shock rounds.

Now, millions of honest blacks might write and say, "Fred, we aren't criminals. Why should we pay for what other blacks do?" Splendid question. But of course whites say, "We don't have any slaves. Why should we pay for what other whites did?" If it is a reasonable question for blacks to ask, as indeed it is, why isn't it a reasonable question for whites to ask?

But while you are in a mood to pay up, Johnny, let me introduce a useful concept: Civilizational rent. You'll like this. It's such a good idea.

A culture is essentially software. No? Sure, there are physical embodiments: positron-emission scanners, high-bypass turbofans, radar with Doppler beam-sharpening. Yet basically a culture is a body of knowledge, like Microsoft Word. (All right, throw in values, which civilizations also have. But I don't want to make this too difficult.)

White guys invented these things at considerable cost. We had to. Europe doesn't have much low-hanging fruit, and it gets cold in the north. So generations of people that I'm sure you're familiar with—Newton, Leibniz, Galois, Gauss, Carnot, Dirac—did work that led to all kinds of useful…you know…*stuff.*

Western civilization, it's called.

As a result of slavery, you have been using our civilization without a license. (I know: You're having trouble with the idea of implied retroactive acceptance of a license I invented five minutes ago. Microsoft would grasp it in a heartbeat. Anyway, I'm writing the column.)

Further, you've been using it for a long time, Johnny. Air-conditioning. Roads. Writing. The wheel. Complicated stuff like that. Medicine. Tractors. Shoes. Houses. I've spent time in Africa, where people live in stick things that look as if a Cub Scout had built a campfire and forgotten to light it. You're getting a deal here, Johnny.

I don't wish stick houses on anyone. I'm glad you have the benefits of electricity, clothes, and daytime TV. I'd love to see blacks study, earn degrees on their merits, prosper. Think of the trouble it would save. But—as suggested by your manly desire to pay reparations—you owe us licensing fees. Granted, it's hard to set a price on a culture. But if Microsoft Office goes for $250 at fire-sale prices, I guess a whole civilization is cheap at $100K a copy.

I believe we can do business, Johnny. I hope so. I can use the money.

The Death Of The Schools

Sometimes a good-humored column is beyond me. This is one of those times. Sorry.

In the *Washington Times* for October 29, I found the following questions posed by Walter Williams, the conservative columnist.

First: "Which of the following is equal to a quarter of a million? (a) 40,000 (b) 250,000 (c) 2,500,000 (d) 1/4,000,000 or (d) 4/ 1,000,000?"

Second: "Martin Luther King Jr. (insert the correct choice) for the poor of all races. (a) spoke out passionately (b) spoke out passionate (c) did spoke out passionately (e) has spoke out passionately or (e) had spoken out passionate."

And where did Williams find these puzzlers? In the *School Reform News* for September first. They are questions to be asked of prospective teachers.

Ignoring the ideological freight of the second question, one asks: What do these questions do? Answer: They distinguish the marginally human from those who clearly need to evolve faster. These are not questions for grown-ups. They are pre-high-school questions. Anyone who can't answer them effortlessly is innumerate and semiliterate. When I was a fourth-grader diagramming sentences in the schools of Virginia, I doubt that any of the kids would have said, "has spoke out passionately."

If you miss this question, you barely speak English. Rocks, mosses, and vegetables have better grammar.

Think about this. Prospective teachers are people who have college degrees. You shouldn't have to check to see whether they can pass a fourth-grade English test. Nor should you wonder whether they have a monkey's grasp of the number system.

Whenever I write that we are putting people into teaching who have barely achieved vertebracy, and that by far the worst are black, I get letters telling me that I've hurt people's feelings, and that I'm being unfair to the exceptions, and that I'm a racist, and no damn good. Exceptions exist, and have my gratitude and respect. But they *are* exceptions. As for the rest: Is it our duty to harm our children so as to help incompetents feel good? Or is it rather our duty to raise our children well? Racism? If the requirement that people be able to do their jobs is racist, I most assuredly am.

This has been going on for decades. The following is from a piece I wrote for *Harper's* in the early 1980s:

"The bald, statistically verifiable truth is that the teachers' colleges, probably on ideological grounds, have produced an incredible proportion of incompetent black teachers. Evidence of this appears periodically, as, for example, in the results of a competency test given to applicants for teaching positions in Pinellas County, Florida (which includes St. Petersburg and Clearwater), cited in *Time*, June 16, 1980. To pass this grueling examination, an applicant had to be able to read at the tenth-grade level and do arithmetic at the eighth-grade level. Though they all held B.A.'s, 25 percent of the whites and 79 percent of the blacks failed. Similar statistics exist for other places."

Similar statistics still exist for practically everywhere. (The author John Perazzo, in his book *The Myths That Divide Us*, in my view the best overview of the racial problem in America, details them on pages 227-228. Not a pleasant read, but worth the effort. Amazon has it.)

When 79 percent of a group fail a very easy test, how good do we think those are who did pass? The whites are better than the blacks, but remember that they, having graduated from college, are being asked to read at a tenth-grade level—i.e., six years behind their formal training. This might be acceptable in a hod carrier. But in teachers?

Much of the problem is ideological. All societies have had serfs, peasants, rustics, or proletariats who have had no interest in education. We are no different. We are, however, perhaps the first society to put our peasantry in charge of the schools.

In the first half of this century, standards for teachers in America were not phenomenally high, but teachers agreed that literacy was desirable. They knew what fundamental schooling was, and imparted it.

Genius wasn't, and isn't, required. It does not take a mathematician to teach multiplication tables and percentages. It takes someone of somewhat superior intelligence who understands these things, and understands that they need to be learned, and will insist that the children learn them. A literate teacher of fair intelligence can teach the writing of a clear paragraph. A great deal of what one needs to master, at least through high school, is simply information.

But a powerful current in education holds that learning is elitist, and to be avoided. Our problem, aside from the fact that on average teachers are not smart enough, is the governing attitude that these things do not need to be learned. Recently a teacher in one of my daughter's schools was reproached for correcting her students' grammar—because she wasn't an English teacher. To the administration of the school, speaking the language well is clearly not something that should be expected of all who graduate. Rather it is, like a jump shot, something that belongs only in its particular venue.

I don't think blacks are responsible for our peasantrification. When you get down to it, thirteen percent of the population cannot impose anything in which the majority is unwilling to acquiesce. Blacks, however, are being used. They have been a potent weapon for those who carry an inchoate hostility to civilization.

Blacks documentably fall to the bottom in any academic setting. Thus any insistence on performance will be disproportionately burdensome to them. Since their evident lack of enthusiasm for schooling parallels their lack of performance, they can be counted on to complain that they are victims of racism. Here we have the charm that never fails for those who want to lower standards—who, more correctly, don't understand why standards existed in the first place. Blacks are not the inspiration, but the excuse. If teachers can't require them to learn grammar, neither can they require it of whites. Bingo.

Year after year, the dismal news bubbles to the surface of national consciousness. Every year it is ignored: Our fear of offending apparently exceeds our concern for our children. Or do we just not care?

Fanny-Swatting As A Felony

I'm gonna break something. It's going to happen. Anything could trigger it. A neutered hamster of a high-school principal is going to complain about the violence inherent in freeze-tag. Or some baffled ditz-bunny in a university will whinny about how Frosty the Snowman symbolizes white patriarchal phallocentric linearity. I'm going to pop, and suffer an access of superhuman strength, and pick up a backhoe, and smack'em into gruel.

And then put on waders and dance in it.

And whoop.

"Espanola, NM—(Reuters) 'A 14-year-old boy could be charged with a felony for slapping a girl's buttocks, officials said.'"

Yeah, the kid did it. Whereupon an assistant principal *called the police.*

When I was a kid, the obvious thing would have been to take Bobby aside and say, "Listen, kid, we don't do that. Quit it. Got that?" Whereupon, unless Bobby was a budding nutcase, the matter would have been closed.

But no. It's "criminal sexual contact." A felony.

The story did not say how the trauma affected the girl. Presumably she is an a psychiatric intensive-care unit, with an IV Thorazine drip, and teams of therapists working around the clock to save what shards remain of her former being. In fact, I'd guess she's in a coma. Maybe worse: She was thwacked on the butt. She'll probably need a respirator for life.

"We have a strict sexual-harassment policy," said Assistant Principal Ruben Lucero. "Any time a person's body is violated, we consider that major."

Savor the somber salacious absurdity. Her *body*...was...*violated.* Yes. It was the moral equivalent of being gang-raped by the Golden Horde. It was just like medical experiments in the dungeons of the Third Reich. Violated. On the playgrounds of America.

The horror.

It seems that Espanola has a police department—barely, I'd estimate. Its chief, Wayne Salazar, says, "The suspect is alleging that this was just a battery, that this was not a sexual issue. But why the buttocks? Why not the arm, why not someplace else? It's the target area that concerns us."

I've always wanted a police department concerned with little girls' bottoms. But, my God, the grim officiousness of these pompous minor Stalins. The *suspect*? I know real cops, undercover guys, actual men who carry guns and go into bad places. Do you know what they would think of a cop investigating felony fanny-smacking in middle school? ("Hey, a Swat Team....") They'd send him a catalog from Victoria's Secret.

Do you suppose Chief Salazar doesn't have enough to do?

A serious question: What will this prurient hysteria—that's what it is—teach Bobby and Sally Sue? These are kids creeping up on puberty. They are going to horse around the fringes of sexuality, like all kids who ever lived. If they don't, something is wrong with them.

The prissy confused in Espanola are teaching Sally that sexual attention from boys is sick, reprehensible, and a cause for calling the police. Gee, that'll make for happiness later in adulthood. And, dead serious, they may put the boy in juvie for two years, destroying his life forever. They're teaching Bobby that females are dangerous, that a man should never trust them.

Think I'm kidding? Reuters: "Salazar said the forensic psychologists would complete their assessment within the next two weeks, after which police would know how to proceed."

I suggest they proceed to grow up, and stop acting like everyone's maiden aunt.

And how is Sally Sue going to feel if in fact the gender rabbitry of Espanola do put Bobby behind bars? She's thirteen, and she's being used by adults to forward weird sexual agendas she doesn't understand. And I don't either.

Europeans laugh at the latent Puritanism in the American soul. That's exactly what this is. *Eeeeeeeeeeeeeeeeeeek*! Don't *touch* me! That's *nathsty*. Note the curious revulsion at the thought that a boy of 14 might have a sexual interest in girls. How...unnatural. It's like, well, dirty.

Huh? What fourteen-year-old doesn't have a budding sexual interest in girls? And if not, why not? What's he supposed to have a sexual interest in? Goats? Endangered condors? Realistically, his options are limited. Girls are sort of what we have, unless we are girls, and then we have boys. And you don't suppose—oh, the gnawing shame—that adolescent girls might occasionally find their minds turning to thoughts of the carnal? Like, oh, about every ten seconds?

Oh, no-*ooo-oo*.

For that matter, do you know how many second dates a boy gets if he's not at least interested? Start with not any, and count downwards.

What is so wonderfully funny here is the irony. In the Sixties, feminists pushed the Pill, and hollered about how women should be able to cat around like guys. Now they can. Oddly, the sexual revolutionaries figured the Pill constituted a triumph over men. The notion that you can triumph over men by making sex more readily available is, uh, lacking in insight.

But now—this is seriously strange—the revolutionaries have reversed their field. Today's comic-opera feminism seems to consist largely of a squeaking horror of sex. They now push exactly the patriarchal attitudes of the 1890s: Women are helpless victims, pitiable, weak-minded, cringing, unable to handle a pass on the playground.

Funny, I've never met such a woman.

Ain't it grand? If a man says a bad word at the office, or glances at her legs, a woman should swoon, deftly dialing a lawyer before hitting the carpet, and maybe get the vapors. Is this not Victorian England all over?

Meanwhile, Chief Salazar has his hands full. Any day now, some deranged crypto-rapist of a boy, doubtless with dead bodies buried in droves beneath his house, is going to snap a girl's bra strap. The thought is ghastly, but…we live in dangerous times. The chief is nothing if not alert, though. He will doubtless have the National Guard on the way in seconds. But is this enough? Sufficient protection against, *eeeeeeeewwww!* ordinary life? Actually, I figure girls ought to come to school sealed in Kevlar barrels, on wheels, with air from scuba tanks, and special headphones that filter out dirty words.

Cooking Rudolph. Drowning Santa.

I figure we ought to abolish Christmas, and then pan-fry those wretched reindeer. Not just Rudolph, either. Donder and Blitzen, Anglo and Saxon, Dancer and Prancer (who sound gay.) They'll all be sausage. And I'll get that fat goober in the sled, too.

I've got no problem with Christmas. Or with Christianity. Either might be worth trying. If people want to decorate the tree, and give the kids a really magical time that they won't find out until later doesn't remotely match the reality of this dismal universe, fine. I like Christmas. For that matter, kids aren't bad.

It's that damned music.

The stuff is everywhere, like sin and phone solicitation. Several thousand times a day comes that insipid song about a White Christmas, and something about a snowman. It never stops. *Chingchingchingaching ringringringading dingdingdinga*, sleigh bells ringing....

Does anyone at all want to hear it? Or have the retailers found that it stimulates the shopping gland? It's probably in the pituitary. Have store-owners learned that, like Pavlov's dogs salivating at the sound of a bell, when we hear Frosty we buy unneeded junk? "It's Christmas. Buy toasters."

The other night I went to a local rib pit that has good barbecue and, usually, good blues. I wanted to get a huge messy pulled-pork sandwich and listen to the great bluesmen, which is what they usually have. Foolish me, I thought I could escape.

No. They had some guy trying to bluesify those reprehensible reindeer. It was ridiculous. Here was a black man, probably grew up on

Chicago's South Side. He knew gin mills and hard times, good lovin' but lots of bad, lousy paychecks and rainy days in the projects and three a.m. in clubs you've never heard of with the dance floor full. First-rate blues guy. And he's singing, "*Dingdingdinga* sleigh bells…." He's never seen a sleigh or a sleigh bell in his life. You could tell he was bored.

Not even Muddy Waters could make Winter Wonderland sound like anything but what it is: lame, saccharine elevator music. I don't know who wrote it, but I'm going to stuff him into a huge red stocking, and push him into an industrial grinder.

I asked the waitress when they would turn off this horror. She looked sympathetic and said, "After New Year. How do you think we feel? We have it all day."

See? It's like the Chinese water torture. I turned and fled.

It's not just the music. To my way of thinking, the country becomes uninhabitable for a whole month in the Winter Shopping Season. You see fifty thousand people milling around in a mall, wandering the aisles with glazed eyes in search of something to give to Ronny, and Billy, and Aunt Elmira with the mustache, and the sound system soughing, "I'm Dreaming of a …."

Me, I'm dreaming of a tire iron. And a mall operator to use it on.

Thing is, the milling shoppers don't really want to get anything for Aunt Elmira. They have to, though, because it's the Retail Season. You've heard of duty-free shopping? Not this month. It's a duty. They make lists, like grocery lists only it's minor relatives: "I've done Rita and Margie and…maybe Bob would like a too-large shirt with an ugly pattern, or a Swiss Army knife that he hasn't the slightest need for, but it's on sale and we gotta get him something…."

The soulless musical joy never ceases. I find myself antisocially completing verses:

"…He's making a list and checking it twice…." I'll get a blowtorch and fry his rice, Santa Clause is turning…brown.

Back when it was called Christmas instead of the Holiday Season, you could at least pretend that it had some meaning other than massive sales of things nobody really wanted. It doesn't. It's a month of compulsory expenditure. The sincerity of Hallmark, the spiritual depth of Disney, the spontaneity of Muzak.

I'm not sure even the kids like it. The idea is that they will go to bed dreaming of what Santa might bring them, some magical thing that is barely possible but will make them happy. What one actually sees every year is spoiled middle-class kids, almost bored, mechanically opening present after present.

"Deck the halls with boughs of holly…" Santa's wife is a half-grown collie.…

I know. I'm going off the deep end. Maybe I listen too much to the little voices. If they start singing Silent Night, I'll blow my brains out.

Even in the grocery stores they have the music. You can't buy pickled garlic and anchovies without bathing in aural sappiness. There's plenty of genuinely good Christmas music, or at least Christian music. The Messiah, things like that. But we get *chingchingchingaching* from crooners with groany-sweet voices. They sound like child molesters.

Actually, I think Rudolph has a red nose because he's a drunk.

The season has the intense spirituality that I associate with tax returns. A giveaway is the phrase, "exchange gifts," as in "We'll exchange gifts in the morning." You don't give Uncle Albert something you think he will really enjoy, because you are deeply fond of him, and want to make his life briefly happier until the regnant miseries of existence reassert themselves.

No. You give him something because you have to, and in return he gives you something because he has to. It's an exchange, tit for tat. (I've always wondered what tat was.) Sort of like a wash sale in the stock market. Calibrated, of course, to Al's place in the pecking order of retail cheer: He's a distant relative, sort of an adjunct member of the family, so we'll only spend fifteen dollars on him, now, what can we find that costs fifteen dollars, maybe this clever shaving soap in the shape of a burro....

It's supposed to be a time of joy, Peace on earth and good will to persons. Yet most adults seem to regard it as an immense nuisance, and the single ones are just depressed. Somehow it has become, for many, a time to feel sad because they don't have the warmth and love that most other people seem to have but probably don't either. I'll bet the suicide rate goes up. And everyone seems so glad when it's over.

I just don't do it. Maybe we should all stop doing it, except for maybe a few treats for the kids. Instead we could get together with people we care about and have a huge meal. That would be it.

And put a bounty on those singers.

Among Los Frijoleros

As the Great Mexican Squid, Tequila, and Lolligagging Bail-Out creeps closer, I gotta decide what to do about this rattletrap column.

A while back, it dawned on me that maybe I'd been in the column racket too long. Since 1973 I've been banging out these pellets of wisdom, one, two, three a week, like rabbit droppings, for this or that newspaper. It wears on you. The blush fades from the dewy petals of journalism. It ain't fun any more. It hasn't been for a long time.

The news racket ought to be, and was, a trade of honest drunks. They'd sit in the dim bar of, say, the Grand Hotel in Taipei, telling lies, except usually they weren't, about obscure bush wars in places most people had never heard of. News ferrets were ribald, smart, ballsy, funny, hard-nosed, and egotistical. Most were born raconteurs. They had met improbable people and done wild things, and talked as if it were reasonable to come roaring out of Angola low over the bush in a rattletrap DC-3 to avoid SAMs. Better company there wasn't.

Now reporters are New Age, prissy, and censorious. The men wear lingerie and the women don't know what it is. You can just tell that if you left them in a fern bar, they would nest, talk about multiculturalism, and lay eggs.

The pressure of a column gets old. You might think writers would get used to deadlines, but you never really do. You're always behind. I once wrote a military column for Universal Press Syndicate, which carries a lot of the heavy names in the column scam. I asked my editor whether the big guns wrote several columns ahead.

"No," he said. "They always file at deadline."

It wasn't just me. Columnists all thought, "Oh my God, it's Friday. The insatiable maw awaits. Dozens of four-color web-offset Goss Urbanite presses wait to inflict my twaddle on the unsuspecting. What desperate fluff, what mental dust-bunnies, what lugubrious sludge can I package as insight? The sky is falling? Been done. The world is going to end? Too obvious. Maybe I can lie. Princess Di seen with Joseph Goebels? Argentine scientists clone Hitler?"

I'm tired of it.

Truth be told, I'm a tad tired of America. I wish I weren't. In the past, I loved the sprawling and variegated asylum north of the Rio Grande. For years I hitchhiked its deserts and prairies, its huge cities and forgotten mining towns. The country was sometimes uncouth but always vigorous and everywhere had its distinctive character. The franchised shopping mall hadn't yet made everywhere exactly like everywhere else. Our people were profligate in their variety, yet ethnicities hadn't become warring tribes. There was an imperfect strength to the country, a sock-hop optimism, a naïve moral radiance of prom queens and jalopies rebuilt in garages. We knew who we were.

That America is dying. It vanishes beneath a coercive semi-Marxist conformity imposed from New York and Hollywood. Stalinism Lite: All the control but half the penalties. We are becoming what we set out not to be. The Bill of Rights erodes. Political speech is punished while illiterate scatology enjoys judicial protection. The country is being remade, becoming controlled, homogeneous, feminized. I don't like it. It isn't the country I signed up for.

In the Fifties we had the vitality of rock and the love ballads of Presley. Music was often sappy but it wasn't evil. Now we have the subhuman grunting of rap. Smiling calendar girls have given way to glossy gynecology. Children in junior high use drugs that, a few decades ago, could be found only in the scummiest precincts of the cities. Kids no longer have childhoods. At eleven they're jaded experimental hamsters who know too much about the sordid.

Some call it sophistication but, if so, it's the sophistication that comes of growing up in a whorehouse. We celebrate casual bastardy, elevate the sleazy and inadequate to high moral principle. We bathe in civilization's bilges. I think a lot of us notice it.

Arguably the place has actually gone nuts. Every week another little boy gets tossed from school for drawing a soldier or playing cowboys and Injuns. Judicial idiots enact more laws to make sure kids don't have families. It appears wanton and deliberate.

I can't stop it, but I don't have to suffer it.

In March, I went to Mexico for a couple of weeks to scope out towns on the west coast. I've always liked Mexicans, and still do. You can breathe in Mexico without looking over your shoulder to see who's listening. True, the country is far from perfect. There are people in Mexico you don't screw with. There is corruption. But you don't have the soft little fingers from afar that reach into minds to instill appropriate values.

Not yet. Our media make inroads abroad.

I figured I'd go back for the summer, which I am about to do, to see whether I wanted to stay. If so, I'd go back permanently—get a small place on the outskirts of a coastal city, with a courtyard and a big gaudy-ass parrot that shrieked vulgarities in Spanish, and maybe a burro to yell *eeeeeeeeeeee*!-honk! so I could be sure I was in Mexico. Take a laptop, plug into the Internut, peddle a few magazine pieces for airfare to Asian fleshpots. Loll on the beach, dive on the reefs. Get on an actual horse and wander through hot empty countryside full of Gila monsters.

A lot of guys think about expatriating. A few actually do it. Some make it, and some don't. Some of them you see in the bars of Patpong in Bangkok, drinking their retirements and waiting for their livers to quit. Others go into the insulated gringo warrens of Lake Chapala, near Guadalajara. Others, wiser, go native, run businesses, acquire girl-friends, meld into the country and live happily. It's what you make of it. You quickly learn to live without surly diversity and lunatic teachers gone limp-kneed because some kid brought a squirt gun to school.

So what to do with this peculious literary eruption?

I pondered dropping it. On reflection, I figure I'll keep writing it as long as anyone reads it. Funny: There's no money in it, but readers have come to be in a sense friends. I appreciate you folks. Maybe writing isn't a curable disease.

I just got a lovely HP laptop. Two-way satellite broadband is going to come in Mexico. But there may be a certain Latin cast to future outpourings, and bizarre tales of doings in remote ranchos. There's no telling. These are strange times.

Paddlin' Where The Water Wasn't

The time Frank Green and I paddled the canoe through the dry hills of King George County in search of water would, I suppose, discourage naval historians. Fact is, we'd have had a better chance of finding water in the Sahara in mid-August of a drought year. I will say, however, that the adventure got us covered with some of the finest ticks bred on the Southern seaboard, which is the best tick country on this or any other continent.

We were fifteen and didn't have a brain in our combined heads. Frank was from a family that made its living by getting up at four a.m. and pulling crab pots on the Potomac, because people in Washington wanted to eat crabs. He eventually became an electrical engineer. King George was wooded hills with fields full of deer and whistle pigs and reasonably poor people who actually worked for a living. I was just me.

I had bought the canoe a few months before with paper-route money. Frank and I had proceeded to do with it every wrong-headed thing we could come up with. We had capsized it in the Potomac and gotten it full of jellyfish. We had loaded it to the gills with Pepsi and paddled the Rappahannock from Fredericksburg to Port Royal. We put girls in it—three of them once, which was more than it would hold, so one of them was always falling out and we had to tow her home, because she couldn't get back in without tipping us over.

At this point there was nothing left to do. The flavor went out of life. We were thrown back on our usual pursuits of reckless driving, purloined beer, and wild, fruitless dreams of lechery.

Then Frank asked why we didn't explore Peppermill Creek. On Route 206 a few miles out of metropolitan Owens, a conurbation with a population of maybe thirty people, the road drops sharply into an outsized ravine and crosses a rivulet running through the woods. As a body of water it is, if not navigable, at least wet.

The hill itself will live forever in local lore. Kids liked to lie about losing the cops on it at 130 miles an hour, generally in unmuffled wrecks that could have made 90, maybe, if you had pushed them out of an airplane.

Friends dropped canoe and us at the reedy marge of the alleged stream. It was one impoverished waterway—about three inches deep on the average. Salamanders lived in it, along with brown scum and the occasional water snake. We found a channel deep enough to float the canoe, but not straight enough: If the stern was afloat, the bow was on solid ground.

We picked up our vessel and carried it fifty yards down the middle of the stream. Here the channel straightened out. Both ends of the boat would float at once—but not with us in it. Our weight pressed it firmly into the mud.

You begin to get the flavor of the voyage.

The United States is a great country, and certainly a marvel to the world, because its citizens don't ask whether a thing is reasonable, or even possible, before doing it. We were as American as you could get.

I heaved on the bow painter, which is technical for a piece of rope tied to the front. Frank shoved mightily on the back. Twigs scratched us. Deer flies bit us. We sweated and swore with fervor and artistry. At intervals we sat in the canoe and drank Pepsis. Clouds drifted past above the thicket and birds made bird noises and dragonflies sat on the paddles and watched us. Life was mighty satisfactory, we said.

It was not travelsome, however. We heaved and hoved and huffed through the undergrowth, a yard at a time. We were establishing that you can go anywhere with a canoe, but not necessarily in a canoe. The rivulet did not behave as in all honor it should have, deepening with distance from its source. Instead it spread out into an almost-marsh of soggy earth, thickly covered with swamp grass. For practical purposes, we were in a canoe on a prairie.

We drank more Pepsis and pondered. Common sense suggested surrender. We couldn't have picked common sense out of a lineup if it had waved at us. We were determined not to accede to reason, mass, topography, or the sheer intransigence of life. Boyhood doesn't work that way. We didn't, anyway.

With great perseverance but little intelligence—and, by now, with a spirit of sheer vengeful stubbornness—we began poling the canoe across the field, rather like demented gondoliers. Exactly like them, in fact.

You can propel a light canoe across slick grass by putting the paddle in the ground in front of you, but at a backward angle, and pulling down on it fiercely, as if chinning yourself. Which sometimes happened: Either the canoe moved, or we found ourselves, so to speak, up the paddle without a creek. It was a new concept in wrong-headedness. One time the canoe slipped out from under me, and I was left hanging on my paddle, and had to walk back.

We expected the creek to resume, but it didn't. Once I actually climbed a tree looking for water, while Frank sat in the canoe. The Pepsis dwindled in number. We started to get tired, a rare state for a country boy. We rested and looked at the swamp grass glowing pale green as the sunlight began to come at it from a lower angle and the shadows of things got longer.

Finally we gave up. We seemed to be heading west and the next body of water might be the Mississippi. We consulted the sun to determine the time. No, we were unlikely to reach California by dinnertime.

We carried the canoe out through a nearby cow pasture and just got covered with ticks. They came to latch onto the cows, and brought all their sisters and granduncles and in-laws, and covered everything, like a speckled rug. I had never seen such robust ticks, or so much dry land.

Going Nuts At Soldier Of Fortune

I came into the weird mercenary vortex of *Soldier of Fortune* magazine when the phone rang in 1980. The voice on the other end was low and conspiratorial, the vocal cords sounding as if they had been ravaged by gargling gravel. Something in it whispered of far places and dark secrets too evil to be told.

"Hi, Fred, you asshole. I need a writer. Seventeen-five and bandages. Interested?"

I had been bumping at arm's length into Bob Brown, the eccentric Special Forces colonel who founded *SOF*, ever since the heady days of the fall of Saigon. Bored after Asia, he had started the magazine in 1975 with about $10,000 as an excuse to go to bush wars. The first press run of 8500 copies looked as if it had been mimeographed in his bathroom by poorly trained gibbons. The photos were badly enough exposed, the grammar wretched enough to give an impression of authenticity—a correct impression.

The first issue contained the famous photo of an African who had taken a 12-gauge blast just above the eyes—say "Ahhhh." Horror erupted. Across the nation, every pipe in the moral calliope began honking and blowing and, exactly as the old outlaw had expected, sales went straight up. This would become a pattern. Brown played the press like a piano.

"Hmm. Lemme think about it."

"OK. Ciao." Click.

I didn't think long. I was barely earning a living in Washington by free-lancing about the gray little men who run the world. A chance to be honestly shot seemed desirable by comparison. Life really hadn't amounted to much since Phnom Penh, and *Soldier of Fortune* had an appealing renegade reputation. What the hell; you only live once, and most people don't even do that. My wife and I packed the convertible.

Crossing the Beltway and setting sail through Maryland into West Virginia, I wondered what we were getting into—not that it really mattered as long as it was out of Washington. Was *SOF* what it purported to be? Was it really the professional journal of questionable adventurers with altered passports, of scarred men of unwholesome purpose who met in the reeking back alleys of Taipei? Of hired murderers who frequented bars in Bangkok where you could get venereal diseases unheard of since the 13th century? Or was it a clubhouse for aging soldiers trying to relive their youth? Or was it, as one fellow in Washington sniffed, "an exploitation rag catering to the down-demo extinction market?"

We crossed Kansas in the old Sixties blear-eyed, coffee-driven, unsleeping push and entered the People's Republic of Boulder, a lovely city of transplanted East Coasters who had gone West to escape the evils of Jersey and taken Jersey with them. *Soldier of Fortune* had its offices at 5735 Arapaho, in a park of egg-yolk-yellow warehouses where people made things like bowling trophies. I had expected a pile of skulls, barbed wire, a mine field or two and maybe a couple of prisoners staked to the earth to dry. Instead, I found a door with a small sign: STOP! BEFORE ENTERING, FILL OUT A CARD SAYING WHERE YOU WANT THE BODY SHIPPED. OTHERWISE, IT WILL BE USED FOR SCIENTIFIC PURPOSES.

Must be the place, I thought.

A suspicious—and good-looking—secretary answered the buzzer lock in shorts and running shoes and took me through the warren-like improvised offices to meet Brown. The walls were lined with pictures of commandos, guerrillas, and Foreign Legionnaires sweating over heavy machine guns in the deep Sahara. In an office, I glimpsed a short, weathered fellow who looked like Ernest Hemingway. Above him was a photo of a Vietnamese Ranger crossing a paddy, holding a severed human head by the hair. Yeah, I thought, this is the place.

I stepped into Bob's office, the Moon Room, and there he was in bush hat, camouflage shorts, and running shoes, with ugly hairy legs propped on the desk and a T-shirt that said HAPPINESS IS A CONFIRMED KILL. The office had previously belonged to a minor aerospace firm, and the walls were covered in a mural of the surface of the moon, a crater of which formed an improbable halo above Bob's head. A pair of H&K 91s—wicked West German rifles—leaned against the wall with night sights on them.

"Fred! How the fuck are you?" he bellowed, his only way of talking. Bob is deaf—artillery ears—and seems to figure that since he can't hear himself, nobody else can, either. Actually, when he talks in his normal voice, people in Los Angeles can hear him. He is also so absent-minded that he is lucky to remember who he is. (This brings out the maternal instinct in women. As a staffer put it, "I never know whether to salute him or burp him.")

"Sit down. Listen, I want you to brief me about some things in Washington." He didn't talk so much as bark. "This is close-hold, real sensitive, but we've got some stuff out of Afghanistan that's going to blow…Washington…open."

The "stuff out of Afghanistan" lay on his desk: shattered instrumentation from a Soviet MI-24 helicopter gunship downed, if memory serves, by Hassan Gailani's men and smuggled out through the Khyber Pass into Peshawar. Brown is always getting terribly important trash from odd places. A staffer once brought in an emptied Soviet PFM-1 antipersonnel mine—the butterfly-shaped kind they drop by thousands on the trails near the Pak border—by wrapping it in a plastic bag and telling Customs that it was a broken asthma inhaler. Anyhow, part of today's booty was a bright-red box, bashed up by the guerrillas in tearing it out of the wreck, with a 13-position switch labeled ominously in Russian.

"Probably the central weapons-control computer for the MI-24,"
Bob growled. "The intel agencies will pay a lot for this. We beat the
Agency hollow on this one. *Hehhehheh.*" Splash.

Bob splashes. He chews Skoal and spits into a water glass—sometimes, inadvertently, into other people's water glasses. You keep your
hand over your coffee cup.

Why, I wondered, was this den of caricatures selling more than
170,000 magazines a month at three dollars a copy?

Popular myth notwithstanding, there aren't any mercenaries today
in the accepted sense of the word: small bands of hired white men who
take over backward countries and fight real, if small, wars for pay. The
reason is that any nation, even a bush country consisting of only a
patch of jungle and a colonel, has an army too big for mercs to handle.
The pay is lousy, the world being full of bored former soldiers. Brown
himself is not a mercenary but an anti-Communist Peter Pan and, for
that matter, has never killed anybody (although he once shot an escaping Viet Cong in the foot.)

True, there are shadowy categories of men who might be called mercenaries, but the word is hard to pin down. Are the hit men and
cocaine pilots of South America mercs? Are the Americans who joined
the Rhodesian army and served with native Rhodesians? Men working
under contract for the CIA?

You do find a few men such as Eugene Hasenfus, recently shot
down flying cargo runs in Nicaragua. Pilots are in great demand as
mercs because, while training soldiers is fairly easy, even for backward
nations, flight training is harder. Finding out who these men really
work for is not easy: the employers tend to be curious corporations,
possibly but not provably owned by intelligence agencies.

So who reads this stuff? Marines, Rangers, and unhappy men,
mostly blue-collar, who are weary of the unimportance of their lives.
What the magazine sells is a hard-core smell, a dismal significance, a
view of life as a jungle where the brutal stand tall against the sunset and

the weak perish. *SOF* may be the only one-hand magazine whose readers hold a surplus-store bayonet in the other hand.

The magazine understands this and fosters it. The stories are mostly first-person accounts of scruffy little wars or how-to pieces on various techniques of murder but always with an undercurrent of approval and written in a low, throaty whisper as of old mercs talking shop. The classified ads in the back, for example: "Ex-Marine lieutenant requires hazardous employment overseas…." "Merc for hire. Anything, anywhere…." "Pyro supplies." "Young man seeks apprenticeship under master spook…." "Uzi accessories." "Merc will do anything, short-term, hi risk." "Laser weapons, invisible pain-field generators…." "Ex-platoon leader, dependable, aggressive, fearless…." "Night-vision scope." "Chemical lance." "Savant for hire, an expert on weapons and demo. Prefer Central America."

Usually these ads are nonsense. A journalist who once tried answering them found that most were placed by poseurs. A few are real. Dan Gearhart, a would-be merc killed in Angola in 1976, got his job through *Soldier of Fortune*. At this writing the magazine is being sued because some mercenaries placed ads ("Gun for hire") and, apparently, were hired to kill a law student at the University of Arkansas.

They botched the job, several times. Almost all mercs who get publicity prove to be clowns. The trade is notorious for attracting neurotics and cowboys and people who think they are James Bond. Being a merc is not a reasonable way to make money. You could do better managing a Burger Chef.

The intriguing thing is the glorification of unprincipled ruthlessness, not of killing per se but of sordid, anonymous killing. The readers do not imagine themselves as knights jousting for damsels in fair fight or as lawmen in Amarillo, facing the bad guy and saying, "Draw." They want to shoot the bad guy in the back of the head with a silenced Beretta. Brown had discovered antichivalry. There's a lot of it out there.

Yet, although the idea was brilliant, the magazine barely hangs together. Despite Brown's proven capacity for doing the impossible, as for example starting a magazine about mercenaries, he has a boundless talent for mismanagement. The staff stays in a state of turmoil and turnover, mistreats its writers and loses them, and barely gets issues to the printer, largely because Bob doesn't pay attention. He won't run the magazine himself, and won't hire a competent editor who will.

Although it may seem odd in a man who sneaks into Afghanistan the way most people go to McDonald's, he is too insecure to delegate authority, yet unwilling to stick around and exercise it himself. For example, at one point, Bob insisted on approving cover photos, but did not insist on being in the country when it was time to do the approving. Typically, everything would halt while frantic messages went out to the bush of Chad. The result made chaos seem obsessively organized.

Time and again, Bob would meet some drunk in a bar who wanted to write for *SOF*. "Oh, yeah, sure, sounds great. Send it to the editor. Terrific idea." Then he would forget to tell the editor and would go off to Thailand for a month, whereupon it would turn out that the guy couldn't write, and Brown couldn't remember what the assignment was, anyway, and the editor didn't know what the hell was happening. Any adventurer with a good line of bull can con Bob out of air fares to distant places and live well for months at his expense until somebody finally figures out that the magazine is being taken for a ride.

Bob doesn't really read *SOF*. He once told me, "Hey, Fred, I really liked that Spectre gunship story you did. We could use some more like that." The story had been published a year before.

Bob misses appointments. He doesn't answer his mail—not surprising, because he doesn't read it. Mail requires decisions and he can't make decisions, preferring to put them off until the problems go away. Sometimes they don't. If the office were burning down, Bob would want to think about the fire for a few days before putting it out. ("Yeah," he would say in that hard mercenary voice, eyeing the flames.

"I don't want to be hasty. Let's kick it around in our heads for a while, see what comes out.")

As I stood looking into that crafty face pocked by shrapnel wounds, lined by many wars, some of which Bob has been to, I began to recognize the horrible truth. *SOF* is not phony exactly—the staff members really do the things they say the do—but neither is any of it exactly real. The magazine is a playground for half-assed adventurers, and Brown was having fun, that was all. I had come to work in Colonel Kangaroo's Paramilitary Theme Park: Step right up, hit the Kewpie doll with a throwing knife and win an Oriental garrote, just the thing for taking out those troublesome sentries. Cotton candy at the next booth—in camouflage colors, of course—and....That was the key to understanding *SOF*—realizing that Bob is not in the business of putting out a magazine. He is in the business of being Bob. He likes being the international mercenary publisher, likes playing Terry and the Pirates, and the magazine is just a justification. Trying to understand *SOF* as journalism merely leads to confusion.

This explains the odd pointlessness of most of what the man does. For example, take the time he and the green creepers sneaked into Laos to see the anti-Communist brigands. In bush wars, they're all bandits, so you choose which bandits will be your bandits. It was a short trip, barely across the border. All that came out of it was photos of the rebel village with a huge satin *SOF* flag (DEATH TO TYRANTS) floating over it—silliest goddamn thing I ever saw. They really went, but it really didn't matter.

The mystery is how anyone as inept as Bob can survive while doing the things he does. In the Special Forces, he was known as Boo-Boo Brown because he couldn't get a drink of water without breaking his leg, losing his wallet, or setting off NORAD alarms. It's hard being a deaf commando with no memory. Bob once left an open bag full of cash in an airport in Bangkok—just forgot it, the way normal people forget a paperback book. Many who know him think he really needs a mother, or a keeper, and the incident suggested that he may have an invisible cosmic sponsor: The money was still there when someone went back for it, which is impossible in Bangkok.

He thrives on conspiracies, but most of them do not quite exist beyond the confines of his skull. I once spent three hours in a hotel suite while he and his ambient maniacs discussed some minor bit of information, so trivial that I can't remember it, whose revelation they thought would prevent the re-election of Jimmy Carter. But you can't blame Bob for not having much idea how the real world works. He has never lived there.

Neither he nor *SOF* can even begin to keep a secret, unfortunate in a man whose hobby is conspiring. I have seen him begin a plot to overthrow a scary foreign intelligence agency by inviting 13 people, including several strangers, into his office to talk about it. The magazine once taped some telephone conversations with me, neglecting to tell me that it was doing so. The editor then sent the transcripts to Thailand, where they ended up in the hands of a buddy of mine who was running cross-border operations into Laos—this was the attempt by Bo Gritz to free some POWs believed to be there. When my friend came back to the States, the FBI photocopied the transcripts.

Bob is the Great Communicator, a sort of one-man CBS.

If, as someone said, the intelligent man adapts himself to the world, but the genius adapts the world to himself, Bob is a genius, living in a world he has built to his own specs. A fantasy world, yes, but Bob knows where reality begins, and usually stops short of getting into trouble. He is crazy by choice, when it suits him—the world's oldest and most successful kid of eleven, with the kid's tribal mentality, deeply loyal to his adventuring buddies but to no one else, playing games in Uncle Bob's sandbox, which happens to be the world. I remember his lying with his head in the lap of his wise and patient girlfriend, Mary, when someone brought up the subject of railroad trains. "I've always wanted to be an engineer," Bob said, looking off into some interior distance. "Maybe I can buy a train. Can I buy a train, Mary?"

"You always want to be everything," Mary said. She understands him.

Mary stays with the old rogue (this is going to be the only real breach of confidence I will commit in this article, for which Bob is likely to have a brigade of assassins come after me) because he is a nice guy. I once asked one of his best friends, who are very few, how vicious Bob really was.

"Well, if you insulted his ancestors, poured beer on his head, and swindled him out of the magazine," the guy said thoughtfully, "Bob might punch you out."

For a few days, my job was to edit the usual nutcake stories for publication, mostly human interest stuff. There was one about how to weld razor blades to the bottom of your car so that a crowd trying to turn it over would have their fingers cut off, and another explaining three handy ways to make napalm with gasoline and simple soap flakes. Most of the staff—smart, funny people—knew the whole business was madness and enjoyed it. A few thought it was real.

The working-level lunacy was plentiful. For example, glancing into red fire-extinguisher boxes, I found loaded 12-gauge riot guns with the safeties off. It seems that the SDS at the University of Colorado had threatened to storm the office, a catastrophically bad idea. You should never storm a den of armed paranoiacs when there is no back door, especially when the paranoiacs have the firepower of a Central American army.

I heard about the SDS threat from Craig Nunn, the art director, a former Special Forces sergeant and street fighter out of Chicago with equal affinities for Bach and blood. To listen to the Brandenburgs, Craig always wore headphones on a long cord in the art room. He looked like a deranged pilot flying an easel. Speaking of the attack by the SDS, he said with subdued longing, the wistfulness of a man who hasn't shot anybody since lunch, "I think they should attack if they believe in it. God, hard times and body bags. I'd like that better than bubble gum."

The assault didn't take place. A local motorcycle association, allies of *SOF*, walked through campus in field dress—scars, missing teeth, gloves with fishhooks on the knuckles, IQs dragging low around their ankles like skivvies at the dip. They announced that if any Commie pervert bothered *SOF*, which was a righteous and patriotic magazine, the bikers would break his arms in 14 places before getting down to detail work. One remark in particular—"Honey, you got pretty eyes. I'm gonna put'em in my pocket"—is said to have directed revolutionary fervor into other channels.

One day I was sitting in the office with Harry, a hulking rightwinger who worried a lot about the Trilateralists. Oddly enough, most of the staffers were liberals. Harry was a prop. (I divided people who hung around the magazine into workers and stage props, the latter being those who twitched, usually couldn't spell, and arrived in the middle of the night. The workers, mostly women, put out the magazine.) A glass wall separated the secretary from Harry's office, where he spent the day roaring and fuming like a volcano. His office was stuffed with guns, one specifically for fending off the SDS.

"Look at the bullets," he said. I did. Green plastic.

"Hollow. Filled with oil and tiny buckshot. They kill but don't penetrate glass. If a left-wing shit-head comes in and I miss him, I won't kill the secretary."

Harry was ever a gentleman.

After much negotiating, we got a Russian language expert from the university to come translate the writing in the red weapons-control computer. She was a tall, horsy lady, obviously unsettled by being in the lair of these horrible killers. We all sat around expectantly, awaiting an intelligence coup of a high order. It looked like a Big Deal. The MI-24 gunship was largely a mystery in the West. The translator picked up the red box and read, with solemn emphasis:

"In case of fire, break glass."

It *was* a fire-control computer, sort of. Oh, well.

Harry, the savior of secretaries, was strange, but he wasn't alone. The staff crawled with real lulus. There was Derek, a brilliant fellow who had been in a spook outfit in Nam (S.O.G., Studies and Observation Group, death-in-the-weeds people. Those in it are called Soggies.) Derek talked to Saint Michael, the patron saint of warriors, and Saint Mike answered. You would be driving along with the guy and he would say, "Mumblemumble, Saint Michael, mumblemumble," with his eyes rolled skyward, and you would say, "Ah, er, nice day, huh, Derek?" "Mumble...yes, quite true, thank you, we are blessed, mumble mumble, Saint Michael...." Vietnam is a hot, sunny place, and maybe there weren't enough hats to go around.

At nine p.m. at the Scottsdale Hilton Resort and Spa, under the puzzled skies of Arizona, the annual *Soldier of Fortune* convention flowed in full throbbing lunacy. The locals were upset: You could see it in their eyes. Across the city, police were alert, parents no doubt sitting up with .22 rifles and the family spaniel to guard their daughters. After all, *Soldier of Fortune* reeked of mutilated bodies in Oriental hotel rooms. It was the trade journal of lurching men with knife scars across their faces and faint German accents. One expected terrible things from it.

And got them. Sort of.

On the parking lot, lit by strategically placed headlights, several hundred conventioneers in jungle cammies gathered to watch Dave Miller, a tiny, fierce martial artist, pull a pick-up truck by a line tied to spikes through his biceps. The conventioneers, by and large, were the biggest collection of hopeless dingdongs ever to trouble this weary earth—twerps, grocery clerks with weak egos, various human hamsters come to look deadly in jump boots, remember wars they weren't in and, for a weekend, be of one blood with Sergeant Rock and his Merry Psychos.

On the tarmac was a cluster of shave-headed Huns, martial dwarfs, and minor assassins—the staff. The hamsters watched, agog. The conductor of this mad symphony was John Donovan, a muscular 270-

pound skin-headed ex-Special Forces major who, it was rumored, manually broke up motorcycle gangs for a hobby. Miller stood with his arms upraised for the spikes, which were actually sharpened bicycle spokes. Nobody asked why he was going to do this. It would have been a hard question to answer. The crowd wanted deeds of desperation and sordid grit, not intelligence. An Oriental guy—of course—swabbed Miller's arms with alcohol.

That afternoon, I had gone with Dave to get the necessary paraphernalia. Dave was the kind of little man who figured that if he couldn't be big, he could be bad and went at it systematically: the Army, Ranger School, Pathfinder School, Vietnam, a dozen martial arts with names like Korean breakfast cereals, knife fighting, all the trinkets. *SOF* attracts large, tottery egos. Dave and I got along. He explained that you couldn't use rope to pull the truck because it stretched, and somehow tore the muscles. You needed fabric. So we sent to a fabric boutique, where the nicest young man, appalled, asked, "What do you gentlemen need?"

Counseling, I thought.

There we were, in worn tiger stripes and jungle boots, bush-hatted, with vicious specialty knives hanging on our hips, all sorts of commando badges and paramilitary nonsense stuck to us. We looked like stamp collections.

"We'd like to see some cloth."

He brought us a hank, or whatever you call it, of lavender-flowered stuff, whereupon Dave told me to hold one end and, unrolling 20 feet, began violently pulling on the other end like a frantic badger to see whether it would stretch. The nice young man nearly went crazy.

Back on the parking lot, the Oriental pushed two bicycle spokes through Dave's flesh ("Oooooh! Ooooooh!" moaned the hamsters) and connected the cloth to the bumper. Meanwhile, a twist had been added. The truck was on boards like rails so that it would roll across some guy's stomach to show how tough he was.

Miller went "Unngh!...Unngh!" and pulled like hell. The truck...yes...no...yes...rolled slowly onto the guy's stomach, and stopped there. Miller had guts but no mass. The guy under the truck was real unhappy. Nobody had said anything about parking the goddam thing on him. He hollered in a rising scream, "*Oaaghgettitoffgetit-offgetitoff!*" and Miller tried ("Ungh! Ungh!") Nothing.

Donovan the Man Mountain walked over, gave the tail gate a little tap, and the truck shot off the guy like a squeezed watermelon seed.

Not everyone took this stuff seriously. At the first convention, in Columbia, Missouri, I and the usual bunch of camouflaged impostors had walked downtown one night in search of a bar. A college girl, not too impressed, asked, "Why are you wearing that silly stuff?"

"It's camouflage," I said, "so we'll be invisible."

"Oh," she said. "I thought you were a potted plant."

One day I went to work and saw someone looking at a peculiar piece of wreckage. More stuff from Uncle Daffy's Used Helicopter Lot? No. It was a Nikon, shattered in a way that didn't make obvious sense. A piece of leather had been driven into the lens barrel and stopped where the mirror usually is.

Brown had gone to Rhodesia and left his camera bag in a shop, which you don't do in times of terrorism. The shopkeeper, reasonably enough, had called the bomb squad. Those gentlemen had tied a long rope to the strap, pulled the bag carefully into the street, wrapped it in det cord—TNT rope, sort of—and blown hell out of Bob's camera. He now owned the only Nikon in the world with the case on the inside.

For a while, Brown espoused survivalism. Survivalists are the folk who dream of burrowing into Utah with radiation suits and submachine guns, awaiting nuclear holocaust. They do not so much fear an atomic war as hope for one, so that they can Survive It, making them the only people on earth with a vested interest in nuclear war. There are entire colonies of these squirrels out West, filling their basements with beans packed in carbon dioxide and arming themselves.

Brown briefly put out a magazine called Survive, which didn't. It folded partly because of amateurish management and partly because survivalists are too paranoid to let their addresses go on a mailing list. Survive croaked early, remembered chiefly for its cover photo of a cow in a gas mask.

Anyway, Bob decided to build a survival shelter. He duly found some land, and had a phenomenally expensive bunker started. He did this with his patented tight secrecy, which meant that everybody in Boulder was talking about it—except to Bob, because people knew he wanted it to be secret. He began choosing people who would go into it and survive while everybody else bubbled into grease and flowed away in the gutters. He approached those elect (I wasn't one) and said approximately, "Are you saved?" Then he told them about Bob's Box. Someone calculated that six times as many were saved as would fit into the shelter.

Unfortunately, it seems that the floor had been badly poured. Water leaked in. And it turned out that the water was alkaline. Bob was the only survivalist in America whose survival shelter contained six inches of poisoned water.

Colonel Kangaroo and his madmen were once playing war in El Salvador. (War in Central America is great for Soldier of Fortune because there isn't any jet lag.) They were out drinking one night with one of the Salvadoran battalions, and things were getting woozy and intimate. SOF wasn't viewed as foreign press; it was part of the war effort, so its reporters got to go places which other reporters never saw. Pretty soon it was amigo this and amigo that, with all the intense comradeship of a war zone, and the wiry brown captain said to someone whom I will call Bosworth, "Come, amigo, I show you something very dear."

The captain proudly flung open a long blue cabinet, revealing row after row of preserved skulls. It seemed that the battalion contained a lot of Indians who hadn't lost their folkways—taking heads, for example. The captain grinned like a child showing his rock collection. Bosworth was charmed: This was the kind of thing he could appreciate. Why, the skulls even had painted on them the names of their former occupants. "Wonderful!" Bosworth said, warmth overwelling in him.

"You like?" said the captain. "I give you!" Whereupon he handed Bosworth a pair of gaping beauties.

So Bosworth went back to the party holding Pancho and Jose in his hands and announced that he was not to be parted from the skulls. He meant to go through life with them. Brown, no fool, stared with an "Oh, shit" expression, foreseeing problems in the afterlife. Customs, for example. ("These? Oh, I found them. No, nobody was in them.") How do you get human skulls into the US?

Finally someone came up with an idea. They mailed them to Bosworth with a note, "This is what happens to you if you come back to our country. !Viva la revolution! Partido Comunista."

I once went to Powder Springs, Georgia, to cover Mitch WerBell's Cobray school of counterterrorism for the magazine. WerBell, who died in 1983, was a legend in the mercenary racket, a veteran of obscure wars back when there really were mercenaries, and he had retired to a small palatial mansion.

Cobray purported to teach the death-dealing arts to professionals (who, in fact, would already know them.) For several thousand dollars, the student got a week or so of training in the arcana of the new anti-chivalry. The instructors were real, but the courses weren't, which didn't matter at all to the students. In the morning, they got Introduction to Small Arms ("The bullet comes out of this little hole here. Point it somewhere else.") In the afternoon, they got Advanced Small Arms and Sniping. Subjects like these take months of study.

So I landed and was met by a former SF colonel and went to watch the classes. Among the students were a podiatrist from Miami, God help us, and his wife and two bratty teenage daughters.

I saw what had happened. Too many years of serenity and other people's feet had gotten to him. He, like the readers, wanted a taste of dark, adrenal-soaked desperation before arthritis set in—his quarter hour with mortar flares flickering in low-lying clouds like the face of God and the nervous click of safeties coming off along the wire, pokketa pokketa. So here he was, $12,000 poorer, with a tolerant wife and bored kids in Calvin Klein jeans, learning Night Patrolling. Women put up with a lot.

When I got there, Footman and the Powder Puffs had already studied Hand-to-Hand Death Dealing. The instructor, Marvin Tao, had told Footman that he had an unusually good radish position, or some such Oriental-sounding thing. This consisted of standing sort of knock-kneed and pigeon-toed, while turning the palms out and bending forward. Marvin couldn't have been serious. Anyway, Footman was charmed, because here was something he could do. A genuine Martial Artist from Hong Kong said so. So every time I turned around, there he was—bent over, pigeon-toed and grunting dangerously.

All this yo-yo needs, I thought, is a string.

Three a.m. at the *Solder of Fortune* convention in Scottsdale. Most of the conventioneers had turned in. Brown and a few cronies sat by the blue glow of the pool, drinking and telling war stories. "Remember that hooker with three thumbs in Siem Riep?...." "So Barrow stood on a moving tank at Pleiku and shot at a dog with an AK. Fell on his head, tried to get disability...." "What ever happened to Jag Morris? I heard he got it in the head north of Au Phuc Dup...." Adventurers at least have stories to tell.

Green smoke was pouring out of one window and somebody was getting ready to rappel from another. I said, "To hell with it," and turned in. A muffled thumping meant the Brown was firing his .45 underwater.

A bit later, I woke up. Derek was handing me an FN rifle. "Found it," he said, and walked off, talking to Saint Michael. I curled around it and went to sleep. It made as much sense as anything else.

Why Mama Doan' 'Low No Self-Esteem 'Roun Heah

If I hear anyone say "self-esteem" again, I'm gonna get my duck gun. What I figure is, we'll catch all the varmints that talk about self-esteem—those pale radishy psychotherapists and feeble-minded educators and enormous talk-show ladies who look like slabs of fatback, only a scientist spilled radiation on it and it sprouted legs. Then we'll get one of those medieval catapults, the kind that can chuck a ton for a mile. I reckon Oprah would carry at least twenty feet. We'll fill it with the varmints. Then we'll put it next to an alligator swamp and invite all the duck hunters, and holler, "*Pu-ll-llllllllllllll!*" What the duck hunters missed, the gators wouldn't.

Then we'd go for beer and ribs.

This self-esteem business has gotten out of hand. Turn on the TV, if you don't have better sense, and you'll probably get some gal talking about how her self-esteem has gone rancid, and has warts on it, and maybe sags where it shouldn't so she's thinking about an implant.

Usually it's a woman. Men doubt themselves, but they respond differently. When a man gets to feeling sorry for himself he drinks himself into a stupor. If he really means it, he loses his job and ends up living under a bench. He may get into bar fights. Maybe he'll just get moody and sulk or inflict a short-man's complex on everybody. But he won't tell Oprah how pitiful he is on national television. He doesn't want anyone to know.

Now, there are reasons for low self-esteem. If you've started a war, for instance, or burned down an orphanage for the insurance and forgot to take the orphans out first, or you're a televangelist and got old people to send you their savings so now they're living in cardboard boxes and eating Vienna sausages. Do the rascals who do these things feel bad about themselves?

No. They're happy as bugs on a picnic sandwich.

The folk with low self-esteem are perfectly good people who can't get dates. (An awful lot of this self-esteem stuff seems to boil down to exactly that.) Or maybe they had unhappy childhoods (who didn't?) or didn't get as far in life as they had hoped to (who does?). At bottom they've got a case of ordinary life, which ain't all collard greens and ham hocks. They don't need low self-esteem. There's nothing wrong with them.

Maybe the reason they have low self-esteem is that people think television is real. If you lived in a small town with no TV, you'd know that everybody was tolerably miserable—the banker was a drunk, the preacher cheated, the mayor and his wife hated each other.

But the fantasy box tells you that the world is chiefly populated by glamorous hunks and gorgeous babes. They live like James Bond and don't have problems. Maybe guys watch this stuff and start thinking, "Geez, I don't have a Maserati, I've never been in a gunfight with international drug lords, and I'm the only man in America who hasn't married Elizabeth Taylor. Oh, how I've failed."

How many of us would worry about self-esteem if the box didn't tell us we were supposed to? Personally, I don't know whether I have any. Further, I don't care. If *I'm* not interested in my self-esteem, I can't imagine why anyone else would be. I've just got other things to do. Honky Tonk Confidential, my favorite bar band, is playing at Whitey's next week. And I've got a new Glock in .45 ACP that I want to shoot.

Now, the way I figure it, if I went to a therapist lady to get my self-esteem checked, and found out I was a quart low, I'd still have the Glock and I'd still want to go to Whitey's. On the other hand, what if she told me I had splendid self-esteem—triple-chromed, with low cholesterol and a good credit rating—I'd still want to go to Whitey's, etc.

Suppose I found that I was nothing special? Just a semi-bald Presbyterian in a cowboy hat? Or that movie starlets were not lining up at my door in wild desperate hopes of carnal knowledge?

I'm used to it.

The whole business gets worse. It isn't just adults. The dumb lobby uses self-esteem as another excuse for making children into whimpering robotic imbeciles. I keep hearing about how teachers want to stop giving kids grades so as not to hurt their self-concept. It's nuts. The schools won't teach the white kids to spell, or the black kids to speak English, because being corrected might embarrass them. Really.

Maybe I'm just a country boy, and don't understand things like I ought. But I have to wonder: Who is going to have the most self-esteem? A baffled semi-literate who reads four years below grade level and isn't sure what country he lives in? Or a high-school grad who reads fluently and has the self-respect that goes with it?

I guess I'm missing something.

It looks as if whimpering is replacing doing. Used to be, a stripling kid might have all manner of doubts about his manhood. So he'd join the Army and become a paratrooper. He'd leap out of airplanes and run seventy miles with a 1200 pound pack, uphill, in a snowstorm. Backwards. That's what paratroopers do. They don't have any better sense, which is why they're good people.

Today the kid would be sneered at, by people frightened of a dark night in suburbia, because he had something to prove. That's exactly what he had. And he proved it. It works. Afterwards he doesn't have to worry about what he's made of. He knows.

Herewith a radical theory, copyright me and trademarked to the gills. It could put therapists out of work. (If the alligators miss any. I'm only going to use alert alligators.) It might restore learning to the schools, grow hair on bald men and eliminate cellulite. This is it: If you want to respect yourself, do something you will respect yourself for doing.

How's that for forty-weight insight? You could lube a diesel with it.

The Attitudes Of Blacks

The letters from blacks come in dribs and drabs to my mailbox, not many, but several a week. They vary. Most are in ordinary English. A few carry the characteristic odd grammar of uneducated blacks. Most are civil. Many are virulent in their hostility to me, understandable given my expressed distaste for racial preferences.

I try to put them together, to piece together from them a picture of black America. It works poorly, of course. My mail isn't a representative sample of blacks. Those who write are those who use computers and, at least occasionally, read Internet columns. That's part of black America, but only part. I don't hear from the projects of South Chicago. What people say in letters to columnists is not always what they say to friends while sitting around the kitchen table.

Yet themes recur. The commonest, not always present but nearly so, is a profound sense of having been wronged by whites, and a corresponding expectation of being given things in return. This isn't news. The intensity of belief, the hermetic impermeability to reason, the apparently implacable anger, are arresting. Whatever is wrong in their lives, whatever woes and miseries they bear—these are the fault of whites. "You people tore us from our homeland and African civilization...."

They regularly ascribe to whites a desire to control blacks, to oppress them, to keep them poor, to deny them education. Drugs in black neighborhoods are a white plot to destroy blacks. I think they really believe it.

Oddly, they seem to define themselves by the sense of abuse, to cherish it, to want to protect it against skepticism. They seem to *like* being angry.

The attitude as I encounter it is usually emotional, at best dimly lit by study, and informed by little familiarity with either history or geography. The oft-invoked attachment to Africa, for example, is unaccompanied by knowledge of the continent. If asked to name the African countries whose capitals are Sulawesi, Patong, and Catarrh, they couldn't. Nor do they care: Since books are readily available, the lack of knowledge implies a lack of interest.

The impression given is of angry people who, in isolation from historical reality, weave a world that isn't there and then live in it. I sense (for what that's worth) a deep discomfort with the values and ways of whites, and a consequent desire to construct a mental universe with explanatory power, as well as power to keep whites at a distance. Part of this world is the frequent assertion that the Greeks were black, that the Egyptians were black, that Beethoven was black, that Jesus was black.

When beliefs become crucial to one's understanding of one's place in the world, they lose all susceptibility to reason. Little point exists in arguing to a Jesuit that the Vatican is merely a collection of buildings, or to a Mohammedan that Shiva is God, or to an evolutionist that much of what he believes doesn't make sense. All of them can, or could, understand the argument. None of them can afford to.

So, I think, with blacks. The sense of grievance, of being owed, seems as central to their notion of the world as God was to Bernard of Clairvaux. Grievance is not a condition but an identity. Without it they would be unsure who they were, and might have to look within for explanations of their problems. And so they protect the grievance, shield it from thought, cherish it as others cherish their children.

This explains the vast chasm that yawns between so many whites and the black mainstream. When blacks demand reparations, a white, acting in the European tradition of logic and analysis, is likely to point that he has never owned slaves, that blacks under 135 years of age have never been slaves, that he supported the civil rights movement of the Sixties, that his ancestors arrived in the US in 1923 from Poland.

He thinks these objections are telling. None of them makes the slightest impression on blacks, whose engagement with the matter appears to be chiefly emotional. They can't look at their position rationally because it doesn't hold together rationally, and would threaten the sense of grievance.

In the background of all of this lies a tendency to think of people in groups, instead of as a collection of individuals. The distinction, coextensive with the fault line between conventional Left and Right, runs through much of politics. For example, conservatives routinely believe that advancement should depend on individual merit, while liberals believe that it should depend on membership in political groups. As Marxism yearns for class warfare between moiling faceless masses, individualism thinks of Marlboro Man tall against the Wyoming sky, alone and self-reliant. The two currents are age-old.

Blacks do not seem to me to be at all Marxist, and in fact do not fit well into the political categories devised by whites. But they do fall on the group-oriented side of the philosophical divide.

Thus blacks as I encounter them appear to regard whites as one large organism, having a lifespan of thousands of years and collectively responsible for all things bad that any of its component particles have done. If Fernando Vasquez of Barcelona was in 1567 a slave trader, then I owe blacks reparations. (That Fernando bought his slaves from other blacks never, ever registers with a black.)

If I told a black man that he was responsible for the atrocities of Idi Amin, because Amin was black, and that the black man therefore owed reparations to Amin's victims, he would regard me as crazy. It would be a reasonable view. But the same black man will quite seriously believe that I owe him reparations for something somebody else did to somebody else long before either of us was born. The illogic means nothing.

Everything is always someone else's fault. I encounter an absolute, unbreachable refusal to concede that they might in any way, however slight, have contributed to their own difficulties. Protecting the sense of grievance seems to take precedence over all else, going beyond the tendency common in argument to fortify one's position somewhat beyond the facts. It seems a desperately held, essential tenet of life.

The reliance on grievance as a universally applicable explanation does not of necessity prevent advancement: One might respond with furious effort to excel the supposed oppressors. ("I'll show them.") But the belief that everything in life is determined by white racists implies that nothing is determined by blacks. Passivity and dependency, I think, result. These haven't entirely crippled blacks, who are indeed making progress, but that progress is slower than it need be.

Tolerating Europeans, Barely

I 'm baffled all to flinders. It happens a lot in West Virginia. (Though actually I'm not sure what a flinder is.) Recessive genes cause it. They flock here, like they were swallows and thought Bluefield was Capistrano, and make it hard for us to understand foolishness. Or Europeans.

On the lobotomy box the other night I found a French gal whooping like a pipe organ about how the United States wasn't Politically Mature like Europe. She obviously regarded Americans as dull-witted rustics ripening in the bumpkin patch. (I didn't mean to say that. The little voices made me do it.) See, she implied vigorously, Americans are inferior to Europeans. We need to grow up, and get some home-training, and learn to tie our shoes, if we have any. Then we'd be civilized and mature, like Yugoslavia.

I watched this moralizing basilisk with a single thought resonating in my mind: Birdshot.

Now, when Europeans get full of themselves, which is any time they're awake, they do it differently, according to whatever odd little country they come from. Brits stand stiff and haughty, like they were hoping for an attack of nobility, or maybe had fused vertebrae, and look solemn as an undertaker with a pair of deuces. The French throw their heads way back like a pitcher winding up for a fast ball and then sight down their noses. That's why the front end of a Concorde looks the way it does.

"You're such a young country," she sniffed. "Europe has been in existence for 2000 years."

And still can't do anything right.

They're *proud?* If they had any self-respect, they'd wear ski masks, and carry their passports in plain brown wrappers marked, "Sex Books." But Europeans are always trying to one-up each other about how ancient they are. Most rocks and any trilobite put them to shame, but they don't notice.

Anyway, let me tell you about America and maturity.

It was about 1776. Tom Jefferson and Ben Franklin and some of the other Foundling Fathers were at Tom's house, drinking bourbon and branch water and playing poker. Tom had a terrible hand and wanted to get out without losing his ante. He sat bolt upright, and said, "Hey! I got an idea!"

Ben Franklin, who was a smart-ass, said, "Treat it kindly. It's in a strange place."

Tom didn't notice. He hollered, "Let's run the Brits off and start a boringly stable democracy that'll run like clockwork and be the envy of the world and take over most of it and invent rock-and-roll and the Internet. Then we can download Pink Floyd on Napster. Is that a plan, or what?"

Everybody looked stunned for a moment. The very magnitude of the idea made it hard to digest, and anyway they been at the bourbon for a while. Then John Hancock said, "Hooo *–eeeeeeee!*" and Ben hollered ""Oh, *baby!*" and they went to get their duck guns and look for Brits. Tom slipped his cards into the deck and shuffled it while they were gone.

That's how America started.

Once the idea grabbed hold of them, they went at it like sled dogs. They wanted the new country to be different from Europe, because the mature Europeans were big on torture chambers and witch burnings and oubliettes and hanging in chains and other features of advanced civilization.

The new country flourished like smallpox in a slum and got rich and was so boringly stable that people had to turn to inventing things instead of having revolutions. The US *was* boring. Generally speaking, if an American went to bed Wednesday, he woke up Thursday with the same government. The country never had a coup, or even an attempted coup, though there was that brigand Lincoln and the tax revolt of 1861. This stability caused astonishment in Italy, where they measure government in rpms. Americans do political polls. The Italians have a tachometer.

Boring stability is maturity. The absolute best kind. Forty-weight.

By contrast, since 1900 alone Europe has started two world wars, not to mention the Spanish Civil War that inflicted Hemingway on the world, and given us both fascism and communism, the two worst ideas the race had ever had except for the designated-hitter rule, and a crop of scrofulous dictators that would embarrass a big-city bus station at three a.m.: Salazar, Horthy, Hitler, Stalin, Mussolini, Honecker, Ceausescu, the Greek colonels, Franco, Kaiser Bill, Tito.

Right now the Yugoslavs butcher each other with vivacity reminiscent of a Burundian soccer match. Maybe they figure it will raise property values.

I don't guess the US is ready for maturity. We don't have enough body bags.

Europe never changes. When they get in a war they can't handle, which is any war, they always come squalling to us like little boys who got kicked on the playground. They want us to be their mother. We have to save them from themselves. Particularly the French.

You do have to concede to the French their place in military history: As warriors, the French have always made splendid pastry chefs. A French war begins with a retreat on Paris, followed by a scream for help, usually American, and four years of peaceful collaboration. They're the only country I know of that has a stack of surrender documents addressed To Whom It May Concern. I've seen fiercer geese.

And they always want us to save them. How splendidly adult.

After 1776 the French watched America for a while. They scratched and looked down their noses and peered wisely off into space and decided that they wanted a boring democracy too. Of course they persuaded themselves that it was their idea all along. So they tried to have a revolution, which they started by attacking a jail. It wouldn't have been the first thing to come to my mind, though I guess it was some better than a men's room.

Thing was, they couldn't tell a revolution from a bloodbath. After cutting each others' heads off for a while they ended up with, yep, a dictatorship, which is embarrassing when you're looking for a democracy. Then that squatty little Corsican, the French Fuehrer, actually won some wars using French troops, showing that they can fight when led by foreigners.

Finally they brought the kings back! They were exactly where they started, but mostly dead. I guess if that's maturity, adolescence must have been a bear.

Now I grant you we're not real smart up the holler in West Virginia, and not too sophisticated. You can't buy *je ne sais quois* at the country store, or if you did it would probably be stale with ants in it. But I've got sense enough that if my history was an unremitting tale of catastrophe, mayhem, and misjudgment, I believe I'd talk about something else.

Blowing Up At Dulles

I wish somebody would invent a transporter, the kind those humorless drones on Startrek use. Or find a way to get to Puerto Rico by dog sled. These days, air travel makes me look longingly at Greyhound buses. It makes me look longingly at being dragged behind a motorcycle.

Now, let me tell you how it used to be to ride in an airplane. And no, I'm not imagining the past as a roseate time when everything was better and Elvis ruled the earth. Lots of things weren't better. The advantages of polio were limited. Dentistry was at a Cambodian level. But air travel was lots pleasanter. How it worked:

You walked out and got on the airplane.

That was all.

No magnetometers, weird beeping gateways, x-ray machines, occasionally surly functionally illiterate third-world affirmative-action prison guards to fumble through your baggage, no nitrate sniffers, no putting your cell phone, change, belt buckle, and fillings in a little plastic basket.

I got to Dulles about three hours early for a flight to Puerto Rico and St. Maarten, knowing that these days anything can screw up, and carrying six hundred pounds of scuba gear and a duffel bag full of tee-shirts and a wet-suit top. Equipment is important in diving. It's a buckle sport, like rock climbing or jumping out of airplanes. Women dive because they enjoy looking at fish. Men don't care about fish. They just want to snap lots of complicated parts together.

Intimidating warnings echoed hollowly from the loudspeakers about being blown up. Like everybody else, I screened it out. I expect to be blown up, take it in my stride. Usually the announcements say, over and over, that if you park your car unattended for a nanosecond, it will be towed away and given to a bomb-disposal unit to be blown up. Oh well. It was just a BMW. Another one says don't put your bags down and go to the john, or they'll be given to the bomb-disposal unit and blown up.

Then there's the one saying that disagreeable panhandling cultists are not sponsored by the airport. Why, I wondered, doesn't the bomb-disposal unit take *them* out and blow them up? That would be useful. But no. The Supreme Court says we have to put up with the larcenous little snits, because they are Expressing Themselves.

How did we get here? To the Fear State, I mean? How many of us notice that we *are* here? (Maybe lots: I don't claim exclusive recognition of the obvious.) We're turning into an anti-terror society. I can't go to my bank now without having my ID checked pointlessly by an inattentive minimum-wage rentaguard as I come in the door.

Next I waited forever in a long line of people resignedly kicking their baggage in front of them to get to the American counter. A bright eighth-grader could probably come up with a faster way to check people in, but never mind. The American lady was perfectly agreeable—many people in airports are, actually—and asked me had anyone given me anything to carry, etc. Translated, this meant, "Are you carrying a powerful bomb or a cleverly fabricated dispenser of nerve gas without knowing it?" Which of course made me think that if I wasn't, somebody else must be. Oh good.

Off I went to the security gate, staggering under the six hundred pounds of scuba gear. You can't check two grand of dive toys because they'll be stolen. They'll be stolen because (a) if morality were oil, this country would be a couple of quarts low, and (b) disciplining crooked baggage handlers would be ethnic discrimination. (Finns. Those wretches. They'll steal anything. I'll bet that's what you were thinking.)

I was walking carefully in hopes that my pants wouldn't actually fall off. I'm serious. My belt buckle always sets off the weird beeping gateway, so I had it in my bag, along with change, watch, and keys. Otherwise I'd have to stand with my arms out as if I had a crucifixion fetish while I got wanded down to see whether I had illegal nail clippers with me. (I picture myself grabbing a stew and hollering at the pilot, "Give me this bird, big boy, or so help me *I'll clip her nails.*")

Things could have been worse. If I'd had a metal plate in my skull, I'd have had to take it out.

The security folk have two new tricks at security gates. One is to make you take your shoes off so they can stick them in an explosives-sniffer or x-ray whazzit. I can't exactly blame them. Some idiot did get on a plane with explosive shoes. OK. But I'm waiting for a woman to be caught with a bra full of Semtex, or a guy with an exploding jock-strap. (If I were a terrorist, personally I'd go with the nail clippers, but I'm squeamish.) After that, hooboy, we'll have some really great searches. Stick around.

I was wearing tropical flipflops precisely to avoid being foot-searched: See? Just toes, no sticks of dynamite, no wires, timers, gre-nades. It didn't work. They still de-shod me and stuck the things in some unfortunate machine.

The other trick is random searches, which tends to mean me. Maybe it's the Harley shirt. There is, after all, a clear pattern of Harley guys who drive airplanes into buildings.

Actually, I think it's social consciousness. Overwhelmingly the ter-rorists have been Mohammedan males, moody representatives of a dys-functional civilization that peaked in the twelfth century and knows it. Now, since these loons are known to be very high risks for blowing things up, it might make sense to focus on them in searches. No?

Ah, but this would be profiling. It might offend terrorists. So we randomly search people we know not to be terrorists, thus avoiding profiling. See? It's like losing your watch under a street light, but look-ing for it in a dark alley.

Oh well.

Finally I staggered aboard the great silver bird, by main force and awkwardness stuffed the six hundred pounds of scuba gear into an overhead bin, and sat in the cramped, compressive little seat with my feet in my pockets. The guy next to me pulled out a magazine and started reading about Jackie O's life in the Kennedy family compound at Hyenas Port in Massachusetts.

Early Sixties. No terror state. You just walked out to the airplane and got on.

Getting Shod At Berkeley

R umor among California's channelers and telepathy screwballs has it that Mark Twain is still alive, like Elvis, and secretly writing for newspapers in the Bay Area. What do you reckon? Nothing else can explain the why the papers are so wonderfully funny.

I guess Twain took some of that Nazi immortality drug that Hitler did before he went to live in Argentina. Most likely Twain actually lives with Elvis in a UFO. Literary types on the Coast figure that once in a while he comes to Earth at a trailer park, in the High Desert near Barstow, to file stories for the *San Francisco Chronicle*. Some think he chose Barstow because his alcoholic brother, Delirium Clemens, lives there in a doublewide.

Anyway, folks at U.C. Berkeley, I see in the *Chronicle*, recently got their innards all in an uproar because the school didn't have enough diversity. Diversity means students who can barely read, don't want to, and haven't the foggiest idea what the purpose of a university might be. The latter point helps them bond with their professors.

Nothing wrong with that, I guess. Everybody has to be somewhere. Berkeley's as good a place as any, being as far from my house as you can get without falling off the continent.

So two thousand activists and progressives and other academic rabble held a great March for Affirmative Action. There was lots of diversity, most of it squalling like train whistles. The high schools let the teen-age diversity out to march. Probably they were doing so well in their studies that they didn't need to be in class. Pretty soon half the earth was bellowing and hollering and waving placards about injustice and oppression and other things none of them had ever seen.

By chance they marched past The Athlete's Foot, a store that sold running shoes.

Whereupon the diversity *looted it.*

Don't you love it?

Quoth the newspaper: "A Chronicle photographer saw about 100 young persons run into the Athlete's Foot shoe store on Telegraph Avenue and about a dozen of the youths run out with boxes of shoes." The others were slower. They probably couldn't find anything in their size.

Wouldn't that make you want more diversity in your school? If you didn't mind going barefoot.

Now, the newspapers somehow neglected to say what the ethnicity of the looters was. I guess they weren't paying attention. There weren't any pictures of them either. Maybe the reporters ran short of film. That happens a lot with professional photographers. But I bet we can all make a pretty good Kentucky-windage guess about who those looters were.

Can't we? And I bet I know what you're thinking right now. The N word.

Norwegians.

Was I right?

I *was.* Why you prejudiced scoundrel, you!

Grabbing those Air Jordans provides an ethnic clue. Norwegians of the inner city are famous for their larcenous predilections regarding footwear. They can't help it, because of their past.

The word Norwegian actually derives from "Norse Weejuns," shoes worn by the Vikings when they went forth to rape and plunder. In fact that's how the French learned to wear shoes, which they saw for the first time when the Vikings came ashore at Normandy. They figured they could run away faster if their feet didn't hurt. (Bet you're surprised a West Virginia boy knew that. The school marm up our holler always said I had potential. She didn't say what for.)

Now I'm trying to understand diversity, and why anybody would want it. Be patient. I'm just a country boy, and slow, and don't understand higher thought. Where I come from, diversity just means you have to lock your bicycle up. And stay in at night, and carry a gun, and watch your daughter and chickens. And I figure that if people loot stores, they just aren't civilized, and don't belong among decent folk, and ought to be in jail.

Like I say, I'm simple.

Then I talked to some sociologist folk, and they explained to me that Norwegians don't have a choice about stealing. Their history makes them do it. This nice sociology lady told me about it. According to sociology, she said, if anything bad happened to anybody related to you, at any time, ever, you got to rape and rob and steal all you wanted.

I can't wait to get started.

Anyway, she said, the Norwegians used to be hunter-gatherers. I think that means they shot turkeys with slingshots and ate wild persimmons and smoked ditchweed. It's what we call shiftless in West Virginia.

But now I can understand about those shoes. When you see a persimmon on a tree in the woods, you don't think it belongs to anyone. If you can grab it, it's yours. When you catch a catfish, you aren't stealing it. It's just there.

So when the diversity see Air Jordans in a store, how are they supposed to know those shoes belong to somebody? To them, a shoe's no different from a catfish. They're just celebrating their Viking heritage.

And they don't mean any harm by it. They just can't tell somebody else's shoes from low-hanging bananas. It's their culture. (Bananas grow down south, in tropical Norway. You didn't know that, did you?)

That's what the sociologist lady told me. And I thought about it real hard, like when the flathead '48 won't start and I'm not sure whether it's bad points or a busted coil. But I guess I'm hopeless. I still figure if their culture means stealing my bicycle, they belong in jail. And my culture says take a shotgun to'em. It's the redneck in me.

Tell you what, though. I'll bet that if you had a shoe store, and put all your sneakers in boxes marked, "Books," the diversity would never come within rifle shot. It would be like garlic for vampires. Maybe that's the best we can do, what with the country going the way it is.

Now I'm going to drive up to Barstow, and see if I can find Delirium's trailer. I've got a copy of *Tom Sawyer* I want his brother to sign, and maybe Elvis will play Blue Moon Over Kentucky for me.

NASA Drains The Federal Udder

Today I'm gonna tell you about the Feddle Gummint and space ships. Then you'll understand everything, and never need to read stuff again.

It's a service of this column.

Used to be we didn't have space ships, or NASA. Didn't need'em. You could sit on a rail fence, listen to Elvis, drink a RC Cola and eat Moon Pies. You didn't need a space ship to do it. You just needed a warm afternoon.

Then in 1957 Russia put Sputnik in orbit. Sputnik was a clunky dingus that sailed round and round like it knew where it was going and said, "*Beep beep beep.*" It was a threat to national security. Anybody with good sense knew we couldn't let the Russians say "*Beep beep beep*" at us. We might turn into robot comminist slaves.

'Bout that time, President Kennedy was low in the polls. He looked at the Moon, and guessed it was like San Juan Hill, only shinier, and hollered, "*Cha-a-aaa-aaaa-ahhh-jj*!" because he was from Boston and hadn't learned English yet. He said we had to get to the Moon before the Russians did.

He didn't say why.

Actually, most folk didn't mind if the Russians went to the Moon. All of'em. Besides, the Moon was made of rocks. We had plenty already. I was only ten, and I knew where lots were, right there in Limestone County, Alabama. I'da sold them to the gummint for a quarter each.

Pretty soon we poured whole trainloads of money into building great big squatty-looking rockets. My father, a mathematician, had his salary double. Before long everybody in the family had shoes. Finally America built the Saturn V, a gy-normous rocket that looked like the Holland Tunnel stood on end, I guess in case we wanted to put aircraft carriers in orbit. Before long so many astronauts were swirling around that we had traffic congestion and then in 1969 Neil Armstrong stepped onto the Moon. And thought:

"What the *hell* am I doing *here*?"

It was a good question. Another question was: What next?

Now, the first rule of gummint work is that, if Uncle Sucker pays you to solve a problem, you have to avoid solving it like the seven-year itch, because then you're out of a job. It's why Washington can't do anything right.

Trouble was, NASA had solved its problem. We had told it to go to the Moon. Unwisely, it did. Now the world's foremost engineering outfit, squashed full to the bilges with superb alpha-geek engineers, who could get rocks from almost anywhere, and who now had progeny and mortgages—faced starvation. Secondary economic effects loomed. If NASA went down, so would the pocket-protector industry. It could have caused another Depression.

Aeronautical designers in the South started slipping away from work to buy big vats and copper tubing. There was always a market for moonshine.

Then some genius hollered, "*Whooooo-eeee*! Let's build a spaceship!"

The idea made no sense. Why go into space? There was nothing there. That's how you knew it was space. The notion was crazier than a duffel bag full of monkeys, but it sounded adventurous and needed mathematicians.

Especially, it needed mathematicians.

Money just sprayed into what came to be called the Space Shuttle, which made it sound like a cross-town bus: Stolid, dependable, practical, like Fed-Ex. If they'd called it Naked Grab At Funds, the public might have noticed.

Now, sure, there was a lot of hooha about how a space ship would answer the riddle of life, cure cancer, and get rid of crabgrass. NASA always says this. Ever notice that, when a space probe sets off to crash on Saturn or somewhere equally depressing, the press handout always starts, "NASA, in an effort to better understand weather on earth, launched a funny-looking dingus with little prongy things all over it...."

Anyone with the brains of a tent caterpillar, which fortunately turned out to be about three people, would ask, "Wait. You want to understand weather on earth, so you study...Saturn. Yes. I see. I reckon when you want to talk to your brother in Orlando, you call your mother-in-law in Chattanooga. Makes perfect sense. Airtight."

The Space Shuttle, like the planetary probes, faced the problem that there really wasn't much to do up there. For a while NASA talked about how we were going to have factories in space to make ball bearings. They didn't believe it: When it costs $20-30K per pound to put stuff in orbit, you have to have a pretty lively markup on ball bearings to make a profit. Congress bought the idea, though. That's what counted.

Now, the trick to achieving funding immortality is, first, to get the country used to paying. In politics, the customary is indistinguishable from the reasonable. Next, you slowly let your boondoggle fade from the papers, so everybody forgets about it. The Shuttle was big news for about three launches. Then it in the back of the papers with truss ads and inner-city murders.

For a while, life was all ham hocks and home fries. Salaries flowed. Research funds overflowed. Then the Shuttle began to get old. It used Sixties technology. If you found the thing in a Neanderthal cave, amid gnawed bones and old teeth, it would look about right. NASA needed a new Brass Ring to chase.

Enter the Space Station.

Most folk needed a Space Station like they needed a rabid raccoon or doughnuts with mustard on them. People had lived whole lives without a space station, and it hadn't hurt them any. Mostly it would just spin like a hamster wheel and cost money. But engineers still needed jobs. So we set to work on it. To improve efficiency, we got the Russians to build some of it. That always helps efficiency.

So now the thing is going up, in chunks and fragments, and nobody cares. Ask the average Joe whether we even have a Space Station.

"Er...ah...heh."

What's it for?

"Well, it's, ah, up there. If it is."

Next—this is being plotted—we'll be told we need to send men to Mars. Unexpectedly, this will cost a bunch of money and require lots of mathematicians. It will, however, teach us about weather on Earth.

Know what Mars has? Rocks. Pink ones, like half of Arizona. I'd still sell 'em to the gummint for a quarter each.

Race And The Inevitability Of Behavior

One marvels that a creed widely doubted in private, unsupported by evidence, and manifestly incorrect, can become compulsory in a society, shape its policy, and arouse furious support. Radical egalitarianism is such a creed—the notion that people, both individually and in groups, are born equal and, preferably, identical. It would then follow that all differences arise from nurture.

What if they don't?

As a matter of daily experience we observe that some individuals are bigger, smarter, better athletes, superior artists, better singers. It isn't all nurture: Raise me as Michael Jordan was raised, and I would still be short and slow. We also observe that some groups consistently excel others. We pretend otherwise because the penalties for not pretending are severe. Most of us know we are pretending.

There is at the University of Western Ontario a scholar named J. Philippe Rushton, much in disrepute among the clergy of nurturism. He is a sociobiologist, a member of an outcast class holding that much of behavior is biologically shaped. His book, *Race, Evolution, and Behavior*, is intensely reviled among the keepers of proper thought. It purports to describe and explain differences in intelligence and behavior among races. This we must never, ever do.

I don't give it blanket endorsement, but its central thrust is sufficiently in accord with daily experience as to be worth pondering. In outline:

The IQ of East Asians (Koreans, Chinese, Japanese) is about 106, of Eurowhites 100, "blacks" in America 85, blacks in Africa 70. He does not in the book deal with Jews, but Ashkenazi Jews average 115. The East Asians have a particular advantage in mathematics.

Why?

The moment one recites the statistics, frantic counterarguments arise. Race doesn't exist or, contradictorily, isn't important. Intelligence doesn't exist, can't be defined, or can't be measured. Tests are biased. In short, anything that gives an undesired answer undergoes summary rejection.

Now, readers may reach such conclusions as they think best. But allow me two questions and an assertion. The first question: Do you not know some people who are unquestionably smarter than some others? The second question: Given that races demonstrably differ in appearance, size, bodily proportions, biochemistry, brain size, and a thousand other things, is there any obvious reason why they should not vary in intelligence? In behavior?

The assertion: The people who devise tests of intelligence, as anyone may discover by reading, are neither fools, nor bigots, nor unaware of the problems of testing. Dismiss them only after much reading and careful thought.

The thesis of the sociobiologists is as follows: Men evolved about 200,000 years ago in Africa. Some migrated to Europe about 100,000 years ago and, then being in genetic isolation from Africa, evolved into the Caucasian race. Roughly 40,000 years ago some of the Caucasians migrated to Asia and, in genetic isolation, evolved into East Asians.

Life in northern Europe, runs the argument, was far more difficult than it had been in Africa because of, if nothing else, harsh winters. Survival required not just the intelligence to keep warm but also cooperation, forethought, planning, and cohesion. The people who would become East Asians, living in still more difficult conditions, needed more of these qualities. Those who survived had them.

This may be true. It may not. In evolutionary circles, plausibility trades as evidence. Yet it fits.

Says Rushton, on the basis of many years of research, there exists a clear gradient in many things from yellow to white to black. Asians have somewhat larger brains than whites who have substantially larger brains than blacks. Measured aggressiveness follows the same pattern of a small gap between yellow and white and a larger gap between white and black. The pattern applies for other characteristics: East Asians are lowest in testosterone levels, latest in entering puberty, lowest in size of genitals, degree of criminality, sex drive, rates of fertility, rates of divorce and promiscuity. Blacks are at the other extreme, with whites falling between.

Rushton is no fool. He knows that some of these things are influenced by variables other than the innate. He knows the pitfalls in cross-cultural measurement. Yet, he asserts, the pattern remains. In the United States, for example, crime is very low among East Asians, academic performance very high, divorce rare, families small.

In short, his thesis is that while environment obviously matters in determining outcomes, our capacities and behavior are very much influenced by genetics. The idea is not new, merely forbidden. Rushton et al however make a careful evidentiary case that is not easily ignored, unless you have determined in advance to ignore it.

Nurturists disagree with the sociobiologists. Behavior that seems racial, they argue, is in fact determined by culture. The question is tricky. Culture may itself be to a considerable extent the expression of biology. If East Asians are by nature less aggressive than whites, perhaps because of lower levels of testosterone, one would expect the lack of aggressiveness to be embodied in the culture. That is, naturally quiet people will raise their children to be quiet and be inclined to value courtesy. The nurturist can then say, "Aha! Just as I thought. Socially ingrained." Maybe. Maybe not.

A shift in the intellectual climate seems to be in the offing. Increasingly we see a clash between the compulsory view that we are all identical at birth, which if true would happily allow the eradication of various inequalities and of crime; and the quietly held but growing recognition that if we are inherently different, as seems to be the case, we will unavoidably achieve different results.

The question cannot easily be studied. The nurturists are politically in the saddle, and so research into racial differences is verboten. One may ask, of course: Why do the correct fear investigation, unless they know, or suspect, that they are wrong? It is assuredly true that, in the past, theories of racial superiority have often emanated from virulent nationalists who have sought to place their own stock at the top of the heap. The inevitable comparison is with Hitler, a dark squatty fellow convinced of the superiority of blonde Aryan supermen.

In Rushton's case we are dealing with something else. A white Canadian who believes in yellow supremacy is hardly aggrandizing himself. I am myself a purebred Euro-mongrel without known trace of Asian or Jewish ancestry. I'd like to regard Scots/English/Huguenot cocktails as the pinnacle of civilization, and those in cowboy hats as the better of the best. I don't see the evidence. Rushton's gradient accords with my observations whether I like it or not. Perhaps we had better get used to Chinese mathematicians.

Queer Studies At Romper Room

I see in the Harvard *Crimson,** once the students' newspaper of what was once a university, that Boston's foremost daycare center, Harvard itself, wobbles toward adopting Queer Studies. Soon, apparently, there will be a Department.

Why, you might ask, does Harvard want to study queers? It doesn't, methinks. I suspect that the adolescents of Harvard, a category which also includes many of the students, merely want to behave disagreeably—to shock their parents or, in the case of the faculty, society. Queer Studies serves nicely. Next year it will be S&M Studies, Pedophile Studies, or a Department of Cannibalism.

On almost all campuses, the behavior of both the studentry and the professoriate is remarkably teenaged in savor. Universities are not the potting soil of maturity. The kids act like teenagers because they are teenagers. Members of the faculty do it because someone once told them that they were intellectuals. It is an odd idea, given the near-total inability of a professor to think anything that all the other professors don't think.

To be an intellectual it isn't enough, or even necessary, to teach competently. One must take to the barricades, any barricades; pose in coffee shops, such as the New York Review of Books; and gambol on the cutting edge, often of fields that do not have a cutting edge. One must Go Forward.

Loitering in the *avant garde,* a favored hobby of minor intelligences, allows them both to annoy others and to congratulate themselves on their advanced thinking. All of this rests on the passive-aggressive hostility of the resentfully inconsequential.

Thus Queer Studies.

A tenured professor cannot stamp his feet, throw creamed spinach from his high chair, or hold his breath and turn blue. Such candor would be thought excessive. He might find himself being forcibly diapered by passersby. Instead of spitting food, he advocates whatever will distress the country, to which he sees himself in a position of tutelary superiority.

What, exactly, is Queer Studies? Part of the impetus behind Harvard's queerward lunge, saith the *Crimson*, is a lecturer in Literature, appropriately named Heather Love. Let us listen to Heather:

"Queer studies is about what thinking about sexuality can teach us about identity and desire in general."

If this means anything, she didn't say what. I'm inclined to think that students unsure of their identity might better consult their driver's licenses instead of turning Harvard further into a den of psychotherapy. And if Heather thinks that college students need a special department to enable them to think about sexuality, she ought to get out more.

She continues, does this beskirted testimonial for Spengler, "Everyone has a gender and a sexuality—this field is not narrow, but rather incredibly expansive." ("Rather incredibly"? Oh Strunk, oh White....)

It is perhaps true that everyone has a gender and a sexuality, despite the asseverations of my divorced acquaintances, but I am not sure this is a reason for studying queers. Everyone has an esophagus. Should we not have Esophageal Studies? Putting it more solemnly, the existence of a group does not obviously make it deserving of a university department.

Which brings us to an important point: The objection to Queer Studies is not that queers are reprehensible—I think they are not—but that the subject is too narrow for a major. Queers are a tiny group of a few percent of the population and of no great importance as a tribe. Yes, they have contributed much to civilization. So have people with warts. We do not have Wart Studies. Yet.

One might as well have a Department of Left-Handedness, or of Amputee Studies, or Balding Presbyterian in Cowboy Hat Studies. (Actually, not a bad idea.) A purpose of a university education is to provide the broad background to allow independent study of narrower specialties. Anyone interested in queers can easily study them at a library or, depending on the intensity of interest, in a gay bar.

But there is yet more in the *Crimson*. Queer Studies has behind it that siege howitzer of appropriate thinking, the school's president. Listen:

"University President Lawrence H. Summers says he agrees that queer studies could potentially effect a broad range of disciplines."

What this means is mysterious. What is clear is that the reporter, writing in Harvard's newspaper, doesn't know "effect" from "affect," and that the *Crimson* needs an editor. Or another editor. It is to me disheartening that the populace of the nation's premier university speaks English with the elegance and lyricism of a bladder infection.

She continues (there is a point in this; wait) with a direct quote from Summers, "I don't think there is any question that issues of identity...is crucial in a range of intellectual areas."

Whether this is more opaque than fatuous, or fatuous than opaque, may be debated by others wiser than I. Somebody should tell the president of Harvard that a verb agrees with the subject of the sentence, not with the object of the nearest preposition. Does everyone at Harvard talk like a concussed recent immigrant?

Now, it may seem that I am being pointlessly snotty about the infelicity of language. No. I am being pointfully snotty. There appears to be a direct correlation between the rise of political hobbyism and the decline of careful literacy, and for that matter of genuine scholarship, in our academic theme-parks.

As best I can tell, the quality of study, and of faculty, in departments varies inversely with the degree of politicization. Black Studies and Women's Studies are scholastically absurd, as many know and few say. (They are also wildly militant, which is why they continue to exist.)

Departments of literature and of "social sciences" (as in "cosmetology science") are nearly as political, and as vacuous. Schools of chemistry and engineering remain healthy: No one has yet suggested that all equations should have the same answer so as to avoid invidious distinctions.

There is a reason why so many purported scholars express themselves so poorly. Good English rests on a precision of thought, a desire for clarity, and an appreciation of language that are inconsistent with enraged self-absorption. Genuine scholarship requires a focus on things other than one's psychic distempers. It does not cohabit easily with obsessive concern with oneself, one's identity, one's stultifying malaises and tedious angers—that is, with the characteristic concerns of teenagers. Succinctly, scholarship is not the domain of academic twerps. But that is who runs the universities.

* "Queer Studies Advances Cause" by Jessica E. Vascellaro, the *Crimson*, February 28, 2002

More Reasons Not To Enlist

The military has fallen apart. It needs fixing. The Pentagon pretends otherwise.

Because until after Desert Storm I wrote a military column that appeared in *Army/Navy/Air Force Times*, men still in uniform recognize my name and email me. The following are examples of their letters, with identification removed. The country will pay in lives for the things they describe.

The problem is not that we have women in the military. There are women in the services who have jobs they can do, who do them well, and who are dedicated to the military. They, and the men around them, know who they are. Rather the problem is (1) feminization of military values, (2) recruitment of low-grade women with no commitment to the armed services, and (3) unwillingness to discipline them.

Fred,

I am (a helicopter instructor pilot) at (a base.) The other day I was sailing along in the simulator with my two flight students when we got into a discussion about 14-hour flying days in combat.

One of the students asked the question "What did you do, pee in a bottle?" Well the female soldier working the console heard this, keyed the mic and said "You better watch it up there, someone said pee in a bottle." The two students were taken aback by this as was I. I quickly told this young Warrant Officer that the female soldier was correct. I can teach you to kill men and women and to blow things up but I can't allow you to say "Pee in a bottle."

Ask any man in the military today what the first thing he does before he opens his mouth and without fail you will hear "I look over my shoulder to see if there are any females in the area." Please don't use my name because I too am always looking over my shoulder.

Fred,

I just read your comments concerning any young man joining the military of today, [I said, "Don't do it": Fred] and I concur 100%. I go to LeMoore NAS for the Base Exchange and the Commissary, and in the process meet many of the base personnel. One thing I notice all the time is that they are either retiring as soon as they can, or are leaving without a retirement, because of the downturn in discipline and morale.

One Petty Officer told me that his relief on watch was three hours late. His Chief asked him not to write it in his report because then the person would have to be put on report, and since it was a black female, the Chief would have his butt reamed by the C.O. for not being more considerate....

Fred,

Here are a few more [examples of what happens today in the military] for you.

"Ma'am do you think when the time comes that you have to pull the trigger going into an LZ you are going to be able to do it?" "Oh no, I could never kill anyone. Since I had my baby my whole outlook has changed." Then why are you here? "I just thought it would be something fun to do."

"Ma'am, could you tell me the definition of this term in aviation." Her reply "Who gives a shit?" The same female student was caught reading a novel when she was supposed to be studying for her checkride. "You're damn right I was reading a novel, I'd have been bored to death otherwise." She busted several checkrides but she is out there occupying a seat today.

"LT, do you understand the Colonel has given a direct order prohibiting you from driving your POV to the flight line?" "So, what's he going to do, keep me after school?"

How about the LT that broke into the Post Golf Courses Pro Shop and stole a golf bag? He cut himself badly when he busted out the window so the MP's checked the hospital on post and caught him. He still is in flight school.

Then there were the two female flight students who were caught red handed shoplifting at the PX and were allowed to finish flight school.

You will love this one. If a student falls asleep during class we are not allowed to wake them up. We have to take their name and send it up through channels. We also are not allowed to say anything about them being late for class, again we have to take their name and send it up through the chain of command and you know how effective that is.

You are right on the money when you say don't let your son join!!!!

Fred,

Your most recent article on gender crap...I mean gap, in the military reminded me of the most ridiculous thing I ever saw in my almost 20 years in this business. It was in the *Stars and Stripes* last year. I was stationed south of Seoul when I read about this MP outfit in Korea that had a...I think it was called a Sympathy Belt? Anyway it was a device that was strapped on to the abdomen of the user...in this case a male captain, 0-3, the unit commander, to simulate a pregnancy late in the third trimester. The idiot looked absolutely moronic in his Maternity Battle Dress Uniform (yes, we have 'em...) The idea is to develop appreciation for what his knocked up soldiers (ugh) are experiencing.

This was part of the mandatory CO2 (Consideration of Others) training required along with our Violence in the Workplace prevention training....honest to God...in the g.d. Army!! Prevention of Violence in the military....kinda like Prevention of Sports in the Stadium....

Fred,

I agree with your opinion about women in the military. But I don't think your proposal for a 'force-march' is necessary to resolve this issue. Every time we conduct a brigade run during PT your point is made. The women in the formations drop out in droves.

I don't understand why these women can't keep up. You would think that an exercise like running would be an equalizer between the sexes, but it's obviously not. It goes back to want you've said about lowered standards coupled with a hesitancy on the part of the chain-of-command to enforce even these sorry standards out of fear with getting slapped with an EO complaint, which in turn can be career ending. The whole situation is rather pathetic.

Keep telling it like it is.

Children In Shards: Tag Did It

I reckon that duck hunters are the only hope for what used to be this country. First, we'll catch all the school principal-ladies who want to neuter boy kids, and we'll make'm disk-shaped. Maybe we can squash them into a special skeet-mold and fill in the empty parts with quick-hardening epoxy. Technology can do wonders these days.

Then we'll take the duck hunters to a really forlorn swamp, and put the principal ladies into a great gy-normous skeet-chucker, and yell, "*Pul-l-l-llllll!*"

Ker-*blaaam*!

Then we'll put piranha in the swamp to eat what's left.

It's getting worse. I read in *The Capital* of Annapolis, Maryland, home of the Naval Academy, that the principaless of West Annapolis Elementary has banned tag on the playground. Yep, tag: You're it. It's for safety. Tag is dangerous. She is going to Protect Our Children.

The principaless in question, Joan Brisco, described the horror of tag.

"They would start up, and inevitably it got too rough. The reason we stopped tag was because we didn't want them getting hurt."

Well, I guess. I can imagine that the emergency rooms of Annapolis have done land-office trade in broken and bleeding children, victims of tag. Probably the halls rattle with the tippy-tap of peg legs. No doubt the children's studies suffer because of missing limbs. That's how tag usually is. When I played tag as a kid, we always had the shock-trauma unit on full alert.

If fact, tag is a leading cause of death in children, ranking just behind meteor strikes.

"Rough" means boys.

89

Now, why do these ladies have their innards in an uproar over tag? Because they are ladies, or at any rate women. Usually when I see that some terrible danger has been ended, as for example dodgeball, or a kid of six has been expelled for drawing a picture of a soldier, a teacheress will be behind it. Occasionally it's a New Age man, apparently a trans-sexual who got stuck in mid passage.

We have feminized the schools. Worse, the teachers don't much like boys.

There is a totalitarian strain in the female psyche. It isn't evil, at least not in intention. Quite the opposite—in intention. Women as a sex want to impose security, stability, and conventionality, at all costs, on everything. They want a tyranny of the safe and comfortable.

For which there is a good reason. Historically, mothers have been women. Their instincts are to keep children alive, which is difficult, especially with boys. Boys favor enthusiasm over judgment. Before they are big enough, they want to climb things, crawl into things, and play with things that bite.

They don't understand about coral snakes. Mommy does. A boy of seven is quite sure it's a good idea to climb a utility pole and hang by his toes from the high-tension lines. His mother is sure it isn't. That's why he survives to manhood.

The trick to civilization is channeling male horsepower into useful directions. Women are good at this. When a man wants to put a city to the sword, or throw his boss from a high roof, she restrains him. "Why don't we nuke China next week, honey? Or you could fiddle with the whazzamajig on your Harley instead."

When the female drive for security ceases to be a useful brake on male energy, and becomes instead the dominant principle of existence, the effect is stifling. That is what we have. A guy principal, unless gelded, will let girls be girls and boys be boys. A gal principal wants them both to be girls. A man will not try to force girls to play football. A woman will try to force boys to stop playing it.

Because what is instinctive seems reasonable, few women have the foggiest idea what makes men tick. (Or, God knows, vice versa.) Some do. Some women scuba dive, jump out of airplanes, shoot competitively. The average teacheress doesn't. She can't imagine why boys like roughhousing, or hard-played basketball, or guns. When she says tag is too rough, she means that it is too rough for her.

And with an intolerance peculiar to the sex, she believes that anything she can't understand must be reformed. I am reminded of that flotsam of wisdom, worn now by much passage over the Internet: When a man marries, he believes that the woman won't change, and she does; she believes that he will change, and he doesn't.

However, says the story, the school will allow tag in PE, "if their teacher chooses to lead a group game." Here is another facet of our attempt to rewire our children: a distaste for things individual.

Now, liberals and conservatives usually amount to twin halves of a national lobotomy, each cleaving passionately to its chosen lunacies, but there are real differences between the two. The left loves groups. Note that it's easy to get the political left to hold a demonstration, for anything at all, and difficult to get conservatives to demonstrate, for anything at all.

So tag is all right in a group, where it can be supervised, and numbingly safe, and controlled, and impart Appropriate Values. Here is what is really wanted: Control, control, control. Don't let kids play whatever the hell they want to, and be kids. No. We must have a group activity. Don't let them play Cowboys and Indians. We must control how they think about gender and aboriginals. No dodgeball: It's competitive, and we must control such an antisocial drive. Forget tag: We must control violence. The schools now seem to be branch offices of North Korea.

And finally the story mentions the school's "no-touching" policy, and the county's rules on sexual harassment. In *grade school.* Always it is there: The twisted prissy Puritanism, obsessed by the fear of sex, yet determined to discover salaciousness everywhere. I think of the spinster afraid that there might be a man hiding under her bed, and equally afraid that there might not be. A profound anxiety underlies the fear of almost everything: sex, childhood games, winning and losing, physical contact, everything.

How can one not feel utter contempt for these frightened, hostile little embodiments of parsnipish mediocrity?

There is some solace in that boys are not required to wear training bras. Wait a few weeks. But you'll have to excuse me now. I'm working on a skeet mold.

Getting Rid Of McKinley

I n the sweltering August of '66 we were in training in Marine Corps boot camp, in the mosquito swamps of Parris Island, South Carolina, getting ready to go to war. The build-up for Viet Nam had begun. We were thousands of kids, from the lower middle class mostly, the nation's usual cannon fodder, young bucks from darkling hollows of Tennessee or hopeless tenements in Chicago or the green twilit silence of the Mississippi Delta or the black-lung fields of the Cumberland Plateau. We were readying ourselves to fight in a country we had never heard of, for reasons we couldn't articulate, against an ideology we could neither spell nor explain.

PI was isolated, flat, buggy, covered with rifle ranges, PT fields, obstacle courses. Today they call them confidence courses, because what matters is how you feel about yourself. What counted then was whether you could get over an obstacle. There was no free time, just running, rifles, bayonet, .45s, running, PT, more running, more PT. Training was tough, for good reason. The DIs knew most of us were going to Asia, and Asia was tough. Many of us would come back in body bags, or gutshot, or blind, or missing parts of our bodies.

The DIs knew it. They wanted us to be as ready as possible. They didn't cut us any slack.

Most of us could reach down inside and do it, sometimes to our surprise. McKinley couldn't. He was a tall, scrawny, doofus-looking kid, almost emaciated. I guess he might have weighed twenty pounds if he'd been wearing a thirty-pound pack. He couldn't do anything right. He marched funny, couldn't get the operating rod back into his rifle, got knocked on his butt repeatedly on the pugil-stick floor. McKinley was weak as a kitten. He always had a wondering expression and his

93

voice was soft. He wasn't a homosexual. He was just…in the wrong place.

The DIs wanted him out. They knew where we were going. A Marine who had trouble assembling his rifle, who couldn't carry the weight, would get killed and get others killed. The DIs didn't dislike him. They wanted him to be somewhere else. So they rode him.

We'd do close-order drill under the blazing sun of South Carolina and McKinley would screw up. The DIs would drop him for pushups, which in his case were more like let-downs. He always got knocked silly with pugil-sticks—just wasn't aggressive enough, didn't have the mass, the muscular power. As the DIs put it, "You gotta want to knock the dog-snot out of the other sumbitch." McKinley just didn't. He got no mercy.

He just flat couldn't do PT. On the rifle range the little red flag usually waved across the target: Maggie's Drawers. He had missed the target completely. In the Marine Corps of the time, you could molest goats, or sacrifice virgins to unheard-of gods, and it would be overlooked as just letting off steam. Poor marksmanship was not overlooked.

Most of us got through, even thrived. A nineteen-year-old boy from Kentucky is hard to wear out. Young studs rise to a challenge. PI was one. I think a lot of us refused to drop out because we weren't going to give the DIs the satisfaction. Besides, the Island was designed to build recruits up. It did. I went in at a wiry 139 pounds and came out at 163.

McKinley didn't build up. He had nothing to build.

By the time my platoon came long, McKinley had been at PI for some time. Twice he had been set back and sent to Strength Platoon. The latter amounted to weeks of heavy PT, intended to bulk up suburban delicates into something resembling men. McKinley didn't bulk.

The DIs wanted him out.

They made him stand on a table and roar.

"*Roar, McKinley.*"

"*Uhhhnnh.*"

McKinley couldn't roar.

"A Marine Corps roar, McKinley."

"Make a muscle, McKinley."

McKinley didn't have a muscle. His tensed arm looked like a broom handle.

The DIs did everything to get him to quit. They told us this later. They offered him honorable discharges, medical discharges, administrative discharges, and maybe even thought of accidental discharges. He wouldn't go. It turned out his big brother had come through PI earlier and been some sort of all-time outstanding super-Marine. McKinley, it seems, wanted to make his brother proud. He wasn't going to quit.

Except he had to.

The DIs knew, as we didn't yet, that after PI came AIT—Advanced Infantry Training—at Camp Geiger, North Carolina. PI built strength. You got plenty to eat and enough sleep. Geiger just beat the bejesus out of you. Day after day after day you hit the rack at midnight, got up at 0345, and humped for mile after unending mile through the greasy clay of a rainy autumn. You humped till your chest hurt and your legs knotted up and cold rain ran down your spine like something evil looking for a vital nerve. On rare occasions when you moved by cattle car instead of on foot, you sat with the butt of your smoke pole on the floor and your helmet over the muzzle, and slept with it for a pillow.

McKinley couldn't have done it. There was no way.

People think that training teaches recruits how to do things—fire a rifle or, in those days, use a bloop tube or rig a stick of C4 with detcord. No. Or yes, but more importantly, what it teaches them, or taught them in 1966, is just how godawful miserable they can be, how whimper-ass, beat-down, oh-God-get-me-out-of-here unhappy, exhausted, almost hallucinating from lack of sleep, and still somehow get things done. A war zone is a bad place to make up for training you should have gotten earlier. We didn't understand this yet. The DIs did.

But McKinley wasn't going to quit. He was going to make his brother proud. It was sad. He had the guts of a battalion of Marines, but the physical attributes of someone in an iron lung. I suspect the DIs respected him. They weren't evil men, or probably even heartless (though you couldn't prove it by me.) They admired guts. But McKinley just needed to do something else.

One day he disappeared. I don't know how they did it. Given how far he got with absolutely nothing to work with, his brother should have been proud.

The Infinitude Of Pedro

Recently I returned to Washington from three months down on the West Coast of Mexico. I found that Vicente Fox, *presidente de*, was in the city. Yep. He was here to demand—*demand*, mind you—that Jorge Arbusto, leader of the US and by implication everywhere else, give amnesty to all the Mexicans who are illegally in this country. Which, shortly, in all likelihood, will be all of them.

So I girded my loins, and wrote Fox a letter, knowing that it would alter his behavior for the better. Managing the world is one of the services of this column.

"Dear Vinny (you can call me Fred),

Now see here, Vin. Enough is enough. We need to sit down and talk turkey about this immigration thing, like men, and not act like State Department types. I mean, we're not transvestites.

Now, I was just in Mexico, and one thing struck me about it: The place was just running over with Mexicans. (And we thought *we* had an immigration problem.) The more I think about it, the more I think both countries have the same problem. Too many Mexicans.

Nothing personal against you, Vin. As Mexican presidents go, you're not bad. Of course after seventy years of the PRI, it would be hard to be bad. And I don't have any objection to Mexicans in reasonable numbers. I like Mexicans. That's why I spend time in Mexico. In reasonable numbers, we could bring them up to first-world standards, and they could teach us to salsa. Fact is, Presbyterians can't dance. A little Latin savor might help.

But what makes you think we want seven million Mexicans? And that's just this year.

Further—if I may speak freely—who the hell are you to be demanding anything at all?

Note, Vinny, we're not talking seven million Mexican nuclear physicists, if there is one. I might not mind a bunch of doctors and engineers. They'd be assimilable. We could tax them, and waste the money on silly social projects that wouldn't work this time either.

But we're not getting doctors. I reckon med school takes a lot of time, and they don't learn to swim.

No. We're getting folks who can't make it in Mexico—the uneducated, the uncultivated, the ones that show signs of staying that way. It's not a brain drain, but more a drain drain. (A little humor, Vinny. Scintillating Anglo-Saxon wit.)

Now, if these folks wanted to act like Vietnamese, and make straight As and go to Harvard, it'd be a different story. But I don't see it. We're getting too many, and the wrong ones. They're going to clump together and be more trouble than Frenchmen in Quebec. Or at least it looks that way.

That's scary, Vin. We have lots of hard-working Latinos here, a lot of 'em from Salvador. The adults seem law-abiding when sober, which is sometimes. They start restaurants, and that's a good sign. I like them fine. But I don't see a lot of books.

Doesn't look good, Vinny.

I've got an idea. What say we talk about things straightforwardly for a moment? Ain't that a concept? Might revolutionize politics. But since this is just a private communication between you and me, Vinny, I figure we can hazard honesty. It's not like I'm going to put it on the Internet or anything.

Fact is, Mexico is outbreeding its economy, and hasn't got the sense to stop. The economy is less than wildly promising. Nowhere in Latin America seems much better. Latin cultures just aren't real dynamic. What worries you, Vin, is that too many hungry people could lead to social unrest and revolution. Think Chiapas. So you want to unload them on us.

Ain't that so?

That's your end of the stick. On ours, George desperately wants to be re-elected, by any means, at any cost to anybody or anything, including the country and his party. So he's sucking up to blacks, who won't vote for him anyway, and to Latinos, some of whom will if he gets them amnesty, and will then vote Democratic for the rest of time. If he has to, he'll turn the United States into an irremediably divided country facing a century of hostility.

Business wants amnesty because it wants cheap labor, which won't stay cheap, and the Democrats want another permanent welfare bloc to control the presidency.

The question, Vinny (and we both know it) is whether Bush can buy more Mexican votes with amnesty than he'll lose from people who, from simple disgust, just won't vote at all. Me, for example.

And we both know that if you get amnesty for today's illegals, ten million more will leak across the border before long and we'll need another amnesty. That's the scam, isn't it? History being driven by inadequate contraception. Pretty.

If I were not as scrupulously courteous as I am, I might ask: Why do you think America has a duty to take your population overflow? Putting it bluntly, if you can't keep your pants up, then you can raise them. (The offspring, I mean. Some metaphors don't work as well as expected.)

I've got in front of me a Gallup Poll that says only six percent of Americans want a blanket amnesty. That may be a majority in Mexico. In America it will pass for a majority, because in our system we do not consult the populace on matters of importance. In the next election here, people who oppose immigration will have a choice between Bush, who favors unrestricted amnesty, and the Democrats, who will favor unrestricted immigration. The ninety-four percent who disagree will be marginalized as cranks.

The real question isn't one that directly concerns you, Vinny. We are in the middle of learning whether there is anything at all that cannot be inflicted on the American public—whether people with cable TV can rouse themselves to resist, well, anything. A greater question is whether there exists any effective means of resistance. I don't think so. But we shall see.

Yours cordially,
Federico"

Talkin' To Hant, Agin.

The other day I went up the holler to talk to Uncle Hant about Democracy. Hant knows everything. Well, nearly about everything.

He lives just past the creek in a double-wide with a satellite dish and his old dog Birdshot. You could call him a mountain man. He's tall and lank, like they made him by the yard and sawed off a piece, and wears this floppy slouch hat, and when he sits down he looks like a hinge folding.

For West Virginia, Hant is rich. Years back he told the Feddle Gummint that he was an African-American with black lung, over ninety years of age, and a small business run by a Native American woman named Sighing Cloud. The gummint sends him truckloads of money. He had to resurface the driveway so they could park.

Anyway, he was setting under his favorite tree with a plastic gallon of Coke and a bottle of Wild Turkey. Birdshot was lying next to him, scratching and watching squirrels. Hant's kind of slow and quiet, and doesn't get excited about much. Ain't much to get excited about up the hollers.

"Hant, explain to me about Democracy," I said.

"Ain't any."

He seemed to think that covered it. Hant's not a man of many words.

I tried again. "I don't reckon that's what that school-lady used to say. Remember her? She came from Wheeling and she went to a real college. She said democracy was the American way, and all advanced, and these old Greeks did it." Of course, the Greeks did a lot of things you could get shot for where I live. "Pass me that Turkey."

101

He did. But he didn't say anything. I wouldn't quit, though.

"She said it was noble, and these important guys like George Washington liked it so much they wouldn't do their laundry without it. She said the best thing about it was that it let the common man run the country."

That got Hant's attention. He thought a little.

"That was the best thing about it?"

"Yeah."

"What was the worst?"

Hant could be hard to talk to.

"Well, she said it was better than stewed rabbit, and how it taught us to respect the wisdom of the people, and the Average Man."

He took the bottle back. No flies on Hant.

"Boy, the average man's barely got sense enough to find his way home at night. I guess we're in deeper trouble than I thought."

I got to worrying about it. About the common man, I mean. There's this show on TV about this enormous fat lady who's always doing specials on things like Dwarves With Three Heads and the Women Who Love Them Too Much, which would be at all. But what was scary was the people that came to watch. They didn't have much shape to'em, and they laughed sort of *hyuk-hyuk*, and breathed through their noses like they'd been inbreeding too much. Whenever that fat lady said something uncommon stupid, they'd yell and clap and stomp their feet, and the women would shriek. I told Hant about it.

"That'd be Oprah," he said. "Looks like five hundred pounds of bear liver in a plastic bag?"

When Birdshot heard the word "liver," he perked up like a Democrat that's discovered an unwatched treasury. I know people with less sense than Birdshot.

"There's another one of them ladies, though," said Hant, trying to remember. "Makes you think of a plaster wall with legs."

I thought about the common people I knew around Bluefield and North Fork. Nice folk, at least until after the thirteenth beer, but, being from West Virginia, they mostly had three thumbs and didn't know who the President was. On the other hand, some things it's best not to know.

Anyway, there was old Robert Weevil up the holler near Crumpler, and Mrs. Weevil, and all the little Weevils. A sociologist lady from Washington D.C. came to give them some kind of test to see how smart they were. I heard they had to put her in a rest home afterward.

I guess I was getting upset. I'd come to tell Hant how good democracy was, and he wasn't having any.

"Hant, what that school-lady said was, elections are like a town meeting, and the candidates express their ideas, and then the people choose the best man. Ain't that better than a Duke or some musty old King?"

I figured I had him now.

"Well, think about the last ten presidents," he said, and got a satisfied look on his face.

Then he said, "I believe if you went to Willy's Beer and Lube and caught the first ten people who came in, you'd do better."

The conversation wasn't going the way I thought it was going to. Democracy did sound better if you didn't think about it too much. Of course, most people didn't. Maybe that was the secret.

By the way, Hant ain't real. He's just a literary apparition. We get lots of them in the mountains, mostly in swampy spots. I think it's something about gas that seeps from the ground.

He passed the Turkey back and said, "People don't care what kind of gummint they got. All's they want is a four-by-four, two bedrooms that don't leak too much, a job that doesn't make them think, and 600 channels on the satellite. Maybe a Bug Zapper and a six-pack on the weekends."

It's a mistake to teach an apparition to argue.

"Think about it, boy. 'Bout a million years ago, they had kings lying all over the place like dead cats, and nobody had much. The only way a king could get more than he was worth was to steal everything from everybody else and put it in a pile. And they *still* couldn't get cable. That's why they had revolutions. People wanted to get their stuff back. They didn't care about freedom and democracy. Still don't.

"Thing is, now everbody's got a four-by-four and satellite. Hell, they mostly don't even know what kind of gummint they got, long's as it doesn't outlaw beer and NASCAR on Sunday. They don't want democracy. They want to sit loose and stay dry. It's all they want."

I figured I needed to stop talking to Hant too much. He passed me the Turkey and I took a big hit. Birdshot cocked his eye at a squirrel on the ground, hunting acorns, but decided against it and went back to sleep. That old dog was comfortable. It was enough.

Latinos, Blacks, And Trouble Coming

As the Rio Grande flows ever more northward, and Spanish grows common on the streets of America, and tacos appear in the lunch counters of high schools along with the usual inedible fare, people worry that "the minorities" may one day be in the majority, and band together against whites. I wouldn't bet on it.

Sez me anyway, the tendency to view Latinos and blacks as essentially identical, or at any rate as natural allies, is mistaken. The browns are more likely to join whites than oppose them. They assuredly don't like blacks.

I listen in the mornings to *Radio Novecientos* in Laurel, Maryland, 900 A.M., a Spanish station with a good morning-talk show. I used to watch Spanish television until I got rid of cable a couple of years ago. It doesn't take much listening, or hanging out in Latino eateries, to realize that blacks and Latinos are more likely to be competitors, or even adversaries, than allies. The cultural gap is enormous, their approaches to life and society wildly different.

To begin with, Latinos want to work. As a rule, blacks don't. *Radio Novecientos* regularly announces to its listeners that such-and-such an automotive repair outfit needs electricians with tools, call this number; or that Whatever Hospital wants cleaning women, or people to take care of the bedridden, or to work in day care, call another number. Latinos want jobs. Any jobs.

I've never heard a black station announce jobs.

Overwhelmingly, testimony is that when Latinos get a job, they do it. Whites respect them for it. I meet a fair number of people who hire unskilled or semiskilled labor. Without exception they report that Latinos show up, work hard, and don't have attitudes. Blacks, say employers, don't show up, don't work hard, quit unexpectedly, and tend to be surly.

The result is that, hereabouts anyway, Latinos have taken over the low-end job market. Blacks resent it. If Latinos succeed in moving up, which they seem to have in mind, blacks will simply be bypassed. No alliance there.

Last week, *Radio Novecientos* asked callers, many of them on cell phones on the way to work, to recount their successes in this country. I didn't transcribe calls. The pattern was, "I'm Juan, and I came to this country eight years ago from El Salvador, and started as a busboy for Hyatt. Now I am assistant maintenance manager, and if I can get a little better in English, I think I will be the manager soon." Thus blows the wind.

Latino crime exists, angry Latinos activists complaining of discrimination, friction between brown and white, Latino gangs, and Latinos on welfare. They are not dominant in Latino discourse. The Latino media do not rail against America. The black media do.

The contrast of the Latino with the black approach to life is stark. Latinos are more active, more assertive, believing that they can improve their circumstances by their own efforts. They are, remember, people who had the drive to make their way from Guatemala and swim the river. You don't hear much self-pity from them. Their energy has consequences. Go into black neighborhoods, and you will find the stores operated by Koreans. Drive the streets of suburban Washington, and you will see Latino restaurants and bodegas popping up. I don't know of a single black business (though there must be a few somewhere).

The passivity of blacks is crippling. They have learned that one gets things not by earning them, but by demanding them. If they demand money from Coca-Cola, they get it. If they demand more black faces on television, television turns black. If they can't pass tests for promotion, they demand that the tests be abandoned, and they are. If they just want money, they demand reparations. I'm not sure how they came to wield their enormous political power, but wield it they do. It works—now.

But Latinos are fast gaining political clout. If the two come into conflict, things will be interesting. Latinos, I think, will feel little guilt over the difficulties of blacks.

The Latino preference for self-reliance over passive complaint appears in many venues. A frequent theme in the Spanish media is the high rate at which their kids drop out of school. The problem is serious, threatening their future in this country, and they know it. According to the host on *Radio Novecientos*, the kids drop out because they want to go to work and buy cars, or because they're intimidated by English. Whatever the reasons, they go.

Conspicuously, however, the Latino response is to ask, "What are we doing wrong, and how can we help our kids do better?" They don't blame Gringos for all their problems. Similarly, alcoholism is a plague among Latinos. When they discuss it in the Spanish media, which they frequently do, the attitude is, "We drink too much. How can we stop?" not, "Whitey did this to us."

By contrast, blacks protest that everything is someone else's fault. Drugs, for example, are a white plot to destroy blacks. In the long run, I suspect that people who face their problems will win over those who don't.

Finally, Latinos want to be here (and want all their relatives to be here, which is a problem). At least in their public comment they speak of the US as a wonderful country, a land of opportunity, where everyone can have "a better life." The phrase constantly recurs: "*una vida mejor.*" (Mexicans however have attitudes much closer to those of blacks than do other Latinos.) Blacks, at least in their public comments, don't like the US, describing it as a fundamentally evil, a land of oppression and lack of opportunity.

I don't see a lot of common ground between the two. To the extent that Latinos succeed, whatever common ground there is will diminish.

If Latinos remain at the bottom of the economy, which I think unlikely, they will compete with blacks. If they rise, they will enter the mainstream. In which case, what's the problem?

California Dreaming

The Great Custom Lawnmower Craze of 1972 caught California unawares. The state is not easily astonished. Still, Mikey Deeter managed it.

Mikey lived in Riverside, one of those pseudo-Spanish Levittowns that dangle like beads from the freeways. He was seventeen. He had long blonde hair, a great tan, and the vacant expression one associates with surfers. His total vocabulary came in at perhaps 127 words, mostly automotive.

It was deceptive. As the world would learn, there was method in his blandness.

One afternoon in August Mikey sat in his backyard. He was pondering the unfairness of life, a phenomenon that always takes the young by surprise. All his friends in high school had cars—deuce coupes and '40 Fords, chopped and channeled, with gleaming hopped-up engines and tuck-and-roll Naugahyde interiors and improbable paint jobs. Cars had practical implications. Mikey suspected his buddies were doing the cheerleaders because of their hot mo-sheens. Mikey couldn't afford a car, even a Plymouth. He pondered suicide.

Then a glint came into his eyes. Maybe... just maybe....

No. It would never work.

But...it just might. Anyway, it was worth a try. He went to the garage and retrieved a deteriorating lawnmower.

All afternoon, and for many consecutive afternoons, he labored over the tired machine. He detail-stripped the beast—took it apart to the bolts, Gunked the engine, sanded the body to bare metal. He sent the motor and blade to Big Daddy Sparkle's style shop to be triple-chromed. Next he painted the body with twenty-seven coats of hand-rubbed Kandy Kolor Lava Mist metal-flake lacquer the color of molten plums. When he finished you could look deep into it, and the little swirls seemed to move. The neighbors thought he was crazy.

Finally he built in an eight-track stereo that played Little Old Lady From Pasadena, added ape-hanger handlebars covered in plastic chinchilla fur and, for ecological piety, installed a plastic recirculating waterfall he found in a flower store. When he was through the thing glittered with little points of ruby light and the engine shot diamonds. It was wonderful, indescribable, and perfectly useless. He put it into his friend Bungie's pickup truck and they drove it to a Kustom Car show in Los Angeles.

Now, Kustom Cars as understood in California have little to do with cars, and nothing to do with transportation. They are a form of automotive sculpture, having vast supercharged engines that won't start because the gas tank has been removed to make room for a refrigerator. Sometimes they won't even roll: The wheels, dismounted so the car will sit rakishly lower, rest beside it on satin cushions. Mikey and Bungie pushed the mower through crowds of aficionados to the Free-Style division and found the presiding official. This worthy was beaded and pony-tailed and had grease under his fingernails. His T-shirt said Duke's Speed Shop. He eyed the mower doubtfully.

"It's a Class-A nontraditional off-road experimental," said Mikey with more confidence than he felt.

He turned the throttle and it played Little Old Lady. The official, though puzzled, was charmed. Then Mikey turned on the recirculating waterfall. The official peered intently and said, "*Far-r-r-r out!*"

"But, I think, you know, it has to be a vehicle," he said.

Mikey countered, "I could stand on it and roll down a hill."

It got in.

To everyone's amazement, it also took First in Class. It was so…different. Further, it was the only entry. Crowds gathered where the mower lay on a cloud of peach-colored glass wool, waterfall trickling.

"It's like, you know, sculpture art," Mikey told a bored reporter from the *L.A. Times*. "Like stuff in museums." The reporter returned to the newsroom, where he mentioned the mower as he might an outbreak of plague. He had been in Los Angeles too long.

Luck had it that the art critic for the Times was on deadline with nothing to write about. He knocked out a piece about how the mower "represented a cross-pollination between the technical underpinnings of modern industrial society and the yearning for a new and meaningful esthetic by the young." He baptized the new movement Kinetic Bauhaus. Then he got drunk to salve his conscience.

The effect was galvanic. Up and down the coast, young males raced to garages. They sandblasted, welded, and painted, surfing on the wave of the new art form. Though few appeared to be repositories of high intelligence, or any intelligence, they were in fact technically adept and imaginative, the kind of young men who had made America whatever it was. They believed instinctively in the Californian principle that if a thing isn't worth doing at all, it is worth doing to wild excess.

Mowerdom flourished. Shows proliferated. Magazines appeared: *Kustom Grassblaster* and *MegaMulcher*. They carried articles like, "440-C Blades vs. Polycarbonate Laminates: Which Is Better?" and "Nitro-Fueled Unlimiteds Take On The Elephant Grass of Northern Thailand."

These were halcyon days for Mikey. He was a guru, in demand on the radio. He explained The Movement, which was now generally recognized as representing a fundamental new direction in artistic expression, and perhaps a basic alteration of Western consciousness.

"It's a new thing and all. If you go to an old art museum, the paintings are, you know, like flat. They just hang there That's the trouble with old art. It doesn't do anything."

However, ominous clouds were brewing. What with being a spiritual leader, appearing on talk shows, and clearing up a backlog of cheerleaders, Mikey was sliding imperceptibly down the slack side of the wave. Already his mower was regarded with antiquarian interest, like the Wright Brothers' airplane.

Others pulled ahead. A post-doc in biochem at Berkeley mounted the engine from a Harley Sportster on a mower modified with dune-buggy wheels. For ecological awareness it had the now-traditional recirculating waterfall, in a cage with a gaudy macaw that shrieked obscenities in Spanish. It would have won the Nationals had not the macaw taken to coughing horribly. The vet determined that nothing was wrong with it. It was just trying to imitate a Sportster engine. By them, unfortunately, the Nationals were over.

Mikey didn't have the money to compete. The death blow came when a wealthy proctologist from Anaheim, with extensive holdings in the stock market, announced that he was going to mount a surplus helicopter upside down on wheels, trumping even the Harley with its confused bird.

It was terrible. Mikey's own movement had left him behind.

So did the cheerleaders. Shortly he was again sitting in his backyard, pondering the unfairness of life.

New York: The Price Of Pansyhood

A few unorganized thoughts regarding the events in New York:

1. We lost. Our moral posturing about our degradation is merely embarrassing. We have been made fools of, expertly and calculatedly, in the greatest military defeat the country has suffered since we fled from Viet Nam. The Moslem world is laughing and dancing in the streets. The rest of the earth, while often sympathetic, sees us as the weak and helpless nation that we are.

   The casualty figures aren't in, but several thousand dead seems reasonable, and we wring our hands and speak of grief therapy.

   We lost.

2. We cannot stop it from happening again. Thousands of aircraft constantly use O'Hare, a few minutes flying time from the Sears Tower.

3. Our politicians and talking heads speak of "a cowardly act of terrorism." It was neither cowardly nor, I think, terrorism. Hijacking an aircraft and driving it into a building isn't cowardly. Would you do it? It requires great courage and dedication—which our enemies have, and we do not. One may mince words, but to me the attack looked like an act of war. Not having bombing craft of their own, they used ours. When we bombed Hanoi and Hamburg, was that terrorism?

4. The attack was beautifully conceived and executed. These guys are good. They were clearly looking to inflict the maximum humiliation on the United States, in the most visible way possible, and they did. The sight of those two towers collapsing will leave nobody's mind. If we do nothing of importance in return, and it is my guess that we won't, the entire earth will see that we are a nation of epicenes. Silly cruise-missile attacks on Afghanistan will just heighten the indignity.

5. In watching the coverage, I was struck by the tone of passive acquiescence. Not once, in hours of listening, did I hear anyone express anger. No one said, coldly but in deadly seriousness, "People are going to die for this, a whole lot of people." There was talk of tracking down bin Laden and bringing him to justice. "Terrorism experts" spoke of months of investigation to find who was responsible, which means we will do nothing. Blonde bimbos babbled of coping strategies and counseling and how our children needed support. There was no talk of retaliation.

6. The Israelis, when hit, hit back. They hit back hard. But Israel is run by men. We are run by women. Perhaps two-thirds of the newscasters were blonde drones who spoke of the attack over and over as a tragedy, as though it had been an unusually bad storm—unfortunate, but inevitable, and now we must get on with our lives. The experts and politicians, nominally male, were effeminate and soft little things. When a feminized society runs up against male enemies—and bin Laden, whatever else he is, is a man—it loses. We did.

7. We haven't admitted that the Moslem world is our enemy, nor that we are at war. We see each defeat and humiliation in isolation, as a unique incident unrelated to anything else. The 241 Marines killed by the truck bomb in Beirut, the extended humiliation of the hostages taken by Iran, the war with Iraq, the bombing of the

Cole, the destruction of the embassies in Kenya and Tanzania, the devastation of the Starke, the Saudi barracks, the dropping of airliner after airliner—these we see as anecdotes, like pileups of cars on a snowy road. They see these things as war.

We face an enemy more intelligent than we are.

8. We think we are a superpower. Actually we are not, except in the useless sense of having nuclear weapons. We could win an air war with almost anyone, yes, or a naval war in mid-Pacific. Few Americans realize how small our forces are today, how demoralized and weakened by social experimentation. If we had to fight a ground war in terrain with cover, a war in which we would take casualties, we would lose.

9. I have heard some *grrr-woofwoofery* about how we should invade Afghanistan and teach those ragheads a lesson. Has anyone noticed where Afghanistan is? How would we get there? Across Pakistan, a Moslem country? Or through India? Do we suppose Iran would give us overflight rights to bomb another Moslem country? [As it turned out, I was sure wrong about overflight. Oh well.] Or will our supply lines go across Russia through Turkmenistan? Do we imagine that we have the airlift or sealift? What effect do we think bombing might have on Afghanistan, a country that is essentially rubble to begin with?

We backed out of Somalia, a Moslem country, when a couple of GIs got killed and dragged through the streets on TV. Afghans are not pansies. They whipped the Russians. Our sensitive and socially-conscious troops would curl up in balls.

10. To win against a more powerful enemy, one forces him to fight a kind of war for which he isn't prepared. Iraq lost the Gulf War because it fought exactly the kind of war in which American forces are unbeatable. Hussein played to his weaknesses and our strengths. The Vietnamese did the opposite. They defeated us by

fighting a guerrilla war that didn't give us anything to hit. They understood us. We didn't understand them.

The Moslem world is doing the same thing. Because their troops, or terrorists as we call them, are not sponsored by a country, we don't know who to hit. Note that Yasser Arafat, bin Laden, and the Taliban are all denying any part in the destruction of New York. At best, we might, with our creaky intelligence apparatus, find Laden and kill him. It's not worth doing: Not only would he have defeated America as nobody ever has, but he would then be a martyr. Face it: The Arabs are smarter than we are.

11. We are militarily weak because we have done what we usually do: If no enemy is immediately in sight, we cut our forces to the bone, stop most R&D, and focus chiefly on sensitivity training about homosexuals. When we need a military, we don't have one. Then we are unutterably surprised.

12. The only way we could save any dignity and respect in the world would be to hit back so hard as to make teeth rattle around the world. A good approach would be to have NSA fabricate intercepts proving that Libya was responsible, mobilize nationally, invade, and make Libya permanently a US colony. Most Arab countries are militarily helpless, and that is the only kind our forces could defeat. Doing this, doing anything other than whimpering, would require that ancient military virtue known as "balls." Does Katie Couric have them?

Women In Combat: Facts From A Closet

O ccasionally I have written that placing women in physically demanding jobs in the military, as for example combat, is stupid and unworkable. Predictably I've gotten responses asserting that I hate women, abuse children, cannibalize orphans, and can't get a date. A few, with truculence sometimes amplified by misspelling, have demanded supporting data.

OK. The following are from documents I found in a closet, left over from my days as a syndicated military columnist ("Soldiering," Universal Press Syndicate). Note the dates: All of this has been known for a long time.

From the report of the Presidential Commission on the Assignment of Women in the Armed Forces (report date November 15, 1992, published in book form by Brassey's in 1993): "The average female Army recruit is 4.8 inches shorter, 31.7 pounds lighter, has 37.4 fewer pounds of muscle, and 5.7 more pounds of fat than the average male recruit. She has only 55 percent of the upper-body strength and 72 percent of the lower-body strength... An Army study of 124 men and 186 women done in 1988 found that women are more than twice as likely to suffer leg injuries and nearly five times as likely to suffer [stress] fractures as men."

Further: "The Commission heard an abundance of expert testimony about the physical differences between men and women that can be summarized as follows:

"Women's aerobic capacity is significantly lower, meaning they cannot carry as much as far as fast as men, and they are more susceptible to fatigue.

"In terms of physical capability, the upper five percent of women are at the level of the male median. The average 20-to-30 year-old woman has the same aerobic capacity as a 50 year-old man."

From the same report: "Lt Col. William Gregor, United States Army, testified before the Commission regarding a survey he conducted at an Army ROTC Advanced Summer Camp on 623 women and 3540 men. ...Evidence Gregor presented to the Commission includes:

"(a) Using the standard Army Physical Fitness Test, he found that the upper quintile of women at West point achieved scores on the test equivalent to the bottom quintile of men.

"(c) Only 21 women out of the initial 623 (3.4%) achieved a score equal to the male mean score of 260.

"(d) On the push-up test, only seven percent of women can meet a score of 60, while 78 percent of men exceed it.

"(e) Adopting a male standard of fitness at West Point would mean 70 percent of the women he studied would be separated as failures at the end of their junior year, only three percent would be eligible for the Recondo badge, and not one would receive the Army Physical Fitness badge...."

The following, quoted by Brian Mitchell in his book *Women in the Military: Flirting With Disaster* (Regnery, 1998) and widely known to students of the military, are results of a test the Navy did to see how well women could perform in damage control—i.e., tasks necessary to save a ship that had been hit. The results:

Stretcher carry, level: 63% of women failed before strength training; 38% after training.
Stretcher carry, down ladder: 94% before, 88% after.
P250 pump, carry down: 99% before, 99% after.
P250 pump, carry up: 73% before, 52% after.

Remove SSTO pump: 99% before, 99% after.
Torque engine bolt: 78% before, 47% after.

No males failed any of these tests, before or after training.

Our ships can be hit. I know what supersonic stealthed cruise missiles are. So do the Iraqis.

Also from the Commission's report: "Non-deployability briefings before the Commission showed that women were three times more non-deployable than men, primarily due to pregnancy, during Operations Desert Shield and Storm. According to Navy Captain Martha Whitehead's testimony before the Commission, 'the primary reason for the women being unable to deploy was pregnancy, that representing 47 percent of the women who could not deploy.'"

Maybe we need armored strollers.

My friend Catherine Aspy graduated from Harvard in 1992 and (no, I'm not on drugs) enlisted in the Army in 1995. Her account was published in *Reader's Digest*, February, 1999, and is online in the Digest's archives.

She told me the following about her experiences: "I was stunned. The Army was a vast day-care center, full of unmarried teen-age mothers using it as a welfare home. I took training seriously and really tried to keep up with the men. I found I couldn't. It wasn't even close. I had no idea the difference in physical ability was so huge. There were always crowds of women sitting out exercises or on crutches from training injuries.

"They [the Army] were so scared of sexual harassment that women weren't allowed to go anywhere without another woman along. They called them 'Battle Buddies.' It was crazy. I was twenty-six years old but I couldn't go to the bathroom by myself."

Women are going to take on the North Korean infantry, but need protection in the ladies' room. Military policy is endlessly fascinating.

When I was writing the military column, I looked into the experience of Canada, which tried the experiment of feminization. I got the report from Ottawa, as did the Commission. Said the Commission:

"After extensive research, Canada has found little evidence to support the integration of women into ground units. Of 103 Canadian women who volunteered to joint infantry units, only one graduated the initial training course. The Canadian experience corroborates the testimony of LTC Gregor, who said the odds of selecting a woman matching the physical size and strength of the average male are more than 130-to-1."

From *Military Medicine*, October 1997, which I got from the Pentagon's library:

(p. 690): "One-third of 450 female soldiers surveyed indicated that they experienced problematic urinary incontinence during exercise and field training activities. The other crucial finding of the survey was probably that 13.3% of the respondents restricted fluids significantly while participating in field exercises." Because peeing was embarrassing.

Or, (p. 661): "Kessler et al found that the lifetime prevalence of PTSD in the United States was twice as high among women..." Depression, says MilMed, is far commoner among women, as are training injuries. Et cetera.

The military is perfectly aware of all of this. Their own magazine has told them. They see it every day. But protecting careers, and rears, is more important than protecting the country.

Anyway, for those who wanted supporting evidence, there it is.

Elvis As A Distributed Algorithm

Today, Napster and the imminent demise (I hope) of the entire entertainment industry.

You probably know about Napster, which is software that lets people exchange music over the Internet. It was invented by this mere kid named Shawn Fanning, who was something like nineteen years old, or twelve, or at any rate barely more than a zygote. Pretty smart zygote, howsomever.

Apparently he was sitting around one day, scratching and thinking about girls, and said to himself, "I guess I'll write a music-sharing program that will explode across the entire earth like a squeezed grape, make all known music available to everyone everywhere for free, drive the recording industry into the gibbering apoplectic heebeejeebees, spawn massive lawsuits, and have teenagers everywhere shrieking for DSL, which their parents don't know what is. Or else I could go to the mall and hang out."

He wrote the code. It worked. In a few months, without federal help, 32,000,000 people (so help me, I think that's the real number) had signed up, and every night many of them were online across the whole earth, gobbling music. Napster had stood the world on its end, which is hard to do with a sphere.

A zygote did this. What's he gonna do when he's big?

But first you gotta under stand what Napster really is. The language will be graphic, but we're all adults here. You probably ought to send children to bed.

Napster is a file-sharing system.

"Why, Fred," you say. "That's fascinating. Like sorting socks." Well, yeah. Manila folders are more exciting.

Practically, however, Napster is, or was, amazing: Tower Records in the Sky, open twenty-four hours, with all the music free. If you typed "Jailhouse Rock" into the little search thingy on Napster, you got a list of computers around the world that had it on their hard drives. You clicked on one of them, and—Hooo-*eeee*!—Elvis His Own Self poured into your hard drive, sloosh. Then, if you were a teenager, you burned it onto a CD. Bingo. You had just stolen Elvis, which is slick because he is actually dead, and taken New York out of the loop. Putting it differently, New York is now everywhere, like larceny.

The recording industry got no end upset, and pretended to see Napster in moral terms: The theft of music owned by others. Actually the industry wouldn't know morals from tadpoles. The real issue, the far greater issue, is control. The entertainment industry is used to controlling music, books, and movies—and consequently, to a considerable extent, American culture.

Unfortunately for the industry, their products are inherently digitizable. This means that all of them, now or very soon, can easily be copied and sent anywhere by Internet. Unless the industry can find some means, legal or technical, to prevent this, all of its property will be de facto in the public domain, oops.

So much for control.

Something that makes things scarier for the industry: People increasingly seem to believe that digital information belongs to everybody, like God and air. Respectable adults, who wouldn't steal a pack of sugar from a diner, now routinely, if quietly, pass around copyright software to friends. They burn copies of CDs checked out of libraries and download gigabytes from Napster. Kids copy CDs wholesale. A moral sea change is occurring. It bodeth not well for the industry.

The flaw in the ointment so far—the fatal fly, so to speak—has been copyright. Most of that music belongs to big record companies. The question isn't as simple as it seems: If you record Jailhouse Rock onto tape from your radio, for personal use, that's legal. If you download it onto your computer, it isn't. What's the difference?

Nonetheless, the RIAA screamed like a scalded eagle. And won, having lots of money. Napster is going away. Well, sort of going away. Maybe. Some of it. Except maybe not.

Sons of Napster are popping up right and left. Try Aimster, for example. While they do the same thing—share music—they do it in ways that may not be legally vulnerable. Which is to say, this war ain't over.

Further, and real important, digital information may by its very nature be uncontrollable—short, anyway, of totalitarian intrusion into people's lives. Many of the music-grubbing criminals are teenagers. If the industry began prosecuting children, it would draw back a bloody stump. Approximately the entire earth uses Napster, and all of the fifteen-year-olds. It is hard to sue the entire earth.

Another, and serious, problem for the industry: Geeks. I mentioned one of the many copy-prevention schemes to my daughter, age nineteen. "Don't worry," she said with unconcern, "the boys will break it." She had a point. All over Berkeley there are rooms full of intense geeks with IQs of 170 and C++ compilers. They eat nothing but potato chips and Jolt Cola, and are anarchists to the gills. They will fall on copy-protection schemes in hunting packs.

The RIAA is filing lawsuits, and its teeth, because it knows that, if the various Napsters aren't killed, the industry will be eyeball to eyeball with extinction. Who is going to pay $33 for two CDs of Credence Clearwater Survival when he can get it for free, and just the tracks he wants? For music, the Internet has already broken the monopoly over distribution. Come broadband, and people will swap movies on DVD, or just flat copy them.

A major money-bucket will dry up, and record stores will vanish, leaving smoking holes in the ground.

Which raises a question. Musicians deserve to be paid. The entertainment industry, however, deserves to be drowned. They are moral sludge who have drenched the country in vulgarity, pore-level sex, and gorgeous explosive eviscerations in slow motion. Anything that hurts them is good for civilization. So how can we pay the musicians, but not the RIAA?

It matters. At bottom, the dispute over Napster isn't about kids listening to godawful rock'n'roll. It's what philosophers call a Pair-of-Diggem Shift. (If they called it something comprehensible, like a Whole Nuther Way of looking at things, they'd never get tenure, and have to work for a living.) We're moving into a new world, whether we choose to or not.

What it comes down to, say I, is whether the cultural splendor of having music, literature, theater, and cinema freely available around the world outweighs the difficulty of finding another way to recompense those who actually produce these things. As for the RIAA—hanging would serve nicely.

A Codpiece For Hillary

The other day I saw a photo of Hillary Clinton going into the Senate. She was, well, rumpled. I have a kind heart, so I won't say that she looked like a teenager's room, but I did conclude that she must have had a better maintenance contract when she was First Basilisk. You could tell that she needed new siding and maybe her lawn mowed and some paint on her trim.

I saw a science fiction movie once, the kind with a twelve-dollar budget and actors they probably found in a bus station. Anyway these scientists were doing experiments with radioactive gunch. It's what scientists do. They'd pour it into test tubes and it would bubble like grits if you don't watch them and turn colors.

I guess it didn't work because they threw it in a landfill and went off to shoot pool. Well, that landfill started to jiggle, and humph, and sort of pile up on itself, and finally set off to eat Boise. It left a trail and looked like it needed combing.

I don't know why I thought of that.

We were talking about Hillary. When she and Bill lived in that nice double-wide on Pennsylvania Avenue, she was sleek, probably because she had terrific make-up people who did injection molding, and she'd say, "Cookies," and "Children," and all the ladies would vote for her so she could be the Senator from New York. It helped that New Yorkers are dumber than rutabagas.

But people who knew her said she was icy cold and crocodilian.

So I reckon we've got one of those profound social questions that you can do a doctoral thesis on:

"Hillary Clinton: Cookie Monster, Walk-In Fridge, Or Dumpster?"

Thing is, you can't look at Hillary in isolation. (Actually, I don't feel a pressing need to look at her at all. But we're being sociological.) If you want to make sense of the Clintons, the best way is to understand them as the revenge of the Confederacy. Nothing else makes them plausible.

My guess is that a secret society, in Montgomery or maybe Chattanooga, figured that the South would never Rise Again, but if they could bring the North low enough, it would be the same thing. I reckon the conspirators meet in a duck blind out in a swamp and drink Franklin County shine ('cause it's the best) and eat okra. Then they plot.

Now, think about this. Suppose you wanted to destroy the Union, and humiliate it, and make everybody cross the street when they saw it coming. You'd probably start by making some hamhock grifter President. You can actually embarrass a country into submission, except maybe the United States. So I guess they called Little Rock, and got What's-His-Porkchop to run. They knew Yankees didn't have better judgment.

Hillary was part of the plan from the beginning. The Committee for Southern Revenge knew that Bill had a character that made tapioca look like reinforced concrete. A vertebrate influence was needed to steady him. Besides, Bill would have to leave office in eight years, taking everything in it with him. They saw Hillary as the iron spine of formless mendacity. She was their hope for continuing the havoc.

It worked pretty well. Ol' Willy Bill came into Washington honking on a saxophone like a cheap rock band and proceeded to grope women and rut and lie more than he breathed. The Yankee Capital had always had the charm of a theater seat's underside. Now it had become ridiculous. Can you imagine what the French thought? They didn't have Elvis or an army that you'd notice, but they did have taste.

The Union had been brought low. It was revenge sweeter than a pair of Moon Pies stuck together with sorghum syrup.

For eight years, Willie was a serviceable embarrassment. In fact he was spectacular. He sold secrets to the Chinese and did chunky interns. He'd look you in the eye like a sincere cow with an uncle complex and say, "Ah feel yore pine," and maybe your leg too. Wise men locked up their daughters and the dog and the whole business was funnier than a toad frog in a milk shake. I guess people in Little Rock laughed and laughed, 'cause they knew it was going to happen.

The next trick for the boys in the duck blind was to get Hillary to be President. I'm serious. They knew she would wreck the Union as Marse Bob and Stonewall never could. She would be like getting a second shot at Gettysburg, but as an inside job.

Sure enough, Willy Bill's eight years ran out, and he left, selling pardons like New Year's at Wal-Mart. (Literary Republicans with a taste for Chaucer began calling Hillary The Pardoner's Tail.) This, what with looting the White House, proved to be a problem. The duck-blind conspirators worried that even the American public might not be crazy enough to elect Hillary after that. She did her best to help. She said that, why, she was just shocked about those pardons, and how she was just a li'l ol' housewife, and baked, and thought about children, and didn't worry her silly little head about politics or what her husband was doing.

Everyone figures that when the White House comes open, she's going to run like bad nylons and, if she wins, then Bill could be first lady and they could steal everything in the White House they didn't carry off the first time. Political insiders in Washington think she'd mostly likely pull it off. She'd get all of the black vote, most of the women, and the men would all move to Canada.

The Committee for Southern Revenge didn't want to take chances. They wanted her to get male as well as female votes. This required a balance between virility and domesticity. Domesticity was easy. She could just say "Cookies" a lot. But ...virility?

So they got a custom-leather store to make Hillary a codpiece, and Fed-Exed it. Suede, with alligator straps, and a little pocket for car keys. It should get here in a week or so. I hear it's stunning, and ought to intimidate hell out of the Chinese.

A Place I Cared About

Dawn comes to the alleys around Tan Son Nhut Field with a faint grey light seeping past the graveyard and up the dusty road toward the banana market. Pots begin to clatter and red charcoal dims in brightening court-yards. A hungry dog sniffs in the ditch. A cyclo, a motor-driven coal scoop equally useful as a conveyance or means of suicide, sputters hungrily down the alley in search of fares. A few women in black pajamas haggle over fresh bananas gleaming like fat yellow and green fingers in the stalls.

For a moment all is quiet. Then, suddenly, ochre swarms of children rush out to begin the day's battles. Swarms of motor scooters appear from nowhere. The sinuous cry of a soup-woman floats over the chaos.

Old Mr. Wang opens the shutters and stands beneath the sign that says, "Wang's Grocery and House For Rent." He folds his hands across his sagging chest, surveys the alley with dignity appropriate to the biggest paunch in four blocks, and smiles broadly. The day is officially begun.

The thoroughfare of the slums is Truong Minh Ky Street. It cuts through the rich decaying life of the back streets like a monotonous grey artery. Hungry and vaguely frightening men in work clothes jostle against hard-faced women carrying baskets of produce. Dirty buses roar and fill the air with choking fumes. Toilets flush onto sidewalks, washing orange peels and rotting vegetables into the gutters. From the counters of little pharmacies and sundry shops the Chinese merchants calmly watch the ebb and flow.

As you move away from Truong Minh Ky along side streets, commerce dies. Tangled alleys twist at bewildering angles. High walls and barbed wire shield palatial residences of wealthy Chinese while bony dogs and endless children play at the gates. Whole apartment houses of chattering prostitutes overlook shacks made of ammunition crates and roofed with tin. Everything in Southeast Asia is made of ammunition crates. Children in Saigon think that wood grows with lot numbers for howitzer shells.

The heart of Asia beats here, among the muddy recesses and noodle stands, in the ever-present smell of fish and charcoal and sewage. Westerners do not come here. They don't like to see rats floating in stagnant pools of green water. And so they never eat rice and fish sauce on the summer rooftops or drink beer and talk away long mornings with the bar girls or see Thao Han playing with her baby. They never see Asia.

By seven o'clock, sunlight streams across the outlying rice lands, crosses the river, and deliberately enters the window of Bill Murphy. Bachelors have their routines just as other people. Every morning Bill tries to hide under the pillow when the sun hits his face. Then he curses a little, rises grumpily, brushes his teeth, and spits over the balcony into the empty lot. Vacant lots are intended as urinals in time of need and places to spit. Bill is fond of this particular lot because he likes its pattern of oily puddles and old crankshafts.

Every morning he forgets the crushed cockroaches on the floor, steps on them, and growls under his breath. Each night at eleven they run from under the walls and rush in mindless circles, making papery noises, until whacked with a shower shoe.

"You oozy bastards," he tells them, and twiddles them by the legs to break the congealed juices. They go over the rail into the lot.

He doesn't discard his roaches at night because he is too drunk. The world is steady if not importunate in its demand for slightly lurid newspaper copy about the East, and the typewriter on the table allows Bill to supply the demand. The secret of writing, Bill believes, is to drink just the right amount of Vietnamese beer. Too much makes the product florid, too little leaves it sparse and dry. With just the right amount, adjectives come with ease and taste, clauses flow in balance and pattern. Unfortunately, the right amount makes it hard to walk with accuracy.

He runs the back of his hand over a stubbly chin and decides that he should shave this week, though not necessarily today. One reason Bill stays in Vietnam is that shaving is optional. The other reasons are women and a lack of alarm clocks. Bill believes that satisfying physiological urges is the end in life. Anything else, he suspects, is going beyond God's intent.

On the cramped landing the Korean family, the only other residents of the second floor, squat around a can of charcoal. Mrs. Li smiles in a glow of gold teeth and waves a limp carp from the six-by-ten room where the Lis and their six children live.

"Murphy-san, fish, have. Him boocoo dead, don't you?" Her English is colorful, if not technically correct.

"A fish, undeniably. Mr. Li get a job yet?"

Her face falls. "No, him no job yet."

She brightens. "No sweat. Rice still have, some little."

Mr. Li has been gone since before light, looking for work. There is no work in Saigon. If there were, Mr. Li could be an electrician, truck driver, second mate of an oceangoing tug, or conscienceless infantryman. He is smiling and deferential to everyone.

The Li children would baffle a platoon of sociologists. They are healthy, neat, and sound of character despite abject poverty. More puzzling to an American is that they are civil and love their parents. The older ones are already learning to read, though they have never seen a school.

The small Lis have decided that Bill's pale skin and odd eyes are aberrations to be forgiven. Kim Li Kuan, who at seven is already a dangerously charming woman, smiles up from her rice bowl. Her eyes flatten into sideways black slits.

"Murphy-san have candy?"

"Unprincipled imp," says Bill, stepping over her into the bathroom. Life is personal at high density.

In the courtyard, the wizened caretaker squats. A discouraged black beret droops across his cropped head. His face is a ploughed field of wrinkles, big gaping gullies, tiny delicate rivulets, middle-sized crevices. They flow across his face in waves, break around his nose, and reflect from his ears. Some catch in the wattles of his neck. He is three hundred years old, and his mother was an earth sprite.

Every morning when Bill Murphy leaves, the old man croaks under his breath and looks puzzled. He is puzzled because there are always crushed roaches on his doorstep, but Bill Murphy doesn't know that. For a man of three hundred he is fiendishly clever. When Bill counts the rent money into his hand, "Four, five, six" the old man takes them in French, "Three, four five," and Bill invariably pays an extra bill.

His mother wasn't really an earth sprite.

In a dim room behind Madame Hai's betel-nut stand, Buddha glitters in chill ceramic complacency at a nude seamstress from Chicago. Why the prostitute who owns him put the god on the gatefold of a girly magazine is a mystery. Perhaps Loan, who could seduce a marble slab, suspects Buddha is not as unreachable as he seems.

On the bed, Loan stirs and opens travel-poster eyes that urge intimacy when she is thinking only of breakfast. Beside her in a forlorn pile are the tools of her trade, glittering high heels, false eyelashes, and scanty dress. She looks better without them, but that isn't how the thing is done. She stretches seductively and glances at the jeweled wristwatch given to her by an American contractor. Eleven o'clock.

Graceful and tiny as a cameo elf, she rises and gathers clothes to wash. By two she must be in Kim Ling's club at the dusty edge of Cach Mang Street. Her life passes among dimness and canned beer, in a gaudy cage of drunken helicopter mechanics. She is free as a force-fed hen.

Bill Murphy, who once lived with her, asked why she didn't marry some sucker and spend all his money in America.

"Then nobody take care my mother. She old now, die soon."

Such sentiment surprised Bill, who thought she was a reincarnated lamprey.

"Can get plenty men," she said, understating the case. "Only have one mother."

Bill goggled.

"When I small, my mother do everything for me. Now I do for her. What men do for me?"

Extremely little.

Bill, tired of having his pockets picked, moved out.

Before starting her washing she meticulously dusts her cosmetic table, a tacky creation of plastic wood and blue polyethylene roses. It has a mirror and two drawers, one of which works smoothly. It is the most beautiful thing Loan has ever owned. She paid three month's savings for it. Sometimes she gazes at it for an hour.

It depressed Bill Murphy to watch her, which is the real reason he moved out.

The noonday sun beats down on Saigon. By the roadside, mangy dogs pant in available shade, wary to avoid a kick. The festering head of one of their friends grins in stale agony from a pool of ditch water. His owners ate him yesterday, but it is too hot for the living to be concerned. Aged mama-sans move more slowly under loads of firewood and vegetables. At the meat market flies hum drowsily around hanging flesh, hardly disturbed by customers' fingers. Even the children seek shelter.

A blind beggar couple in their eighties hobble painfully by Loan's gate. The small boy with the alms cup pulls respectfully on the rope which ties them together. The old man tries to help his wife with a ropy blue-veined hand on her shoulder. Both totter with the effort.

Downtown, tourists drink gin and tonic and gaze at martial statues.

On the dark walls of Kim Ling's club a lizard hunts, dragon eyes smoky with fly lust. Kin Ling counts the month's bribe money at the bar. At 35 she is tough, infinitely shrewd, and still pretty.

She riffles the big orange bills with a practiced thumb, dragging a finger to test the texture of the paper. It is a slow day, and the girls won't come until two. The glasses over the bar lack the gleam that colored lights will give them and, without bottles of beer, tables look cracked and stained, tired almost. Kin Ling doesn't notice, being immune to illusion. Illusion is in the minds of foreigners, who believe anything you tell them. Kim Ling deals in substance.

Traffic rushes past on Cach Mang. Kim Ling lights a cigarette and reclines against the bar, her face tired. Smoke curls to the ceiling, disturbing the lizard.

Twenty years have passed since a swarthy French lieutenant led Kim Ling into a bungalow in the northern village where she was born. In the ensuing exchange, he took her virginity and she got his wallet. The pattern persisted, though now she deals in the innocence or experience of others. The years, while profitable, have been wearying. She continues because there is nothing else for her to do.

The East takes a practical view of sin. Kim Ling gives order and comfort to what otherwise would occur in dark alleys, asking only half a girl's take in return. She nurses her girls when they are sick and dismisses them gently when they are old.

The bills go into Kim Ling's brassiere to await the police chief's agent. She stares at the wall, thinking about nothing. There is nothing to think about.

By mid-afternoon the life of the alleys imperceptibly begins to wane. In front of Nguyen Thao Thi's ramshackle barbershop, the leather-faced peasant women mechanically swing their picks in the road-building project. The wizened caretaker at Bill Murphy's house empties Bill's trash in the courtyard and examines it piece by piece with senile concentration. In Wang Chi's pool hall, which floods knee-deep in the rainy season, the cue ball cracks against the floor, to be pursued by small boys.

Caught in the merry-go-round of a failing economy, people who have little to sell try desperately to sell it to people who can't afford to buy. In the shade of the broken wall by the graveyard, withered women sit in endless patience beside a dozen peanuts or three balls of rice paste. Nobody wants rice paste. Small boys beat *tock-tock-tock* with pieces of bamboo to advertise the soup their mothers are selling.

At a bomb-bomb stand on Truong Minh Ky, a thin white man and an athletic black from Georgia sit over warm beer, a picture of contented lethargy, gazing at the life of the streets. Their careless slouches suggest unfamiliarity with jobs and responsibility. Midas Randall leans back and looks at the sky in sleepy speculation. With a long drag on his cigarette he says to Bill Murphy, "I may put up a hotel downtown. Some friends of mine and me. Something to do on the side, until I get back on my feet. Big money in it."

"Suppose?"

"You know it ain't the money. As much money as I've had, I don't like to bother with it anymore."

His pained expression indicates the burden of money.

"Yep."

"Of course, it all depends on the Greek shipping interests."

"Reckon?"

Midas shrugs with the air of one to whom high finance is crystal. The lapel of his coat, stolen from the coat rack of a tourist restaurant, is stained with six weeks of breakfast. Hs own clothes were left behind when he deserted from the American navy seven years before.

"We got the debenture collateral and our management associates—between you and me, now—they're gonna drop the TWA contract and work with us. That's how big it is. But it's the fealty assiduities, you know."

Bill stares at his beer with furrowed eyebrows, struggling with the fealty assiduities.

"Yeah...yeah, assiduities are rough these days. Damn those assiduities."

Men who have been badly used by the world must manufacture their self-respect. Many of the American derelicts on Truong Minh Ky have made and lost millions and been familiars of royalty. Many speak several languages, though not, of course, any which anyone else is liable to speak. The iron-clad rule is that you never question the other man. You let him be a magnate down on his luck, and he lets you be a CIA agent on a secret mission of unspeakable importance. It is a generous system and saves a lot of effort.

Midas hits the table in a theatrical outburst of sorrow.

"Dammit, Bill, this region has so much potential! It hurts when the big interests ain't interested. But they just won't listen...."

His eyes are tragic.

"Yeah, the big interests are like that," says Bill, paying for the beers, and wondering how a liar as good as Midas could have failed to make good.

In late afternoon the sun gleams blood red on the rusting tin roofs of the alleys. High overhead the clouds glow pink and gauzy in the deepening sunset of Asia. Beyond the city, green rice fields grow suddenly dark in the red light. The alleys dim. Activity slows. The lights come on in Wang's Grocery and House For Rent as Mama-san Wang begins the evening shift. Bill Murphy crosses the dusty way to buy his nightly three quarts of beer.

Beneath rows of dried fish and cans of condensed milk, beside brown sacks of rice, Mama-san Wang sits with patient calm. At Bill's entrance the wrinkles of her plump face flow in a ritual smile of welcome. The foreigner has three bottles, so he must want three beers. With slowness partly of age and partly of character she rummages in the leaky galvanized icebox that keeps the drinks lukewarm.

Beneath the fish sauce, a thin pretty girl sits on a case of Hong Kong crackers with her baby. Her name is Mae Li and she is always serious and a little sad. At Bill's entrance the baby gurgles and crows excitedly with much waving of small arms. No dolt, he remembers that the large stranger will sometimes give a fellow chocolate or other good things from the glass case beside Mama-san Wang. The trick is to get his attention.

"Gitchy-goo, kid," says Bill awkwardly, unused to children. With an experimental finger he pokes at the squirming child. He suspects there must be other things one may say to a baby.

His mother speaks the only grammatical English in the alleys, learned from her American husband before he decided he wasn't really married to her and went back to California. She plans to marry Bill though he, an obtuse male, suspects nothing.

"He is a very fine baby-san, is he not? He satisfies me very well."

"Nice little fella," says Bill peering curiously. "Reckon he'd like some chocolate?"

"Oh, yes, I do think so."

Bill removes his finger from the sticky grasp and supplies the chocolate, which is wetly eaten. He wishes Mae Li weren't trying to marry him. Being Western, he doesn't realize that it isn't very important to her. Life will go on in any event. It always has.

Mama-san Wang hands him the brown bottles with their green-eyed tigers and gives him his change.

"Night, mom. Night, Mae Li. You too, kid."

Mama-san Wang smiles, wondering whether foreigners mean anything when they speak. Bill Murphy crosses the alley and doesn't count his change until he is out of sight, which is the furthest any sane man will trust a Saigon shopkeeper.

Sunset wanes. The sky darkens. The air cools. Wind rustles in the trees and there is a hint of rain. In the courtyard below Bill Murphy's balcony, a slender girl walks through the darkness to the peak-roofed shrine beneath the flower tree. By day it is a mass of green and gold dragons, by night a dark outline obscuring the moon rising in the still-cloudless west. A faint smell of incense floats into the night as she lights joss ticks. The glowing points trace cherry arcs as she bows again and again.

From the distance comes the lingering thump of artillery, a movement of air more than a sound. The nightly fighting is beginning in the countryside. A young girl bowing to Buddha while the guns roar in dark forests—thirty years of Vietnam.

The Times Magazine of Army Times, 1975

How I Was A Big-Time Drag-Racer. Pretty Nearly.

In high school I was a nationally ranked drag racer, almost, and nearly went to Bakersfield in California, to race against Don Garlits and Swamp Rat II. Garlits was then the king of high-revvin,' screaming, blown, nitro-fueled, bored-and-stroked, ported, polished, and wildly over-cammed rocket sleds running on exotic chemicals, big rubber, and the raw edge of metallurgy.

I might have won. I really might have.

You need to know this.

This was in 1963 in King George County, Virginia. The county was a wooded region of the Southern mentality where nothing mattered to teenage boys except cars, beer and, of course, that. The country boys were muscular and unpolished, accustomed to hard lives. They worked shifts in gas stations, changed their own transmissions, and hunted deer in autumn. They knew cars. Some of them got their cobbled-together old jalopies to do things you wouldn't have believed possible. Such as start.

In those days, drag-racing held the male mind in a greasy but powerful grip. Dragging meant putting two vehicles next to each other on a straight piece of asphalt at least a quarter of a mile long, saying "Go!" and seeing who got over the finish line first. It appealed to an intense and primitive competitiveness in young males. There was no point to it, no reason behind it. We figured making sense was an overrated virtue.

I guess I still do.

Anyway, I was then driving a 1953 Chevy the color of two-tone mud. The engine was an inline six that had perhaps at one time run on all of its cylinders. Now it usually seemed to want to keep three in reserve, perhaps as spares. The suspension made me think of drunken cattle. The tired warrior didn't so much have compression as remember it, as an octogenarian reflects on the ardors of youth. You could tune the engine, as a musician probably could tune a clothesline. It mattered about as much.

Another kid named Butch, dark, saturnine, and sometimes a rival, drove a '53 Ford painted white with barn paint. I forget whether one of the windows was broken or one of them wasn't. The tires usually showed more fabric than a tailor shop. One night Butch and I and some others fools made a high-speed run to Colonial Beach along a winding narrow road, only to have a rear tire sigh and go flat as we pulled into the parking lot of a dance hall. It had worn through.

From time to time we'd run into each other out on the forested roads of Saturday night, maybe in a gas station on Route 301, maybe at the high school, maybe at HoJo's in Fredericksburg, where we drove in endless circles with other kids and ate Mighty Mo's to get a head start on plugging our arteries. We worked on The Look. You know, arm draped casually in the window with a confident but jaded smirk. It was Brando meets Presley in the testosteronal evening, young studs on the prowl. The trick was not to park under a mercury vapor lamp, because it would make your zits turn purple.

We did The Challenge: Stared at each other with cynical assurance, the slightest trace of a sneer disturbing the peach fuzz, sizing each other up. Actually we spent all day together in school, and we were buddies—but that's not how the thing was done. Then we'd tap the gas pedal, *rudden*-udden. The other would push the rpms up a bit, *rudden-udden-udden*. Then the first would really push it, *ruddenuddenuddens-ceeeeech*! which was no end impressive. Actually, the *sceeech* meant you had a loose fan belt.

You know those nature shows where the male swamp birds flap their wings like crazy and jerk their heads back and forth and gurgle, so the girl swamp birds will love them? The same principle holds with teenage boys. And it works. Men ought to be grateful that women don't have any more sense than swamp birds. If they did, we'd have to date possums.

One night Butch and I finally drew down on each other at Winterduck: The shootout. There was in those days a commercial dragstrip called Summerduck. Winterduck, where kids dragged illegally, was a stretch of 206 out of Dahlgren in King George, where it crossed Williams Creek in the woods. One midnight we met there, just the two of us.

Showdown. One of us wouldn't come back. We both knew it.

The night was pitch dark and star-studded. Bugs shrieked in the trees, thinking it would get them laid. An occasional fished jumped *plonk*! in the creek. There was no traffic.

The way you lined up next to each other was by stomping the gas and then stomping the brakes, so the car lurched. This was to give the impression that you had 1,532 horsepower with twelve pounds of overpressure on the blower and beefed-up clutch springs. A really hot car was twitchy, goosey. We knew that much. We'd read it somewhere.

There we were, side by side, cocky, ready to rumble. We gunned the engines against soft automatic transmissions and held the brakes on, trying to get the jump on each other. Butch blew his horn. Go! I let go of the brake, as close as I could get to popping the clutch, and waited to be thrown against the seat by blasting acceleration. You know, like a catapult launch from a carrier deck.

Whirrrrr. *Ummmmmmmm*. Sougghh.

At bottom, the fitty-three sounded like a vacuum cleaner. I looked anxiously at the trees in the headlights. Was anything happening? Yes, they were beginning to move. I was sure of it. Less and less slowly we went. We hit twenty-five miles an hour...thirty. Butch was beside me, lifters ticking like castanets. Thirty-two, thirty-five, headed toward destiny and valve float.

But...*nooooo*! The barn paint was pulling ahead. It was inexorable. Fate was against me, robbing me of my shot at the big time. Slowly the white blur gained ground and I....

Lost.

That one defeat was all that kept me from national importance. I know I could have taken Garlits and the Swamp Rat. At least I could have if you'd stolen one of his rear wheels, chained the Rat to a fire plug, and filled its cylinders with linoleum cement. And given me a five-minute head start.

War And Cities

I wonder whether we hadn't better think about the military. A lot of people, both in and out of uniform, suspect that we have become complacent, that we have grown accustomed to bloodless wars, that the country is no longer prepared to accept casualties, nor our troops, in many outfits, to endure the hardships of combat. Again and again these men worry that the military is concerned too much with sensitivity, too little with the hard training that saves lives in combat.

Underlying the debate are two differing ideas of the nature of war. The first holds that war has changed fundamentally in recent years, that henceforth it will be Nintendo. That is, the United States will fight from a safe distance, using technology instead of men. Automated weapons controlled from computer consoles will take the chances and the casualties. The enemy will not have weapons that can threaten our aircraft or our distant carriers and bases. War, for us, will therefore be safe, antiseptic, remote, and physically effortless.

Recent wars lend plausibility to this view. The Gulf War entailed few American casualties and was largely fought from the air. The mini-war in Yugoslavia and the current campaign in Afghanistan continue the pattern: Aircraft and overwhelming technological superiority have allowed victory almost without loss to friendly forces.

Certainly the technological trendline points in the same direction. Remotely controlled, expendable aircraft now have sensors and data links good enough to allow them to find targets and fire serious missiles at them. These weapons as a class are in early development and, to judge by frequent stories in *Aviation Week*, improve rapidly. Surveillance of battlefields by drone aircraft at high altitudes further decreases the need to have men on the ground. Sensors get better, computers faster. Each year it becomes harder to hide.

Soon, say those who accept the theory of war-as-Nintendo, GIs will sit safely in air-conditioned comfort on ships safely at sea, drinking coffee and driving unmanned aircraft five hundred miles away. There will be no danger, no casualties.

Nice if you can get it.

The second school holds that the recent easy wars were, if not freaks, then not typical. We are, they say, lulling ourselves into unpreparedness that will cause disaster if we get into a real war. Recent wars haven't been. They point out that Iraq set itself up for catastrophic defeat by fighting, with a fifth rate military, exactly our kind of war, at the peak of Reagan's buildup, after giving us all the time we wanted to get our forces in place. As military stupidity goes, it ranks with invading Russia. Afghanistan had no modern weapons. And, crucially, no industrially competent adversary is supplying our enemies with advanced weapons.

What if this changes, or we come up against a better enemy? In circumstances not conducive to Nintendo war? Can this happen?

Oh yes.

The way to defeat a superior enemy is to force him to fight in circumstances that keep him from using his superiority. The question arises: In what conditions would our technical mastery cease to be decisive?

Cities. The Marine Corps has noted that a high proportion of the world's population now lives in cities or city-like conurbations. Many of these are near oceans, which makes them of interest to the Corps. The Marine Corps Warfighting Laboratory in Quantico, Virginia, has consequently given a lot of thought to urban warfare. I interviewed some of the men involved a few years back on a story for *Signal* magazine, which covers military electronics. They were sharp. They knew about Stalingrad, knew tactics, knew that fighting in cities has historically produced lots of dead.

There are reasons for this. To begin with, normal weapons often don't work well in cities. You can't easily use artillery because the buildings get in the way. Finding the enemy is difficult when he hides in buildings. A bomb hitting the top of a ten-storey building will do little to urban guerrillas on the first floor. Tanks are easy targets as they move down streets in what the Marines call "urban canyons." Every window is a potential sniping post or rocket site.

It's spooky. In a former life as a military reporter, I patrolled with the Marines in Beirut (weeks before they were blown up) and with the British Army in Belfast. No fighting was going on in either place. Still, you find yourself watching windows carefully, looking down alleys. There's too much cover, too close to you.

There are other problems, ones that soldiers don't always quite grasp. For example, civilians. The enemy would likely be mixed with the normal population, and perhaps use them as shields by not letting them leave. In today's world you can't kill thousands of civilians to dig out the bad guys—particularly if you have been invited in to eliminate terrorists or revolutionaries.

Like it or not, global television is now a force to be dealt with. The enemy would make sure that every little girl screaming with her entrails hanging out would be on the five o'clock news around the world. This does matter, and the Marine Corps knows it, though I'll get lots of mail saying who cares, nuke'm, let God sort'em out and suchlike *grrr-woof-woofery*. It wouldn't take much of that kind of footage to turn the public against intervention.

The only practical way to defeat a capable urban enemy holding the population hostage, without killing large numbers of civilians, is the hard way, with disciplined and trained small units on the ground. This is bloody, nasty work, physically demanding, and slow. As the Marines were perfectly aware when I talked to them, technology can help. For example, small-unit leaders would profit by being able to get quick access to maps of utility tunnels and so on. But men would still have to clear areas building by building. It's not a job for the sensitive.

In short, there are places where gadgetry isn't enough. If we get involved in such places, and have to send non-elite troops, GIs will come back in body bags and, if units aren't psychologically prepared and well trained, even more will die. Can the military, or the country, any longer handle it? Some think so, and some don't.

Now, if you said, "Fred, what city are we going to fight in?" I would answer without hesitation, "I don't know." Maybe we never will fight in a city. I hope not. Yet wars are not easy to predict. Ten years before any of our wars, probably five years before, we didn't know it was coming. Iraq and Afghanistan erupted from nowhere. Others may and probably will.

And we don't seem to get to choose the location.

Hant Explains Women

The other day I went up the holler to see Uncle Hant. I figured he could teach me to understand women, because he knows everything. Hant lives in a double-wide with a '54 Merc on blocks outside, and a fuel-oil tank painted silver, and a three-legged coon dog named Birdshot. A couple of years back, old Birdshot stuck a paw under a lawnmower to catch whatever was making all that noise. I guess it worked.

I knew I'd find Hant working the moonshine still he has farther back in the woods. Everybody figures he makes the best shine west of Roanoke. Flatlanders out of Washington just about fight each other to buy it. Sure enough, he was slouched against the cooker, wearing that hat he has that looks like he found it in a cow pasture, and working on the condensing coils.

"Hant," I said, "You know everything. I'm trying to figure out women."

"Get along, boy. The Lord God Almighty hasn't got that far yet."

Hant doesn't actually exist. He's a Convenient Literary Device.

He went back to fiddling with some copper tubing.

"How's that panther sweat selling?" I said to change the subject for a bit. He nearly went out of business a few years back. Then he started putting cocaine in the mash and a little LSD. Sales went up so much he had to double the price to keep from having traffic jams. On Saturdays a line of Volvos backs up almost to Wheeling. They could have bought good bourbon for half as much, but they thought they were getting something special and authentic. They were, too.

"I reckon I can live with it. 'Cept two damfool yuppies drank the stuff on the way home, like I told'em not to, and kilt theirself on a telephone pole."

Yuppies are dumber than inbred possums.

"Guess you feel kinda bad."

He got that smug look he has. "Nope. I guess I'm just a filter in the gene pool."

Hant always was modest.

"I don't know what's got into women," I said. I was determined to get some pearl of wisdom out of him if I had to drag it out with a back hoe. "You know, these days you can't even get in a fight in a pool hall, and smack hell out of somebody with a pool stick, without some woman starts hollering about violence. I don't understand it. Why else would anybody go to a pool hall?"

"I can't imagine," he said, looking sorrowful. "The female mind works in strange ways. They don't like riding drunk on a motorsickle at night with the lights out either."

"They must be crazy."

"Like a big dog."

You can't teach a woman reason. I used to date this old gal in high school, pretty as a deer gun that's just been blued, and smart too. She couldn't have been nicer if she'd had a passel of angels to show her how. Only problem was she didn't want me to shoot road signs with a twelve-gauge.

I mean, I was that close to perfection.

Hant cocked his head back and looked hard at the condenser coil. He had the air of a man who was starting to be satisfied with himself.

"I reckon you got it fixed," I said.

"Weren't broke."

"Then why work on it?"

"Marketing. Gotta look authentic. You know, like that old Merc by the trailer. I had to go all the way to Bluefield to get one beat-up enough. A yuppie won't buy shine from anybody that drives a Toyota."

That was Hant. Always figuring the angles.

I said, "Another thing I don't understand is how come women always want commitment. Seems like just about the time you're having a good time together she gets all lit up about it. How come they always want to get married? I wanna keep *my* trailer."

It's the lord's own truth. First it's commitment, and then it's marriage. Nothing ruins a couple like matrimony. You got no reason to behave anymore. Five years later you hate each other and she's got your kids and satellite dish.

Hant must have been satisfied with the coil. He spat a stream of tobacco juice and sat on a stump. Nothing's more authentic than tobacco juice. I saw a camel spit like that on the Discovery Channel. I reckon Hant had better aim, but that camel had him hands down on throw-weight.

"Nothing wrong with commitment, boy. I always thought it was good stuff. About an hour at a time. I wonder if I need more tube."

I was starting to like marketing. "I got an idea…" I said.

"Treat it kind, son. It's in a strange place."

Never give Hant an opening.

"You need a stoneware jug and some Mason jars, *I* think."

He pondered, like he always does when money is on the line.

"I guess you might be right. There's this company in New Jersey, makes'em for the tourist trade. Maybe I'll git some." He pulled a bottle of Jim Beam from behind the cooker and sat on a stump. Hant knows better than to drink that rattlesnake poison he makes.

"There's gotta be an answer, Hant. I was talking to Bobby McWhorter the other day. Sally's mad at him again. She says he needs to stop keeping his crankshaft in his kitchen sink. Well, where else is he going to put it? The engine block's in the bathtub. I mean, it seems like women just don't know how to think. Bobby's got a race in two weeks."

"Figures. Well, I guess it could be worse."

"How?"

"I don't know."

When a man can't keep his car in his own sink, something's wrong, I reckon.

"She says he ought buy table cloths."

"What's a table cloth?"

I was beginning to realize that maybe Hant didn't know quite everything.

We gave up and got to talking about things that made sense, like bass lures and monster trucks and how to sell more shine to the yuppies.

"I'm thinking either Ecstasy or PCP," he said. "Probably won't be a telephone pole left between here and Washington. I never cared for telephone poles anyway."

I gave up and went home. Hant's pretty smart for a literary device, but some things are beyond him.

The Politically Correct Also Die

The current hostility toward the churches puzzles me. Almost daily one sees new decisions by the courts apparently aimed at eliminating any manifestation of religion. Yet in almost all places and all times, faith has inspired admiration and respect, and been taken as improving the likelihood that a man could be trusted. Today the slightest whiff of religion is cause for lawsuits and calls for extirpation. When Joseph Lieberman ran for vice president, the objection was not that he was Jewish, but that he might take it seriously.

Why?

I should say that I am not a believing Christian, or believing anything else. Yet I think that the decline of faith has seriously depressed the moral tone of society. It also constitutes a gigantic evasion.

The arresting fact about life is that it doesn't last. As someone said, nobody gets out of here alive. One day the elephant sits on your chest, or the drunk runs the red-light, or the blood vessel bursts. We become definitively dead, smell terrible if not embalmed, and turn into unattractive bones. This would seem to be more fundamentally interesting than the standing of the NASDAQ.

Yet we do not discuss, do not think out loud about such matters. Where do we come from? We don't know. Why are we here? We don't know. Where *is* here? We don't know. Where do we go next, if anywhere? Isn't it a trifle odd that we find ourselves on a small blob of dirt, spinning around a largish spark, in a vast emptiness?

So why the hostility? The secular do not quash religious observance because they think it foolish. Disney is foolish, yet not attacked. Why, then?

Because it offends a particular turn of mind that has been around for a long time, most recently being called Marxism, cultural Marxism, or political correctness. It is a recognizable philosophy, characterized by a desire to remove from public life such concepts as free will, individual autonomy, and any trace of the spiritual.

Proponents of the pseudo-Marxist matrix of modern thought, or avoidance of thought, invariably invoke the separation of Church and state. They are not opposed to religion, they say. Rather they are concerned about constitutionality. Though this is transparently not true, it is tactically effective. A nativity scene in a town square does not remotely constitute the establishment of a religion. The authors of the constitution plainly didn't think it did. It doesn't matter. The Supreme Court simply imposes things that would never survive a popular vote.

Another reason for the hostility is that the faithful are not governmentally tractable. The first loyalty of believers is to things higher than government. A healthy church can resist the encroachments of temporal power. A believer is capable of saying, "No. That is wrong. I won't do it." For him the dictates of God are categorical. The crafted diktats of the Court are not.

This isn't to say that the behavior of believers is always moral, only that it is a threat to the totalitarian aspirations of modern government. A vast catalog of crimes committed in the name of religion can be adduced. Yet the pseudo-Marxist is concerned not with morality, but with power. To him, the crime of religion is not crime, but the allegiance it inspires.

Another and related sin of religion is Sin itself, a subject with which the secular are exceedingly uncomfortable. It is not that they are brutal, callous, or lacking in common decency. The politically correct share with non-psychopathic humanity an inchoate sense of right and wrong. They do not knowingly hurt children or mistreat their dogs. But they do not want to speak overmuch of right and wrong, because it tends to elide into good and evil, and then into Good and Evil.

Good and Evil, in the upper case, imply outside standards, moral rules that cannot be changed by human authority, and carry spiritual overtones. All of this is intensely unsettling to the politically correct. The essence of all forms of Marxism is simply control, control, control. The correct don't want competition.

The current PCism is perhaps just another step in the historical reduction of humanity to parts in a vast machine. In classical antiquity, the world lived in paganism, now mysteriously regarded as bad. The whole world was held to be numinous. Gods in mad variety ruled from the skies. Satyrs and dryads moved half-glimpsed in darkling glades. Marcus worshipped the moon. Lavinia worshipped her sacred grove. Sempronius worshipped a weirdly shaped rock. It sounds foolish, but it wasn't, quite. They were all responding to a sense of Something Beyond. This offends the Correct.

Come roughly the Renaissance, the march toward mechanism began in earnest. Copernicus showed that we moved around the sun. So much for the centrality of man. Newton showed that angels didn't push the spheres in their orbits, but that they followed monotonous habits that one day would be called Newtonian mechanics. Darwin said they there was no plan or design to the world, but that it was all a sort of gorgeous accident. Sea horses and tulips and Manhattan were just what one would expect when leaving a large cloud of hydrogen unwatched for a long time.

Freud appeared. From his maunderings could be deduced, and was, a sort of psychological Newtonianism: All that we do is driven mechanically by (in Freud's case, weird) impersonal psychological forces. Marx did the same for economics and history in general, making people into flotsam bobbing helplessly on the currents of history. His focus on "the masses" instead of individuals has the flavor of statistical chemistry.

Thus we come to our current pass. The gods are banished, maenads become social workers, and churches turn into fellow travelers. Mechanism rules, and the politically correct mean to pull the levers. They brook no competition. Why should they? Are they not the measure of all things? Those of the mechanistic persuasion have an arrogance of phenomenal dimensions.

One may ask whether the tinker-toy conception of existence, in which there are no morals but only evolutionary predilections, in which we are not free agents but just vector sums of external forces, is more nearly accurate than the religious and spiritual understanding. Is there more in heaven and earth, or is there not?

Take your pick. The choice is between the hideous tediousness of cultural Marxism, and the flaming sunsets of Arizona, with the night wind rising and glowing legions of shapes arrayed in waves across the fiery sky—the sense that there may be more to this mad dream than social construction and the midget pedantry of the Supreme Court.

Anorexia. It's Fred's Fault. He Did It.

I'm dreaming of army ants. Big, nasty ones, like pliers with legs. I'm going to feed all the feminist-psychologist ladies to them.

First I'll get a bodacious nest of 'em from Brazil, the kind that strip a bull moose to the bones in 4.3 seconds, or could if Brazil had moose. (It did, but the ants ate them.) I'll breed them in a swimming pool till they're twelve feet deep, and spray them with rum 'cause not even an army ant will eat a feminist if it realizes what it's doing. Then I'll wrap those gals in bacon and tip them off the diving board.

Hah.

The other day one of these harpies told me something else that men are guilty of. I was surprised, figuring there wasn't anything left, but there was: Bulimia and anorexia. Yep. Men. Me. I did it. It's my fault.

It's because my male patriarchal linear-thinking hierarchical gender-hegemonic colonial objectification of women got their self-concept out of alignment, like when the front end goes bad on a '53 Chevy because you drove it across a corn field. See, the bulimic gals watch TV, which is my fault, and TV tells them that men want bony wrecks without hips. Personally, I'd rather have infected warts, but never mind. Anyway, said this psychological vampire bat, women "perceived themselves" as fat. So they decided they had to starve themselves silly so men would want them.

That's what causes anorexia. And I thought they were just nuts.

Actually, the psychologist lady was mad at me, because when she got growly and said, "Do you know *anything* about eating disorders?" I said I'd never eaten a disorder, but I reckoned that if you pan-fried one and sprinkled vinegar on it, it would be pretty fair. That isn't funny, she said. I told her it was the best I could do.

Now, she was right: Men don't understand about eating disorders. We'll gobble donuts and drink beer till we look like petroleum bladders, but we won't starve ourselves for love or money. It's just not something we do. And most of us have never heard of eating disorders.

When I was a kid in the countryside of Virginia, we didn't have any. Girls ate when they were hungry. So did boys. When they weren't, they didn't. It seemed to work. We mostly weren't fat because we walked around a lot, the way people do in the country, and probably played basketball. The girls were pretty, which a young woman has to work at not being, and no crazier than the baseline for the sex. The boys sure liked them, because feminism hadn't yet turned women into giant shrews. They seemed happy. So they didn't need eating disorders.

I guess I'm just slow, and don't understand things. When my daughter told me about gals that ran into the girls' room to upchunk after lunch, I reckoned it was food poisoning. And the girls doing it weren't the ones that needed to. You got some bodacious mamas out there that look like inflatable boats with eyeballs, mostly working in talk-shows, and you'd think that if there was a market for anorexia, they'd be it. Naw. *They're* gobbling pork chops dipped in mayonnaise. It's gals that don't need to lose weight that want to.

It didn't make sense, bulimia especially. If you're just going to upchunk something, why eat it in the first place? I figured an anorexic was just a bulimic with foresight.

Do young men, or any men, really want spindly funny-looking girls with bulgy knees from not having any meat on their bones? Of course not. This stuff is sheer malignant fantasy, one of our intermittent national hysterias, like Hula Hoops or Prohibition.

If you want to see what college boys want, pick up a copy of *Playboy*. You will find gorgeous airbrushed bimbos, who say non-threatening things like, "I'm studying Cosmetology Science and I want to be an actress some day, but right now I just need to learn about life, *ooooooooooo*." (Actually, lots of them aren't bimbos. But it wouldn't do to say, "I'm majoring in astrophysics at CalTech and I'd rather have weasels in my bra than date a retarded preppy with bad skin." The college boys would all commit suicide.)

Anyway, the *Playboy* girls aren't flat-chested stick figures being fed intravenously. They are shapely, as in curved, and run the mammary range from reasonable to Georgia watermelon patch. Try *Penthouse*, which is *Playboy* with real women. Same thing: Curved and breasty, but less air-brushed.

So who does like stick figures? Easy. Homosexual fashion designers in New York. They'd really like little boys for runway models, but people would notice, so they use linear flat-chested freaks as surrogates.

But men do yet worse things. While some girls starve themselves till they look like overcooked ribs, others shove baggies of silicone into themselves. I guess they really want to be taxidermists, but can't find a sailfish or a duck, so they stuff themselves. This too is my fault. It's because men want rounded curved women, and this makes gals spend thousands of dollars in search of cantaloupe-hood.

Starve or stuff, men do it. It's kind of sad, because what most guys want is a reasonably cute gal who's fun to hang around with.

I've got a theory. Maybe it's wrong, but you can't be a columnist unless you have theories. Best I can tell, women these days are just bewildered, but don't know it. Not all of them, but enough to bewilder men too, because we can't make a grain of sense of any of it. (I know, I'm going to get mad letters. Send them to Antarctica.) I swear it's true. Women can't decide whether they want to be bombshells or stockbrokers, sirens or SEALs, and keep landing in between.

In Washington, the fashion uncapital of the earth, women dress for the office like Brooks Brothers manikins so they'll look like the city's browbeaten men, and grow chips permanently attached to their shoulders (which actually show on x-rays) because they aren't going to be oppressed. Then they complain that men are afraid of commitment.

Next they wear push-up bras and tight sweaters so men will look at them, and then sue for harassment when it works.

If that ain't puzzled, I don't know what is. And, you know, they don't seem real happy, though they won't admit it.

Granted, we men don't amount to much, and don't clean up after ourselves real well, but at least we know who we are, or don't care, which is just as good. It let's us eat.

Octopus Woman

Manzanillo, Mexico—

From the restaurant on the beach at La Boquita it's an easy swim, even in scuba gear, to the stern of the wreck. La Boquita is a local Mexican beach, the restaurant really a thatch roof over sand with a kitchen shack attached. The owners let Susan and her dive parties stage their gear from its tables because they know the divers will return hungry and run up a good bill. It is a symbiotic relationship that has worked for fourteen years.

Under a sun beginning to be hot with late morning, we walked into mild surf, inflated our BCs, put on our fins, and started swimming backward toward the wreck. Besides Susan and me, there was a family of four Mississippians on vacation. They had found her dive operation, Underworld Scuba, the same way I had: The Internet, which roars along in Mexico.

The San Luciano was not my idea of a wreck. I was used to the deep wrecks off North Carolina, the Papoose and the Aeolus and the U-352, that start 110 feet down and many miles off shore. The San Luciano was in all of twenty-five feet of water. I thought it was probably a good first dive for people Susan deals with. A dive shop gets all sorts of divers, from loud and clueless to reserved and comfortable. All have C-cards, but you can't tell what they really know. Ninety feet down on a night dive with low vis is not the place to realize that a diver is in beyond his abilities. She can accommodate anybody, but she likes to know who she is accommodating.

We grouped up and went down. Blue sky ceded to dappled green, soothing in its dimness, occasional fish watching with their usual expression of cold forlorn brainlessness. Maybe they are Little Richard fans in the privacy of what minds they have, but they look bored and stupid. We stopped just above the bottom at what my computer said was twenty-four feet. The Luciano stretched away into nothing, crumbling into ruin, holes gaping where steel plates had given up the struggle, covered with the weird growth that takes over everything in the sea.

At that depth, air lasts forever. Until Susan began digging, I just floated along, sssssssssss-*wubbawubbawubba*, reflecting that if nuclear war began, or the Black Death broke out again in Europe, or radioactive vampire bats from space ate Tokyo, my editors couldn't get in touch with me. It is one of the consolations of diving.

Susan is a tall blonde and looks like a Valkyrie, but in fact has a lot of Indian blood. Perhaps she is one of the Oslo Cherokees. She dropped to the sand next to a disintegrating girder, went negative to peg herself to the bottom, and peered beneath the steel. It was her Octopus Response. You know how a bird dog alerts on a partridge? That's Susan. Only it's octopuses. She just, you know, *likes* them.

And has an affinity for them. Some months back the Discovery Channel wanted to film underwater here and asked her to guide them. She has logged over 3000 dives around Manzanillo, and so knows the ocean hereabout. She quickly found them an octopus eating a puffer fish, which is impossible. You don't just find things like that. Except she does. It isn't luck or skill. It's more like telepathy. The camera crew wouldn't stop filming and almost drowned.

I planted myself full length on the sand next to her, and the Mississippians hovered above. I couldn't see squat. She could. Moving slowly, she reached under the girder, removed a piece of shell, reached into the hole up to her wrist. Nothing. She pulled out a piece of rock, and reached farther in, very slowly.

I don't reach into holes under water. There are moray eels in them. All of them. Huge morays. I'm sure of it. Not to mention fire coral and deadly venomous sea urchins unknown to science. On the other hand,

Susan has been doing it for years and she still has two arms. Of course, I don't know how many she started with.

Next, so help me, she took her glove off, and reached back in, halfway to her elbow. There's a reason for this. Actually, there probably isn't, but she says there is. Octopuses don't like the texture of gloves.

"They like the feel of flesh," she says.

If that's not comforting, I can't imagine what might be.

At first, she says, they barely touch your fingers. Then they get exploratory, and suck on to you, like amorous bath mats. There's no hostility: They can bite if they want to. They're probably just thinking, "Gosh, wonder what *this* is?" And maybe, "Do I want one?"

She slowly pulled her hand out and, ye gods and little catfish, a sureenough octopus was wrapped around it. He (sex is actually a bit arbitrary in octopuses) looked like a dirty gym sock: The concept of shape isn't well developed among octopuses.

He had a certain appeal. Call it aesthetic insouciance: He was perfectly content to look like a gym sock, and wasn't about to wear designer jeans to get on the cover of GQ.

He ran up her shoulder, clambered over her regulator hoses, and attached himself to her tank. Then he sat, formlessly, and sucked onto my finger when I offered it to him.

Maybe he thought he had caught Susan, and was no end proud of himself. Or maybe he didn't know what to do with her. I figured octopuses proved the theory of evolution, since nobody would design one on purpose. On the other hand, nothing so profoundly odd could happen by accident, either. There may not be an explanation for octopuses.

After a bit he decided he didn't need further human company, and jetted back to the wreck to pry things open and eat them. We swam off to investigate other improbabilities. I actually missed him, and wished I could take him home and stick him to the bathroom mirror. The effect on drunks at parties would have justified the expense.

That was my adventure with Octopus Woman. Any time you think you have existence excessively figured out, and grow bored, and sink into ennui, get Susan to find you an octopus. It'll fix what ails you.

Housebreaking Our Young In St. Louis

Fall comes. Across the country leaves turn, the morning air grows crisp, and nuts ripen, chiefly in the public schools. In the St. Louis *Post-Dispatch*, I see that a school kid of 11, Paul Volz, got suspended for three days, because he drew a picture of the World Trade Center on fire.

Yep.

It was your basic 20-second kid drawing on lined paper. Versions differ as to whether he stuck a paper airplane on it. He then put the picture on the wall of his study cubicle. Bingo. Outta there.

Have we lost our tiny little minds?

It gets better. From Jeff Boyer, the principal: "When I asked him why he did this, he just looked at me and smiled. This is totally inappropriate and Paul's behavior has to change."

"Inappropriate" is the word used by schoolmeisters when a kid hasn't done anything. If Paul had attacked a schoolmate with a machete, he could have been called "dangerous." If he had stood on his head and screamed for three hours, "disruptive" would have fit. But he did nothing wrong at all, so it's "inappropriate." This conveys disapproval without specificity, leaving the child with no defense.

("Inappropriate" actually means "I'm a hopeless priss, and you aren't, so I'm going to get even." Honest. It's in the Oxford English Dictionary.)

Things get better yet. Apparently there's a whole hive of of gooberish control-freaks in St. Louis. Ben Helt, the district spokesman—whatever that means—said it wasn't the picture that engendered distress. No. It was Paul's grinning.

Yes. We now have the grinning police.

There's no end to this. Said Helt, "How a child handles that drawing could be just as important (as the drawing itself). Some drawings can be therapeutic and others can be offensive."

I pondered this, crossing my legs. It's not just the English. Therapeutic? Since when do pictures by children have to be therapeutic? Who asked the wee timorous beasties who run the schools to do therapy? Why the assumption that kids need psychological care because a couple of buildings blew up? Why is a picture of a news event offensive?

We have here one of those pair-of-diggem shifts I read about. We used to have sexual prudes. That doesn't work any longer. It would be like being a water-prude in mid-Pacific. So we now have violence-prudes. All the prurience, but half the fun.

Now, why did Paul grin? I'm not sure what else a kid is supposed to do when asked a preternaturally stupid question. Kids draw pictures. They draw what interests them, what they see around them, what's on television, what piques their imagination. Spacemen. Cowboys. The Trade Center. They don't know why they draw things. I don't know either. It's what people do.

If this were an isolated case, we might figure that there was a really serious hole in the ozone layer over St. Louis. But it's not isolated. It's everywhere. A friend of mine has a (large) son of twelve, who couldn't find his jacket one morning. Dad was at an early meeting on Cap Hill, so the kid borrowed his leather coat.

Bingo, suspended: It was a Columbine-style coat.

The same kid, after the recent adventure in New York, wrote a note to a classmate: "Westernport is next. Ask me how I know." Westernport is a tiny place of no interest to anyone who doesn't live there. The kid, being a kid, was kidding. Days later the note fell out of the recipient's notebook, and a teacher found it. Bingo: Another suspension.

Before thinking about what all of this is, let's think about what it isn't.

It isn't about safety. A kid who draws a burning building, or borrows his dad's coat, is not a dangerous psychopath. If he were, would a three-day suspension cure him? Maybe the idea is that an angry killer, having been humiliated by being tossed out of school, will respond by becoming well-adjusted. I expect so. Any day now.

When a child writes that some crossroads is next on Bin Laden's list, one of three things must be true: (a) the kid is perilously bonkers; (b) he is a member of an Islamic terrorist organization (common among Anglo pre-teens in remote Maryland); or (c) he's a kid. Pick one.

If you really thought a kid was dangerous, you would try to get him out of school permanently, which would be entirely sensible. The parsnipocracy didn't, which establishes that they know these kids aren't terrorists.

What, then, is the point of this bullying? Which is exactly what it is.

This is a judgment call, but…these people bring to mind the good-goody little girl in third grade, the pasty tattle-tale boy who would run up and say, "Teacher! Ricky made a spitball," and then watch in triumphant disguised hostility as Ricky got chewed out. They were kids who really didn't like others, but didn't have the courage to assert themselves directly.

The teachers who throw kids out of school for pointing chicken fingers at lunch and saying "bang," or for drawing GIs (both in fact happened), feel to me like the same kids gotten older. (Incidentally, I expect one day to see a book by a principal, "Fear of Chicken Fingers: A Survivor's Guide.")

These delicates are not conspicuously overburdened with courage or character. A man who gets his innards in an uproar because Johnny drew a soldier with a gun—*squeeeeal!*—isn't up there with Churchill, Jim Bowie, and Gordon Liddy. Further, though with many exceptions, teachers are the dregs of the colleges, and they know it. They know that others know it. Throw in diversity hires and it's worse.

The resentment borne by the consciously inadequate goes quickly to vengefulness.

And that, I think, is where we are. Today, the little rat-finks of third grade are Teacher, and in charge. They want to squash what they aren't. I can't find a better explanation. They have the totalitarian instincts of the empowered negligible, the desire for control, control, control that characterizes the vaguely frightened.

Control is indeed what they want: To browbeat kids into conforming, into complying with their pallid sanctimony over imagined peril. The totalitarian outlook invariably leads to puritanical moralizing. One doesn't easily imagine Joe Stalin getting a lap dance or Franco swinging from a chandelier. Thus dodgeball is violence, playing soldier is "unacceptable," drawing a burning building is "inappropriate."

We have consigned our offspring to anxious mental defectives.

I'll say this to the Pauls of American: Don't let the bastards grind you down. It isn't you. It's them.

Questioning Integration:
Thoughts Antecedent To My Lynching

Always we are told that we must integrate, but may not the virtues of racial integration be exaggerated? Might a degree of separation serve us better? What has integration produced other than ill will and strife? Might we not we be happier with greater distance between us? Such thoughts are publicly heretical. Yet they are privately common. May there not be a reason?

The crucial question about integration is simply this: Does anyone want it?

The evidence suggests that no one does.

Appearances can deceive. If at lunchtime you walked along Connecticut Avenue, a business thoroughfare of Washington, you might believe the country to be in the throes of racial amity. Blacks and whites of prosperous mien throng the streets without evident friction, sometimes dining together. In offices they work side by side. All seems well. What is less obvious is that they have no choice. A vast federal machinery of suasion and intimidation exists, disposing of heavy sanctions, to repress the slightest disinclination to mix.

When integration isn't forced, it barely happens. At quitting time, blacks go home to black neighborhoods, whites to white. Mixed regions are few and unstable, with one race usually moving out when too many of the other arrive.

As the races live apart, so do they play apart. Whites go to white clubs and blacks to black. Crossover is minimal, yet there is no discrimination. Private social life remains highly segregated, even among

167

those who most decry segregation: Although Washington is predominantly black, parties held by liberal whites are overwhelmingly white.

Is this not everywhere the pattern? We pretend otherwise, pretend to want integration, and speak of racial progress, but it is pretense.

Upon comparing the endlessly preached with the observably practiced, one might easily conclude that integration was an abstract political goal being imposed against the impulses of human nature, one of which is the desire to be among one's own. Integration seems not to be something we want, but something we are told we ought to want.

For half a century we have sought to compel mixing by legislation, judicial diktats, quotas, goals, busing, affirmative action, legal terrorism, and remorseless indoctrination of our children. We remain stubbornly segregated. Blacks have made great economic progress, yet their hostility toward whites has not visibly abated. Whites, to judge by their actions as distinct from their dissimulations, do not crave the company of blacks.

Certainly blacks want a comfortable standard of living, equality before the law, a degree of respect, and so on. These are not integration. Do blacks want to spend more time with whites? If so, they conceal the urge well.

The truth, I think, is that the races do not care for each other. If this is not the truth, show me that it is not. We may think we ought to like each other, but we don't quite get there. The question arises: What do we gain by compulsory togetherness that seems chiefly to encourage antagonism?

The United States has never made the experiment of civil and voluntary separation. Until 1954, the doctrine was separate-but-equal, which was in fact separate, but not at all equal. Then, as we are so often reminded, the Supreme Court decided that separate but equal was inherently unequal. Desegregation, and then integration, became the law. Once we couldn't mix. Now we have to.

Here we need to bear in mind a couple of points. First, a thing is not true because the Supreme Court says that it is true. The ukases of the

Court, while perhaps sometimes tainted by the Constitution, reflect the political prejudices of a given court and its sense of what it can get away with. In 1896 the Court found in Plessy vs. Ferguson that separate but equal *was* constitutional. Same constitution.

Second, imposing a rigid segregation intended to repress differs from allowing a degree of separation by mutual consent. If people choose to live separately, or somewhat separately, without thereby being subjected to legal disability, why should it not be their business?

The root of our racial impasse seems to me to be that blacks and whites are very different peoples, and want different things. For example, I am of European descent, and want my children to study English literature, European languages, mathematics, the sciences, English grammar, and European history with reasonable attention to Asia. I want high academic standards. I care about the GREs.

By contrast, blacks note that they are not European and do not want to study things European, that they prefer their own to Standard English, do not want calculus or what I regard as high standards, but do want Black Studies. They detest the GREs.

Our approaches are inherently irreconcilable.

Our choices are (1) to force blacks to study things they do not care for and about which, whether by unconcern or incapacity, they seem to learn almost nothing; or (2) to lower standards for my children and teach them things which I regard as worthless; or (3) to allow people to send their children to separate schools and raise them as they think best.

I don't care what blacks study, as long as they are happy with it. The second clause needs emphasis: I do not propose to force anything on anyone. If blacks want to learn calculus, German, and Roman History, I will support them. If they want to learn Swahili, Black Studies, and Ebonics, or anything else or nothing at all, I may think that they are making a mistake, but I will respect their choice. I presume that black parents are better judges than I of what their children should learn, just as I think that I am the better judge of what mine should learn.

Might not such a policy of mutual noninterference greatly reduce tension?

Having said these things, I will, with a predictability exceeding that of gravitation, get mail saying that I hate blacks and want to do them harm. No, actually. If I could magically move all blacks into the middle class, inspire academic frenzy in their children, and make them happy, I would do it. I gain neither pleasure nor profit from the difficulties of others. But I don't know how to do these things. As I don't want my culture destroyed by that of blacks, any more than they want theirs destroyed by mine, I wonder whether it might be wise to do neither.

The Virtue Of Discourtesy

It's going to happen, I tell you. Once too often I'll go into one of those suck-up restaurants that spread now like dry rot in old tires. It'll have the nauseating cutesy-sweetsy menu. You know the kind: You can't get ham and eggs, side of grits, some really nasty greasy toast. No. You have to buy "The Hearty Frontiersman—two USDA Grade-A eggs especially selected for your dining enjoyment, cooked just the way you like them, drizzled with fresh Monterrey Jack cheese, with a mouthwatering touch of ...."

Those places make me want to kill something. The food sounds like a moist perversion. I don't want my eggs drizzled on. I'd rather not think about it.

It gets worse, though. The waiter will say, "Hell-*ooo*, I'm Steve, your waitperson! *Oooo-oo-ooo*! I'm going to do everything to make you visit with us enjoyable. We're so glad that could come...."

I know myself. I'll whip out a bolo knife, chop Steve into chunks, and beat the kitchen staff to death with them. Then I'll wait for the police, glowing with the inner peace that comes of having found meaning.

That's why I like New York. People there have enough respect for each other to be honestly rude. You can read a menu in Manhattan—most places, anyway—without feeling imaginary fingers on your knees. In a breakfast dive in Brooklyn, the waiter, who isn't concerned about your inner being, says, "Yeah." You say, "Two over medium, whole wheat, cuppa mud." He says, "Got it." That's all. It works.

Of course you can't ask for grits in New York. It's a nice place, but limited.

The rudeness of New Yorkers is almost a tourist attraction. It's a phony one. New Yorkers at least have the consideration not to subject you to saccharine smiley-facism. They're not cuddly. That's why I like them. You can talk to N'Yawkas without feeling as if you had grabbed a sticky doorknob. The city can be rough, but it's human.

Now, it's true that a New Yorker doesn't want your life story. There are too many people, all with life stories. You don't say to him, "Hi! I'm from Busted Fork and, gee, it sure is a big city, and, you know, we aren't used to tall buildings. Just look. They're everywhere. Tall. You know, buildings...."

A resident of the city will listen to this performance and think, "Yeah. OK. Yeah. *Whaddaya want?* What, I gotta wait for the Ice Age? Come on, spit it. Hey, is this guess-my-secret or something?" He's perfectly willing to help, but he believes in same-day service. He wants to see his kids again. He doesn't care about your mama's spoonbread in Bug Tussle.

But if you just say, "Hey, where's Davidoff's Bolo Knives?" he'll say, "Eighth Avenue, two blocks on the left." That's genuine courtesy—answered the question, no therapy.

New York doesn't tolerate sick self-absorbed do-goodery, for which God bless it. If you told a waitress in Brooklyn, at least anywhere in Brooklyn that I know, that you wanted a Hearty Frontiersman, she'd probably send you to a gay bath. Don't even think about drizzled anything. She'd regard you with the look New Yorkers use upon discovering that they are talking not to a human, but to a giant decomposing carp. It combines horror, resignation, and loss of faith in the essential rightness of things. It says, "How do you exist? Have you thought about stopping?"

Another manifestation of the general decline is the phrase, "Have a Nice Day," which justifies decapitation. I find myself perversely wanting to say, "No. I don't like nice days." Or "Actually, I'd rather have beri beri." Or "May I attack you with my bolo knife?"

When one stranger meeting another says, "Good day," it means, "I acknowledge your existence, and wish you well to the extent that strangers can be expected to." But have-a-nice-day is meddlesome, hortatory, contrived, like, "Have a, *yuuummmmmmmm*! mouthwatering day exactly as you like them with just a sprinkle...." "Good day" is courtesy. "Have a nice day" is factitious solicitude. It gives me the creeps.

The modulated insincerity and meretricious goodwill savor of the PC plague. See, the world isn't what we know it to be—a vale of imperfection with occasional bright spots. No. It's a pinball machine with grinning Smiley Faces rolling around like yellow marbles. Breakfast isn't breakfast. It's a heartening Traditional American Experience that you deserve, with dollops of tasty fresh Grade-A Unction...."

What about a couple eggs, bacon, hold the smarm?

I saw a builders' catalog once that listed toilets. So help me, they had names like "The Cerulean Princess" (cyanotic, no doubt), and The Woodland Dawn. Then you get those syrupy recordings over and over when you're on hold for forty-five minutes. "Your call is very important to us. A customer-relations executive will shortly stroke you like a starving masseuse...." The tone invariably suggests that she wants to sit in your lap.

The sense of being managed galls, especially of being managed by idiots. The implication is that, if you call a toilet the Roseate Verge of Morn, I won't know it's a toilet. I'll think it's a sister piece to the Nike of Samothrace, and keep it in a glass case filled with helium. Call a Belgian waffle the *Charlemagne avec Crème des Mouches*, and I won't have the brain to notice that it's a waffle like every waffle ever made—pancake, with little square holes. No. I'll think I'm doing the squat-and-gobble with Louis XIV, right there in Howard Johnson's.

New York can give you a cold shoulder or a hard sell. Go into a discount camera store and the salesman will be on you like a buzzard on carrion. "Hey, best camera ever made. Gotta lens. Lotsa buttons, see? Little thing on the side here. You need this camera. Buy it." It's straightforward commercial bullying, but that's OK. It's what salesmen do. He's trying to con you about the camera. He isn't trying to con you about yourself, to shape your character, or make you feel empowered.

I tell you, it's part and parcel of the whole gummy zeitgeist that urges you to eat plenty of roughage, drink nothing but purified water, slather sunscreen on yourself till you feel like a Vienna sausage in mayonnaise, and never, ever offend anyone. The Mommy State, the PR society. Insufferable niceness. If instead of calling the old, poor, crippled, and blind what they are, we instead call them Senior Citizens, underprivileged, mobility-challenged and Differently Visioned, why, then, everything will be better.

I could live with being crippled. If anyone called me mobility challenged, I'd pull a gun. Which I may do anyway.

Pondering The Chinese

We should think about the Chinese. We are going to hear more from them.

Several lives ago, after Saigon fell, I was free-lancing around Asia, and went to Taiwan to await the next war, which didn't come. I'd been there before, to visit friends in the military. This time I stayed, and signed up for intensive Chinese at *Gwo Yu R Bau*, actually a newspaper but with a language school attached. My abode was an apartment shared with a tiny Japanese mathematician named Sakai, two Chinese graduate students, and Ding Gwo, a local kid who wanted to be a rock guitarist.

It wasn't the golf tour. In the winding warrens and back alleys, gringos were sparse to none. I struggled for four months against four hours a day of Chinese conversation, and gutted out the written language in off hours. It was work, but soon I spoke a subset of the language, and could plough through a pulp novel with lots of help from the dictionary. This allowed me to acquire a girlfriend, a nurse whose family lived down-island in Pin Tung.

As an introduction to the Chinese, it was nothing if not direct.

These folk can be packaged as exotic. The sounds and smells of those densely peopled labyrinths, the bustle and press, the open-fronted workers restaurants with the flat white sheets of fish and tiny squid like gray vitamin pills with fingers—these carry the credentials of the exotic. And my God, *Wan Wha*, relic of a far older China, where the snake butchers worked. (The name means "Ten Thousand Glories," definitely a whitewash.) There, snakes hanging in stalls were skinned and the blood squeezed into a glass to be drunk at a high price by superstitious workers. "*Dwei shen-ti, hen hau.*" Good for the body.

But this would be literary fraud. In truth the Chinese were as exotic as potatoes, though not as mysterious. There were agreeable, courteous without being neurotic about it, and concerned with the same things that concern us. The girls were interested in the boys and the boys were interested in the girls, who were not loose but certainly warm-blooded. Children played at soldier and space men. People worried about paychecks, kids, grandma's heart condition. Presbyterians are stranger.

They were smart, though, and studious, and showing marked signs of economic competence. This we need to think about.

Of an evening I'd come home through tortuous alleys, where housing was cramped and intimate and would have appalled an American, There, sitting at crate-desks in the narrow ways to avoid the heat, children did their homework. You don't see this in Brazil. We've all heard about Vietnamese valedictorians in America. The difference between the Vietnamese and the Chinese is about a billion two hundred million.

At the time, every patch of jungle with a colonel and a band of torturers had a Five Year Plan for economic development: Uganda on the march. Taiwan, almost uniquely, had results. I saw the steel mill in Gau Sheng, the Jin Shan reactors. On a story for the *Far Eastern Economic Review*, I interviewed a few of the directors. Some Harvard, mostly MIT. Taiwan is now a serious high-tech manufacturing power. Russia can't make a decent personal computer.

The Chinese have all the pieces for a ferocious competitiveness. Hong Kong is New York with slanted eyes: They can do entrepreneurial cut-throat hardball business. The better American universities are heavily Chinese. They can do academics. They fit naturally into a techno-industrial world.

None of this is true of Arabs, Latinos, Africans.

China is an enormous, old, and talented world that we know little of. When Chiang Kai Shek fled the communists from the mainland, he brought a fabulous amount of art. This was well, as the communists would have destroyed it. I spent days in the museum in Taipei. This isn't the place for a disquisition on Chinese art, but for subtlety, polish and, particularly, a feel for the natural world they can match anything the West has done. Their work is different, but it's very good. Even the writing, while awkward—they missed an important boat by not going with an alphabet—has an odd beauty. Hand-written characters almost wiggle and swim on the page.

They are not a lightweight people.

How the West got the jump on them, I don't know. Modern civilization is a white European invention. Yet until, say, 1700 the Chinese were ahead. If the mainland has in fact found the formula for sustained economic advance, as it seems to have, in fifty years they will be ahead again. Yes, China has a lot of peasant stupidity still, and inefficiency, and it's still a poor country. So, not so very long ago, was Japan. So, not so very long ago, was the US.

We are not going to like their rise. They can be every bit as domineering as Caucasians, and will be. They are racially and nationally arrogant. So is everyone else, but we are not accustomed to being on the receiving end. As a nation they bear no love for us, remembering our participation in their humiliation by the West in the 1800s. Few of us know of the Opium Wars, the Boxer Rebellion, the legations. The Chinese do.

We would be wise to be circumspect about military confrontation, particularly over Taiwan. By linguistic convention we are a superpower. In reality we are far weaker than most of us realize. The Chinese fought us to a standstill in Korea, and the Vietnamese beat us, when we were militarily paramount. Today we have neither the troops nor the will to fight a land war in Asia.

By sufficient effort, by virtue of better airplanes and the Taiwan Straits, we could hold off China for a while. Once committed, we would have no way of leaving. There are bluffs to call, and bluffs not to call.

Years after my time as a back-alley orientalist, I returned with my then-wife and tow-headed daughter of maybe a year and a half. We stayed at the Grand Hotel, a gaudy and wonderful confection on a hill in Taipei.

The Grand swarmed with pretty Chinese maids, who were smitten by our yellow-haired girl-child. They took her from my wife, not quite asking permission, and for several minutes a golden tassel bobbed up and down on a sea of dark hair. She disappeared into the kitchen, I think it was, reappeared. All the staffs wanted to see this apparition. Finally they returned our golden puff to us. She was cooing and laughing. One of the girls said, "You have a beautiful daughter."

I said they were intelligent.

Posing In The Pluke Bucket

Tell you about my Fitty-Sedden Chevy with the leaky radiator, bad wiring, and the mattress in back.

Maybe you thought you didn't need to know about it. Life is full of surprises.

In the early Sixties, every kid in high school knew the Fitty-Sedden Chev was God's favorite car. Nothing looked better, not even Annette Funicello in mid-development. It was lovely, sleek, and powerful. The tail fins rose like chromed transcendence and the whole car had a road-hugging muscularity to it. That smooth 283 V-8 rumbled mellow as Godzilla on Quaaludes, and for those days a Fitty-Sedden (or, sometimes, Fitty-Sudden) was quick. For a country boy who had one, it was home, bar, hunting lodge, girl attractant, and manhood amplifier. And you could go places in it.

The Fitty-Sedden was an American icon, like the flag, Babe Ruth, and McDonald's. Boys figured that when their time on earth ran out, and they went to the great Southland in the sky, they'd find Elvis and Carl Perkins parked in front of the soda shop in a bad-ass Fitty-Sedden convisible—top down, hair slicked back with eight pounds of Ace-Hold Duragrip pomade, and singing Jailhouse Rock to a gaggle of poontang sweeter than Karo syrup.

Oh yeah.

My Fitty-Sedden was baby blue, falling apart, and called the Pluke Bucket. "Pluke" was a local coinage from King George Country, Virginia, that meant carnal knowledge that you hadn't really had but could lie about. In those days it was the commonest form of carnal knowledge.

Anyway, it was 1965 and I had become a student, or something vaguely resembling one, at Hampden-Sydney College, a small school in central Virginia. The place was the suburbs of nowhere, green and forested. The Bucket was with me. (Like rural Star Wars: "The Bucket be with you.") In a fit of mechanical imagination I'd taken out the rear seat and put in a mattress that extended into the trunk. It was so I could go camping. I said.

Now, nothing is more fun than showing off. Well, almost nothing. There's nothing wrong with showing off. You just have to avoid beating other people over the head with it. You should do it by overpowering inference instead of waving your arms and yodeling. If you have to tell'em you got it, you probably don't.

For college kids, showing off was all balled up with sex. They were trying to figure out how to be men and women. The boys wanted to swagger and stick their chests out, and the girls wanted to swivel and stick *their* chests out. (I think today it's the other way around, but the principle holds.) Love meant looking cool and hoping. It's why male birds ruffle their feathers and flap a lot.

Shirt was my girlfriend. Actually her name was Shirley, but for evident reasons everyone called her Shirt. She was a cute brunette and nice as the day was long and went to Longwood, the state teachers college seven miles away in Farmville. You probably don't think anywhere could actually be named Farmville, but it was. It was a drowsing little burg with one street that amounted to anything, a statue of a Confederate soldier, and tobacco warehouses that smelled so good you almost wanted a chaw.

Anyhow, Shirt. This was before girls decided it was empowering to be wildly disagreeable. So when she stepped into the trash can of cold water on the floorboards, she was good-humored about it.

Reason was, the radiator leaked. I had sense enough to know that the Pluke Bucket was the pinnacle of earthly meaning. I didn't, however, have money enough to maintain it. Only about a third of it worked at any given time. The transmission leaked, for example. The electrical system shorted strangely, and sometimes I had to almost hot-wire it to get it to run.

I put oatmeal in the radiator. That plugged the leak for a while, but it started again. I took the radiator cap off to reduce the pressure. Still leaked. So I got a plastic trash-can, filled it with water, and kept it on the floor on the passenger's side. I thought it made perfect sense. I had a kind of scoop made out of a Clorox bottle or something that I used to dump water into the radiator.

Except Shirt forgot about it one night when we were going to a dance. And stuck her foot in it. I told her I'd get her some waders for her birthday.

One day the accelerator-return spring broke. I'd step on the gas and the Bucket would go faster. I'd take my foot off and it would keep on going faster. This could obviously be bad if I wanted to slow down and the Bucket didn't. I tied a string around the gas pedal and pulled up on it with one hand while I drove with the other. Probably I looked like I had a small dog on a leash. When Shirt was along she'd sit with the water bucket between her knees, pulling the string.

Her parents had sent her to college so she could be a return spring.

Come one day in May, the sun was bright and the breeze blew soft as a Yankee's brains and the whole glowing world called to your hormones. I figured I'd get Shirt and drive down Main Street, pretty much the only street, and look no end studley. Sometimes a stripling wants to get ahead of himself. There's no harm in it.

For a while it looked as if it would work. Shirt was in a pretty dress and sweet as a dream raised on Moon Pies. I didn't really have a tattoo that said "Death Before Dishonor" or a pack of Camels twisted into the shoulder of my tee-shirt. I'd tried, but they always fell out. Anyway, I didn't smoke. Still, that was the spirit of the thing.

So I cruised down the street, left elbow cockily out the window, Shirt beside me pulling the string. I hoped nobody would notice that string. "Ticket to Ride" blared from the speakers. Farm boys posed on the sidewalk, and I posed back at them. Shirt looked like a million dollars after taxes. I was unspeakably studley.

Thing was, every time I turned a sharp corner, the transmission went into neutral and the horn blew. I've tried to explain it. I guess the transmission fluid was low and the sump didn't have slosh baffles. Turn, honk!, *Swooshhh*, dying sough....

Shirt kept giggling. No respect. It probably scarred me for life. But if I were going to do it again, and I would, nothing would do but a Fitty-Sedden. *Ba-a-ad* mo-sheen.

It Looks Downhill To Me

O ne must be careful in remembering better days. Memory presents an improving mirror, smoothing rough edges of rougher times, giving a warm glow to things that were less roseate when they happened. Like a good editor, it revises things for the better. Thus one recalls, or half-imagines, the idyllic boyhood in Mississippi, the favorite grove where one played in the slanting afternoon sunlight that probably wasn't as golden as one recalls, with childhood companions who perhaps weren't as admirable as they now seem. One forgets, or half forgets, the drunken parents and the poverty and hookworm.

And so one must tread cautiously when pondering a past in which all things were better, cleaner, and purer. Yet...yet sometimes things *were* better, and sometimes things do decay. Sometimes a society does go from better to bad to worse. I wonder.

In 1964, I finished high school in King George County, Virginia. The anomie and hopelessness of the Sixties hadn't arrived. KG was rural and relatively poor, poor enough that a couple of dressed deer in hunting season made a difference in the family diet. The country people worked for a living, doing real work that involved actual effort. They farmed, many of them, squeezing crops from the county's marginal land. Many crabbed in the Potomac, rising far before dawn to pull pots in the Potomac for a few bushels of crabs to sell to the restaurants at Pope's Creek. Life wasn't easy. And yet....

And yet there were no drugs. At all. We in high school had never *heard* of them. Today, middle schools are awash in chemical surcease. Kids of fourteen get strung out on crystal meth, drop huge amounts of acid, swap Ecstasy for concert tickets. We think it normal.

In 1964, we didn't lock anything—the house, the mailbox (it didn't lock), the car wherever we parked it, the garage. Today we lock everything.

In 1964, kids dropped their bikes in the front yard, or left them unwatched on the bike rack at the pool. People didn't steal bikes. We would have thought it absurd to keep a bike in the living room. Today, my bicycle stands at the end of the sofa. The diversity has stolen three bikes from me and a couple from my children. They cut cable locks as a matter of course, break into storerooms, snatch-and-bolt everywhere. This too we accept.

In 1964, pornography meant airbrushed *Playboy* models, Vargas girls, lingerie ads. Now it means pore-level gynecology in macrophotography. It means worse. Any ten-year-old with a computer, which means any ten-year-old, can find sex with dogs, bloody sadomasochism, animals being tortured for sport, and people defecating on each other.

In 1964, the SATs were at their peak. Teachers, being white, could be held to standards. Ours weren't geniuses in King George, just reasonably intelligent people who understood that their function was to impart information. They did. Today kids graduate without being able to write a clear sentence, lack any grasp of the language, have to count on their fingers. Teachers, too many of them, are useless affirmative-action hires who can't be criticized.

A few years back in a middle school in the suburbs of Washington, I saw a poster made by a child to celebrate the contributions of Italians to America. In huge letters it mentioned Enrico Fermi's work in, so help me, "Nucler Physics." And it was *on the wall*, uncorrected.

Behavior? In 1964 kids were smart-asses, especially the boys, who performed in class for the girls. Kids mouthed off, tested the limits. But there *were* limits. When Larry Roller, the steely-eyed principal, said No, it was No. There were no cops in school (the idea would have been thought barbaric, as it is). No cops were needed. Had any of us cursed a teacher, or threatened one, expulsion would instantly have followed.

Society would have supported the ejection. Today, in many schools teachers are afraid of the students.

In 1964, sex was rare in high school and, for most of us, nonexistent. The girls said "no." Society backed them up. Pregnancies were few, illegitimacy rare—even, I think, among blacks. Now blacks are at 70% plus and whites around 35%. We become a nation of bastards. Today early teens, unwatched and uninstructed by parents chiefly interested in their jobs, rut like barnyard animals.

Boys, then as now, were immature, exploitative, horny little monsters whose sex drives had the nuanced understatement of police sirens. The girls, then as now, were too young for too much intimacy, emotionally ready to be hurt by it, and in search of affection more than carnal delights. But, because the girls said "no," and society backed them, they didn't get hurt. The boys didn't really expect otherwise, and dated girls because they liked them. Now girls are commodities, cheap as Seven-Eleven frankfurters. The boys know that if one doesn't say yes, another will.

I spoke recently with a young woman of twenty. She was highly intelligent, an A student, beyond her rebellious years, neither trying to seem advanced nor to shock. She told me, a bit sadly but with acceptance, that she wanted children one day, but assumed she would have them without benefit of marriage. She wasn't an angry feminist. She didn't like feminists. She just viewed divorce as inevitable. She knew it was very painful, especially for kids—this in particular she knew well.

Bastardy has become a reasonable choice, not just a reflex among welfare brood-mares.

In the Fifties, violence on television meant the Lone Ranger shooting the gun out of Slade's hand. In 1964 it meant Paladin bloodlessly shooting a somewhat more believable evil-doer. Today it means Hannibal Lecter eating the brains of a living man, disembowelings in loving close-up, and nauseating beatings.

In 1964, kids seldom stole from employers. Today, theft is accepted and close to universal. The ingrained prejudice against dishonesty has weakened.

On and on it goes. In the Fifties I lived a long walk away from my present address. There was no crime. In the last couple of years there have been two murders within three blocks of my door. Washington now is dangerous almost everywhere, especially at night, having had in one year more than 400 murders.

The churches are dying. Buses don't give change, as they formerly did, because the diversity learned to rob them. Books advocating sex with children appear, and are solemnly reviewed. Schools promote homosexuality, expel boys for playing cowboy and Indians, discard grammar as elitist.

Thirty-five years. That is all it has taken. Half a lifetime. Things move fast now.

Looting In Cincinnati

As I write, Cincinnati is under curfew. A white police officer shot and killed a black man. Blacks have been looting and burning. The media imply that the shooting was unnecessary, an example of police brutality. Perhaps it was. I don't know. I wasn't there.

Over and over it happens. Something upsets blacks, and they loot and burn. Usually, these days, the precipitating event is a shooting by the police. There have been other reasons. Blacks burnt Los Angeles because they didn't like the outcome of a trial, and engaged in further burning in 1968 because an assassin shot Martin Luther King. But usually it is the police. Usually it is a white policeman. No one cares if blacks kill blacks.

Can anything be done to prevent these outbursts?

To answer the question, I think we need to understand a few things.

First, though we pretend otherwise, race relations in this country are very bad, and do not seem to be improving. Blacks hate whites. Yes, there are sparse exceptions, and degrees, but the hatred is there. Particularly the blacks of the deep city hate whites. If the animosity were diminishing, wise counsel might be to grit our teeth and wait. I see no sign of a diminution.

The feelings of whites are harder to read. The penalties for public expression of dissatisfaction are heavy. Whites by nature are more controlled than blacks. Yet there is an impatience, and it may be growing.

Second, blacks are profoundly convinced that whites discriminate against them in every conceivable way, and ascribe most of their difficulties to the malevolence of whites. In particular, they believe that white cops single them out for mistreatment. I think this is largely nonsense, but it doesn't matter what I think. What matters is that blacks believe it to the depths of their being, believe it with bitterness and barely repressed fury. Reason, evidence, analysis—all mean nothing to them. This isn't changing either.

Third, the media remorselessly play up offenses perpetrated by whites against blacks, while concealing race when blacks attack whites. The editor of any paper will tell you that I'm wrong. Believe him if you like, but I'm in the business. As the saying has it, you can bullshit the fans, but you can't bullshit the players. The spin is without remission, and encourages blacks to think that they are always victims, never malefactors.

The media will continue to fan the flames of racial discord. It is a dangerous policy.

Now, if these things are true, and I believe they are, urban outbursts will continue. This too is dangerous. In my best judgment, racial animosity, though heavily repressed, is easily great enough to fuel an explosion of irremediable effect. Should the looters finally invade the white suburbs, as sooner or later they may, a shooting war will begin. Should the impatience of whites ever reach the point of expression, Northern Ireland will seem pacific.

It would be ghastly. How do we prevent it?

Perhaps the wisest course is to get white policemen out of black neighborhoods as quickly as possible. I don't suggest this as a punitive measure, as most white cops are guilty of nothing, but in simple recognition that the races do not mix well. As a beginning we might offer white cops early retirement, and hire only blacks as replacements. We might set up exchange programs to encourage black officers in the white suburbs to swap jobs with white officers in the cities. We might stop hiring black officers for work in white regions. Let each race police its own.

Nothing short of separation, I think, will work.

By habit, we explain the conflict between white police and black citizens as a consequence of unrequited racism by whites. Reform of the department is typically recommended. Other standard remedies are counseling, review boards, training in sensitivity, more care in recruiting, and greater supervision. None of it will work because none of it addresses the root of the conflict, which is that the cops are white.

Racial hostility exists, in both directions, which clouds the issue, and incidents of racism by police, black and white, can be found. Yet if white police were perfect, little would change. Any white police whatever, seeking to control a population that detests them, including a violent and heavily criminal underclass, will be involved in clashes. The impasse is inherently racial. The underlying problem is that blacks regard themselves as a separate people, and white police as an occupying army. Perhaps we should accept their view.

If on the other hand white police were replaced by black, then blacks would be responsible for their own neighborhoods. Within reason, how they chose to exercise the responsibility would be their business. Presumably a black government would be better able than a white to conform the style of policing to the cultural patterns of blacks. A powerful source of tension would vanish. If black officers shot anyone, as would certainly happen, the incident might take on juridical tones, might lead to investigations and calls for reform, but it would not be a racial incident. The cities would not burn.

Objections to the segregation of police will inevitably be raised. Segregation would be said to reverse progress toward integration, to acquiesce in racial division, to turn the United States into two nations occupying the same territory. But …what progress toward integration? Where does integration exist when not compelled? Do we not already have racial division?

We have always been two countries. We merely choose to pretend otherwise. The division does not seem to be changing. On television last night I heard that 28 percent of the whites in Cincinnati have fled the city in the last year, or five years, or ten. (I was in a noisy bar.) Cincinnati is getting blacker. After the current riots, you can be sure that whites who remain will be looking at ads for real estate elsewhere.

No happy resolution of today's racial incompatibility appears possible. The best we can hope for is the least unsatisfactory of several bad outcomes. Permit me a heretical thought: Maybe less integration would lead to less hostility.

Friction is proportional to contact. The greater the extent to which blacks govern themselves, and the less authority whites wield over them, the fewer explosions we will see. Letting whites police whites, and blacks, blacks, would reduce contact, and particularly the inevitably confrontational contact with police. Given the potential consequences should an uprising become general, maybe a degree of separation is worth pondering.

The Maserati Of Tanks

To an observer on one of Fort Hood's flattened prominences, the M1 Abrams tank would seem a dark mote below a high plume of dust, a glint of periscopes, a small furor lost in the vastness and pastels of central Texas. Not even the grandest of tanks can intimidate a landscape. By day and night tanks rumble across this land, seen only by tankers. Armor is a private trade.

There were in the tank with me the tank commander, the driver, and the loader. You still feel alone.

From low in the turret in the gunner's seat, the tank (depending on what it is doing at the moment) is a terrific clatter of tracks, a howl of big turbine, a shriek of hydraulics, or a welter of strange oscillating noises of no obvious origin. Everything vibrates. Talking is absolutely impossible except on the intercom, where it is relatively impossible.

The effect was almost nautical. Stuffy air, smelling of paint and oil, and heavy machinery filled every available space. There were turret controls, the primary sight, the auxiliary sight, switches, hydraulic lines, cables, the machine gun, and most notably the breech of the main gun inches to my left. Intermittently, we lurched sharply sideways. A tank steers simple-mindedly, by slowing one of its two tracks, with the subtle result one would expect. There is a certain directness about a tank, a lack of understatement. One knows intuitively that Proust would not have wanted one.

In the strange isolation born of dimness and cacophony, I braced my forehead against the brow pad and peered through the round eye of the gunner's main sight. A glowing pink reticule floated slowly, deliberately across the land; pale green Texas drifted by in the eerie clarity of good optics. The stabilization system held the turret rock-steady despite the bucking of the tank. I laid the empty gun on a distant steer—Fort Hood is open range—not from any hostility toward cattle but because some limbic instinct wants to aim at living things. Beneath a huge sky we careened on, with me, two gyroscopes, a laser range finder, a remarkably precise turret drive, a fire-control computer, and a 105mm high-velocity gun fixedly watching a cow.

The public attributes a great many qualities to tanks that they do not have. It is easy to think of a tank as a sort of terrestrial torpedo boat, dashing rapidly and invincibly about and blowing things up. Unfortunately, some who harbor this notion are armor officers, who tend to be frustrated cavalry officers and believe a tank to be an intractable but noble form of horse—which is one reason why in war, tanks are so often seen in flames.

In fact, tanks are big, hard, solid, fragile, unreliable, temperamental, and vulnerable. When possible, they are carried to battle on enormous trucks called tank transporters in the hope that they will function when they arrive. They break, bog down, and cannot go very far without something going wrong. They fall into holes and can't get out. They are a superlative pain in the neck.

Tanks ought to be obsolete, but they are not. Civilians said tanks were obsolete when I was in armor school with the Marines in the late 1960s, and later as I followed them through three Middle Eastern wars as a correspondent for various publications. Yet they were always there, always dangerous, and always decisive. I watch them today and see no change.

The voice of Sergeant San Miguel, the tank commander in the turret with me, roared from the headphones of my CVC helmet (the initials stand for something like Combat Vehicle Crewman). The army could never bring itself to call a headset a headset. "You gotta TC a M1 different from a A3." TC, Tank Commander, is both a noun and a verb, and an M60A3 is an older tank than the M1. "In A3s you stay high out of the hatch, but in M1s you keep low. You gotta be careful about your face." He demonstrated, lowering his seat until only the top of his head cleared the steel coaming of the hatch. "You gotta think about your teeth," he said. "You can smash them."

Tanks are dangerous to their crews, and much effort goes into avoiding injuries. They are also brutally uncomfortable. After a few hours in the hatches, you ache, unless you are nineteen and too dumb to know when you are uncomfortable. Fort Hood is uneven, pitted, ravined country. Tanks, except for the M1, which has a limousine's suspension, do not race across rough country. They pick and baby their way, like an automobile on a badly rutted road. The driver slows as he reaches a declivity, and the tank—*whoops!*—pitches downward, checks sharply at the bottom, accelerates, rocks back to the horizontal. Each step throws you against the hatch coaming unless you brace against it. At high speed, you have to resist with muscular tension, bend your knees, sit back hard, press your arms against the side. The world rocks *u-p-p-p-p*, tips sharply over, down, thump, roar of engine, bump of upslope, surge, hour after hour.

The M1 is a feline tank, quick, agile, with a smooth, honeyed ride—for a tank. This means that the crews hot-rod M1s over rough ground, being after all American kids, so you still get thrown around. Somewhere the army is said to have a photograph of an M1 firing in mid-air. The stabilization is certainly good enough.

We pulled into the firing range. The range-control people were on a low hill behind us, working from an armored personnel carrier fitted with radios. A dozen dirty M1s clattered about, squeak-squeaking, rattling, turbines howling like mournful lost vacuum cleaners. Tanks are exciting for about an hour, after which they are obtuse tractors that need fixing. The are also incredibly ugly and throw up a lot of dust. For the next several hours we did endless minor maintenance. The M1 seems to need a lot of it. Like yachts, tanks never work perfectly all at once.

The sun was hot. A constant wind from the hills desiccated without cooling. I leaned against the turret and waited. From somewhere down the line came the sharp crack of firing tanks, the putt-putt of their machine guns. I wasn't sure what we were waiting for. In the Army, waiting is intransitive, without an object.

I watched the crews, aware of the yawning gap of twenty years. These days they are smart, competent, and cheerful, which is astonishing to one who remembers the dregs of the late 1970s. And they can use their tanks. Yet there is a terrible innocence about them. It is a curious paradox that reporters go to more wars than soldiers do. I wondered whether the junior officers, who are conscientious, or their men really understand the business they are in. They have never looked inside a gutted tank. They were children during the Vietnam War.

From *The Sharp End*, an excellent book about soldiers in World War II:

"A tank that is mortally hit belches forth long searing tongues of orange flame from every hatch. As ammunition explodes in the interior, the hull is racked by violent convulsions, and sparks erupt from the spout of the barrel like the fireballs of a Roman candle. Silver rivulets of molten aluminum pour from the engine like tears…When the inferno subsides, gallons of lubricating oil in the power train and hundreds of pounds of rubber in the tracks and bogey wheels continue to burn, spewing dense clouds of black smoke over the funeral pyre."

Not the stuff of recruiting posters. The tank crews do not know of these things, not really. Armies don't read. Even the officers have never seen the horror of a burning tank. Fire is the hideous, unspeakable nightmare of armor. So many things burn in a tank: ammunition, fuel, hydraulic fluid vaporized by 1,500 pounds of pressure. The crews don't always get out. Hatches jam, the wounded can't move, sheer panic and agony prevent escape.

The M1 uses fire-retardant hydraulic fluid and a Halon gas fire-extinguisher, which are said to greatly reduce the likelihood of fire. One hopes they work.

The gun is the soul of a tank. The M1 is computerized, electronic, designed for accuracy at long ranges and for firing on the move. The wisdom of this design can be argued on complex grounds, yet the

Israelis, presumed to know something of tanks, have remarkably similar equipment on their own Merkava. So do the Germans.

Firing is easy, although there is an ampleness of buttons. Before battle the gunner should enter into the keyboard on the turret wall to his right the bore wear, the barometric pressure, and the temperature of the air and of the ammunition, all of which influence the strike of the round at long range. There is a gadget to offset the droop of the gun as it softens slightly in the sun. Sensors automatically account for crosswind and for the cant of the turret in case the tank is parked on a bump. Some of this works, some doesn't always. At normal ranges, it doesn't matter.

Next, depending on what he is firing at and whether it is day or night, the gunner sets various switches mounted in boxes of industrial appearance and labeled in abrupt, technical *Gotterdammerungian* language: NORMAL MODE DRIFT, AMMUNITION SELECT/ SABOT/HEP/HEAT. FIRE CONTROL MODE. EMERGENCY/ NORMAL/MANUAL. POLARITY BLACK HOT/WHITE HOT. The words reek of Wagnerian drama and insulation. I found myself with wild visions of Beowulf standing in dented armor, high in the cold hills of Denmark, holding a calculator from Hewlett-Packard and figuring azimuths.

There is a peculiar appeal, perhaps original to the late twentieth century, in being low in the cramped bowels of a tank, secure behind the armor and surrounded by all manner of fierce, cryptic controls. Major weapons always seem to me to be as much civilizational Rorschach blots as reasonable solutions to problems. Beneath a superficial rationality, all of them—tanks, fighter planes, submarines—are too obviously the toys I wanted when I was eleven. They call powerfully to the male's love of controllable complexity, and they are too much fun for coincidence. They too readily offer to a romantic the grey adrenal satisfactions of doom. And soldiers, God knows, are romantics.

Few of us have room to psychoanalyze others. Still, I suspect that if tanks came in decorator colors, pink and baby blue with satin trim and leopard skin, and the switches said BIG BOOMY GUN and LITTLE PUTT-PUTT GUN, war might stop.

Anyway, you set AMMUNITION SELECT to SABOT. This prepares the computer to fire a thing like a heavy metal arrow at terrific velocity. In the sight, the ominous circular pink reticle hangs in space. A pair of handgrips, universally called Cadillacs by the troops, raise the circle or move it sideways. Squeezing the grips turns on the turret stabilization so that the bucking of the tank does not affect the gun.

You put the reticle on the target, press the laser button to feed the range to the computer, and squeeze the trigger. There is a jolt, as if a giant boot had kicked the tank. Outside the noise is terrific, but inside it isn't loud. The shell case ejects onto the floor with a clang. Modern tanks can hit each other a mile away.

Earlier in the dust and heat of Fort Hood, I had watched as Sergeant San Miguel tried to start the tank. The turbine cranked around with a rising howl and sighed to a stop. An abort. He tried again. No go. She wasn't going to start.

He called another tank over and it jump-started ours successfully. Yep, batteries. Many of the ailments of tanks are depressingly similar to those of the family car. We pulled the armored cover from the back deck and discovered that two batteries had been rebuilt badly. There was nothing to do but wait for new ones.

I chatted briefly with a couple of soldiers about Killeen, the town just outside Fort Hood. Tankers see an awful lot of Killeen, and an awful lot of Germany. Killeen is the usual nasty little strip of burger joints, beer halls, motorcycle stores, and loan sharkeries, all engaged in the patriotic business of separating a GI from his paycheck. Signs blare NEED MONEY? SEE HONEST JOHN THE CASH SPIGOT. Denny's, Roy Rogers, McDonald's, Arby's—all the way stations on the road to coronary occlusion are there.

I was told that Killeen has improved in recent years. For example, the prostitutes have been chased away to Austin. I said I was glad to hear this, being sure that several thousand single men would respond with gratitude. "Ain't but one hooker left," a tanker told me. "She's so ugly I wouldn't take her to a dog fight if I thought she'd win."

The principles of tank gunnery find perfect expression in the age-old military prescription, "Do unto others, but do it first." The armor may help, but no one depends on it. The tank that doesn't fire first is likely to have a finned arrow of depleted uranium, moving at a mile a second, come through the turret in a burst of metallurgically complex finality. When a tank fights in what the military euphemistically calls a target-rich environment, the result is a terrifying controlled ballet as the loader slams 40-pound rounds into the breech, while the gunner desperately floats the pink circle onto an enemy tank that is trying to do the same thing to him: *boom*, load, *load*, goddamit....

The Soviets have experimented with an autoloader which unfortunately displayed democratic tendencies, promiscuously loading crewmen into the gun along with ammunition. ("Once more unto the breech, dear friends....") This is said to have been corrected.

Once, while in the jumbled rock country of the Golan Heights covering the aftermath of a war, I drove along a winding road cut into a hill. The curves were so sharp that it was impossible to see more than a short distance around the hill. Suddenly, a Soviet-made tank loomed into view; there was a neat hole at the base of its turret. Farther around the turn was another dead tank and, farther still, yet another. As nearly as I could tell, Israeli and Syrian tank columns had met unexpectedly, and the Israeli lead tank had fired first and loaded fast. The Syrians apparently had not realized that they were in a fight.

Earlier, I had passed a small plain, green against the high crags and rocky hills. A Syrian tank army seemed to stream across it, almost pretty, pennants flying from aerials. They had been dead for a week. Where tanks had paused to take on ammunition, great piles of cardboard canisters and splintered crates lay in sodden piles. Nobody thinks of war in terms of trash. There is a lot of it.

In peace, the tanker's life is the curious combination of boredom and resignation to lunacy that has always characterized militaries. The army is ridiculous in ways beyond civilian comprehension, and tanks are ridiculous even by army standards. Attending a military exercise in Korea, I witnessed the guarding of a bridge by a tank. The exercise was hopelessly unrealistic, as most are, being intended to show our highly questionable resolve to come to the aid of Korea if need be.

It was mid-afternoon. Mountains sloped sharply to paddies frozen to steel and a frigid wind raced up the valley. We guarded the bridge by parking beside it, pointing the gun in the presumed direction of the imaginary enemy, and pawing through C-rations for the edible parts.

The day dragged on. For a while we stood in the hatches and watched in awe as Korean kids played in freezing water. Next we made wretched C-ration coffee and lay on the ground with our heads against the tracks and talked. As a pillow, a tank is flawed. Then we watched some soldiers building a barbed-wire enclosure to fence in nonexistent prisoners.

From the driver's compartment came a lugubrious wail from Hoover, the driver: "Heater's broke."

With night falling in a Korean winter, that was a knell. The tank commander responded with the natural leadership of a good NCO. "Hoover, fix that goddam thing or you're on watch for a week!"

Hoover tried. The heater began to emit thick black smoke but no heat. The sun sank behind the mountains and the temperature began to fall in earnest. Smoke poured from the hatches of our 58-ton smudge pot. We leaned overboard, caught in a coldly burning tank, coughing like consumptives, Korean kids staring in stark wonderment....

From war movies it is easy to imagine that fighting in a tank is something like Luke Skywalker's exhilarating rush into the entrails of some death star. This sentiment killed many men in World War II and still kills, there being a profound tendency for tankers to regard themselves as diesel cavalrymen at Balaklava. Given the capacities of anti-tank weaponry, tankers who regard themselves as cavalry usually meet the same fate as those who charged with the Light Brigade.

In fact, the first element of ground combat, armored or not, is not élan but exhaustion—grim, aching weariness that actually hurts, that saps the will to resist, turns fingers to rubber, makes a standing man blank out for a second and catch himself falling. Eyes go gritty, armpits get raw from stale sweat, and the mind has trouble with simple things.

Then, in armor, there is the paranoia, the weird sensory deprivation that swathes a tanker in his own dim world of nerves. He can hear nothing above the racket of the tank, except through the intercom. An infantryman hears small arms fire, shouts, crackling of bushes, his own breathing. A tanker hears none of this, only the voices of the other crewmen hissing and roaring metallically from the headset, and the voices of other tanks over the radio. But even these have an odd disembodied quality. They don't come from anywhere in particular, for example. All voices seem to hang six inches behind your skull.

When the tank is buttoned up, with the hatches down for protection, it is almost blind. The driver, low to the ground (almost lying down in the hull of the M1) can see nothing at all in dense vegetation. The gunner has only the narrow field of his sight to connect him to outward existence. The loader sees nothing. The tank commander is slightly better off, but not much. Behind every bush there may be an antitank rocket that will explode through the side armor and make mush of all within.

And so tanks, the ones that survive anyway, are diffident, timid things. Except perhaps on flat desert, they advance fearfully and, depending on terrain, perhaps escorted by infantry that screens the hedges, kills the rocket men, roots out mines. Tanks stay under cover whenever possible, dislike open ground, dash from shelter to shelter like frightened fawns. This is why the Army chose the turbine engine for the M1, trading fuel economy for acceleration. A bold charge of massed armor, racing across open terrain with streamers flying, often leads to many flaming tanks.

A preferred way to use tanks is to put them in holes with just the turret showing. Another is to stay on what the army calls the reverse slope of hills (meaning the other side), climb into sight to fire quickly, and reverse back down. It is almost embarrassingly ungallant.

The tank remains critical to war, yet one somehow feels that it shouldn't. The mood of a tank, if you will, is not suited to the times. The thing belongs in an age of blast furnaces and raw national force, in an epoch of dreadnought navies when guns that a man could crawl into flung projectiles weighing a ton. The tank is a characteristically Soviet weapon—crude, brutal, but effective. You imagine them crawling like dark beetles from roaring factories deep behind the Urals.

Tanks are heavy machinery at its heaviest and simplest in a time when respectable weapons abound in microcircuitry, frequency-agile radar, focal-plane arrays, and near-sentient electronics. Modern tanks have many of these gewgaws and sometimes use them well, but they are essentially an encrustation of glitter. Remove the accretion of advanced whatnots, and the tank is still a hard object with a large gun. No matter how silly tanks may seem, no matter how archaic and unreliable, when one heaves out of the smoke and comes at you, you have a problem.

Do not think that because tanks are something of a blunt instrument, no thought goes into them. A tank is a cosh, but a highly engineered cosh. Open a book on tank design at random and you are likely to find a swarm of second-order partial differential equations. Lethal details are fussed over. For example, engineers give careful attention to the best ratio of length to diameter of long-rod penetrators—the "arrows" fired by the main gun. X-ray flash radiographs stop the penetration in mid-act for examination. The mechanics of plastic deformation are considered with great mathematical sophistication.

The engineers try to maximize behind-armor effects, or BAE, a technical term that encompasses burning and mutilation of the crew. Pressure transducers measure the "overpressure" as the tank is hit to see whether the lungs of the enemy will be ruptured, a desirable effect if you can get it. The probability of flash burns and their likely severity is studied. The following paragraph is from a report on an anti-armor warhead tested at Aberdeen Proving Ground, Maryland, but could have come from the labs of any civilized nation:

"The pressure transducer was the Kistler type 6121 piezo-electric gauge. This gauge, having a frequency response of 6 kilohertz, was used to measure air-shock pressures generated in the compartment. The incapacitating effects of temperature were assessed using the burn criteria presented in figure 7."

I once lay across from a pair of scorched tankers at the Naval Support Activity hospital in Danang. I couldn't see them because my face was bandaged, but we talked. They had been hit with a rocket, they said. It didn't penetrate, so the crew, having no idea where it came from, began to fire at random, this being the embodiment of American strategy in that war. Unfortunately, a hydraulic line had burst, and the fluid had ignited. Two tankers got out. The others stayed behind, screaming. This is sometimes called secondary or delayed behind-armor effects.

The fear a tank inspires in infantrymen is hard to grasp. A tank is far faster than a man. The M1 hits 45 miles an hour on good ground and doesn't get tired. The infantryman knows that it will run over him to save ammunition. Unless he is beside it and has exactly the right weapon, there is nothing he can do about it. He knows this. And if you haven't heard a big gun fire close up, you cannot imagine what a shattering thing it is. Seasoned troops who know a tank's limitations will stand up to one in reasonable terrain. Others will run in blind, squalling panic.

Once, late at night, I was out on the rolling dunes of Camp Pendleton with a platoon of infantry. The night was foggy, the moon a glow through dripping mist. We were in good spirits, listening to the soft swish of waves. Then we heard it: *squeak-squeak-squeak.*

Tanks. They weren't supposed to be anywhere near infantry at night, but somebody had slipped. I could feel unease go through the platoon. The squeaking grew in volume over a deep rumble of diesels, growling and dying, growling and dying as the crews rocked them over the dunes. We couldn't localize it; in the fog the sound seemed to come from everywhere.

We all thought the same thing: My God, they're going to run over us. They wouldn't even notice until they found the meat in the tracks. The roaring grew and grew, and with it came the seeds of panic, a panic that didn't know where to run. The fog shuddered with belching exhaust and—*whumph*—they rose over the dunes and stood there, idling, growling, waiting....

Three a.m., Fort Hood. Down the hill from me the tanks were firing into the blackness. Armies don't stop at night. There was no moon. The wind still soughed through the brush. From other ranges around us came distant detonations, streaks of fire across the sky, the brilliant white light of magnesium mortar flares dangling under their parachutes. From the invisible tanks low on the slope erupted violent yellow blasts and the cherry streak of main-gun tracers slashing across the unseen land. Behind us a spotting tank called on the radio, "Target...target...target..." The troops can shoot these days.

I waited for a lull and asked whether I could look through the thermal sights that allow firing in the dark. People and tanks are hotter than other things. The thermals pick up the heat and turn it into video, allowing fighting at night. They are also complex, delicate, and, it seems, prone to break down. A lot of them were burning out. The new ones from another manufacturer don't, the crews say, but they don't have them yet.

We made sure that tanks weren't going anywhere for a moment and walked down the hill with a flashlight. The night was pleasant, the company good—whatever one's political delusions, GIs are likable. For men who enjoy being outside and are not driven by the devils of the ego, tanks are not a bad field of endeavor. We found the step and hauled ourselves up the slab side-armor and lowered ourselves through the hatches. The inside was dim with battle lights. A pile of hot shell casings lay on the floor.

The sergeant turned on the refrigeration and we waited for the noisy little unit to cool down the thermal sensors. After ten minutes I crawled into the gunner's seat and peered through the lens. Nothing. The field was a meaningless jumble of flicker and snow. We slued the sensor head, and suddenly I was looking at clear, white silhouettes of troops. The effect was strange: The surrounding land didn't exist because it wasn't hot enough, so targets appeared to hang in fuzzy nothingness. But they were shootable.

I walked back up the hill and lay on the bleachers. The radio blared and chattered. A tank had slipped sideways into a hole and thrown a track. The men repaired it. The flickerings behind the neighboring hills continued. The red streaks flared from the dark tanks, hour after hour.

Harper's, February 1986

Why White Men Prefer Asian Women

There is near me an Asian sushi-beer-and-dinner establishment that I'll call the Asia Spot. The region is urban, so the clientele is a mix of some of just about everything, but the waitresses are all Asian, principally Japanese, Indonesian, Vietnamese, and Thai.

The Spot is a neighborhood bar. A large after-work crowd, many of them regulars, gathers at happy hour. The social dynamics are curious. It would be an exaggeration to say, as someone did, that the black guys come to pick up white women, and the white men come to get away from them—but it would be an exaggeration of an underlying truth. The waitresses are a large part of the Spot's appeal.

A common subject of conversation among male customers is how very attractive these women are when compared to American women. It is not a thought safe to utter in mixed company. It is a very common thought among men. American women know it.

Why are the Asians attractive? What, to huge numbers of men, makes almost any Asian more appealing than almost any American? The question is much discussed by men at the Spot. (I should say here that when I say "women," I mean the majority of women, the mainstream, the center of gravity. Yes, there are exceptions and degrees.)

American women of my acquaintance offer several explanations, all of them wrong. For example, they say that Asian women are sexually easy. No. American women are sexually easy. The waitresses at the Spot are not available. They date, but they cannot be casually picked up.

Another explanation popular among American women is that men want submissive women, which Asians are believed to be. Again, no. For one thing, submissive people are bland and boring. In any event the waitresses aren't submissive. Many compete successfully in tough professions. Among Asian waitresses I know I count an electrical engineer who does wide-area networks, and a woman with a master's in biochemistry who, upon finding that research required a PhD and didn't pay, went back to school and became a dentist. Both of these wait tables to help out in the family restaurant.

At the Spot I know a woman waitressing her way through a degree in computer security, a bright Japansese college graduate making a career in the restaurant business, and the manager of the Spot—not a light-weight job. Submissiveness has nothing to do with their attractiveness.

Why, then, are they so very appealing?

To begin with, look at the American women in the Spot. Perhaps a third of them are stylishly dressed. The rest of the gringas run from undistinguished to dumpster-casual: baggy jeans, oversize shirts—often male shirts—with the tails out. They seem to affect a sort of homeless chic, actually to want to look bad, and do it with more than a touch of androgyny. Too many are at least somewhat overweight. (So are the men, but that's another subject.) The Asians, without exception, are sleek, well-groomed, and dressed with an understated sexiness that never pushes trashy.

Further, the Asians are what were once called "ladies," a thought repellant to feminists but so very refreshing to men. Listen to the American women at neighboring tables, and you will frequently hear phrases like, "He's a fucking piece of shit." In what appears to be a determined attempt to be men, they have adopted the mode of discourse of a male locker room and made it their normal language. The Asians, classier, better students of men, do not have foul mouths. They presumably know about body parts and bathroom functions, but do not believe that a woman raises her stature by referring to them constantly in mixed company.

Men at the Spot, I have noticed, instantly understand that cloacal commentary is not wanted by the Asians, and don't engage in it: In the presence of the civilized, men adopt the standards of civilization. Men also tend to think of women as women think of themselves. The Asians, without displaying vanity, clearly think well of themselves. And ought to.

All in all, they give the impression that they do not want to be one of the guys. They want to be one of the girls. Here we come to the core of their appeal. Let me elaborate.

The default position of American women is what men refer to as "the chip," a veiled truculence, mixed with a not-very-veiled hostility toward men and a shaky sense of sexual identity. The result is a touchiness reminiscent of hungover ferrets. There is a bandsaw edge to them, a watching for any slight so that they can show that they aren't going to take it. They are poised to lash out in aggressive defense of their manhood.

As best as I can tell, they don't like being women. Here is the entire problem in five words.

The Asians at the Spot show every indication that they do like being women. They do not seem to have anything to prove. Being happy with what they are allows them to be comfortable with what they are not—men. They are not competing to be what they can't be with people who can't be anything else. They don't have to establish their virility because they don't want it. They do not assume, as American women tend to, that femaleness is a diseased condition to be treated by male clothes, gutter language, and bad temper.

I've spent many dozens of hours chatting with the gals at the Spot, and never seen a sign of the chip. For a man, the experience is wonderful beyond description—smart, pretty, classy women, who are women, and are not the enemy. As long as American women carry the chip, the Asian gals will eat them alive in the dating market.

Note that the espousal of hostile obnoxiousness as a guiding philosophy appears to be an almost uniquely American horror (though other English-speaking countries are catching up.). It certainly isn't requisite to independence or self-respect. I recently met a quite attractive blonde who, among other things, was smart, a long-haul motorcyclist, a student of the martial arts out of sheer athletic enjoyment of it, and an excellent marksman. She was also heterosexual, feminine, delightful company, and had no trace of "the chip." I was astonished. How was this possible, I wondered?

She was Canadian.

Nekkid In Austin

The day carnivorous reptiles almost ate me in the skin bar in Austin was hot and breathless, with a relentless sun hanging over the city as if waiting to drop. It was maybe 1971. I'd hitchhiked in from New York or maybe Minneapolis to see my friend Carol, who lived in a shack on Montopolis. Her boyfriend, a psychology student of some kind, suggested that we grab a cold beer, and several of its friends and neighbors, and grandchildren and second cousins, at a girly bar he knew.

Cold anything worked for me, though I only went to girly bars to read the articles.

The brew and view, which was on a densely trafficked main vein through town, was called the Sitting Bull, or maybe Wigwam or Tipi, or anyway one of those Indian words you live in.

The place was a certifiable western bar that could have gotten a USDA stamp: dim, smoky, with sprawling curved longhorns mounted on the wall, a cherry-red Bud sign that looked as if it meant it, and cowboys. A purple jukebox twanged about how momma done got runned over by a damn ol' train. The cowboys were big, rangy, and broad-shouldered, like Robocops in Stetsons. Texas has never quite figured out unisex. They were hootin' and hollerin' and swilling cold ones and telling lies. It was, like I said, Texas, than which it don't git no better.

Pretty soon the bartender got on the stage, which was six inches high, and said that now the "internationally known exotic dancer Kandy Pie" would entertain us. I think that was her name, though I once knew a stripper named Noodles Romanoff. You can't strip west of the Mississippi if you're named Mary Lou Hickenlooper.

Anyway, this clippity-clop music started and Kandy Pie came out wearing a horse. I guess it was plastic. It looked like she'd stolen it from a merry-go-round, and had a hole where the saddle was so she could wear it around her waist. That horse was about all she was wearing.

She wasn't too exotic, but she was pretty near nekkid. I had to give her that.

Which had its appeal. Kandy Pie was a bodacious blonde who looked like a watermelon patch in Georgia, except she wasn't green. She was also on the wrong side of thirty-five. The make-up didn't hide it. She drooped where she should have perked, and had a few more pounds than she needed, and just looked tired. The cowboys didn't like it. Catcalls erupted.

They were louts, I guess, but they weren't really mean-spirited. Thing was, they hadn't paid to see an enactment of the Onslaught of Middle Age. Yeah, they should have been more gentlemanly. She should have found another line of work five years earlier. Fact is, Kandy Pie seemed to be on the receding cusp of her international career. Which probably spanned three cities in central Texas.

She clipped and clopped and the horse grinned its idiot's grin and the catcalls increased. She bore up under it, but you could see the pain in her face. It wasn't fun being laughed at for fading looks when looks were all she had. On the other hand, there's something to be said for knowing when to quit.

She clopped and bounced and hollered things like "Yippy Yi Yay" and "Yeehaaa," and then pulled cap pistols and fired them in the air.

Blam!

Kandy Pie froze. I believe she thought a cowboy had shot at her. Actually a light bulb had fallen from the stage lighting and exploded.

That was all for dancing in a horse. She stepped out of ol' Trigger and just walked off the stage.

And came back with a cobra.

About two feet of cobra, gray, with hood flared. It had cold black eyes that augured nothing good and a low, empty forehead like a network anchorman. It wasn't a happy cobra.

Dead...silence...fell, thump, like a piano from a tall building. Nobody had expected a cobra. I supposed a sign somewhere averted to Kandy Pie and Her Merry Scary Animals, but I hadn't seen it, and apparently neither had the cowboys.

Kandy Pie was suddenly a different woman. Sort of goddess-like. She held that death-rope up and peered into its eyes, let it wrap around her neck, and peeled it off. A confidence had come over her, as though she were somehow in her element. Then she put the cobra on the stage. It set out toward the cowboys. Apparently it had plans for them.

Thirty chairs scraped simultaneously. Another second and those cowboys would have climbed the supporting poles and hung there like bananas. I planned to exit through the nearest wall.

Sure, I knew the beast had been defanged. So did the cowboys. Probably defanged, anyway.

Just before that length of gray extinction left the stage, Kandy Pie put out her foot and gently pinned its tail.

"Anyone wanna hold it?" she said softly. It was a challenge. My turn now, she was saying.

Cowboys have their virtues, such as courage, and they really weren't bad people. In fact, they were actually pretty good people. One said, "Shore." He did hold it. You could tell he thought it was a really fine snake, even if it looked like Dan Rather. Others followed. Soon Kandy Pie was surrounded by masculine hunks who had decided she was quite a lady. I thought somehow of Tom Sawyer whitewashing the fence.

Turns out she was an act unto her own self. Soon she took the cobra backstage and returned with a boa constrictor. I won't tell you it was 400 feet long. I'll tell you it looked 400 feet long. A lot of fire trucks would have envied that thing. We all took turns draping it around our necks. About sixty pounds of it.

"Whatcha feed it?"

"Chickens."

"Live'uns?"

She smiled. "Yep."

The final act was a tarantula, a big hairy orange-and-black sucker, like a yak hair pillow on stilts. Did I want it to crawl up my arm? No, but I said yes. It was a manhood issue. She put it on my wrist. Those rascals are heavy. She poked it so it would crawl. I knew it was going to bite me and carry me off to a hole to lay eggs on me. The cowboys clustered around, enthusiastic. They wanted a tarantula to crawl on them too.

I don't think it could have happened, except in Texas: One bearded long-haul road freak, buncha cowboys in dressy boots, large blonde in, if not the altogether, at least the mostly together, and a sprawling tarantula the size of a tennis racket. It was splendid, I tell you.

Democracy. But Not So's You'd Notice It.

Perhaps the oddest idea regarding democracy is the belief that more than five people want it. Other curious notions are that it quite exists, or ever did, or is particularly desirable, or likely to endure.

Few say this. We are all subjected in high school to advertising slogans about Truth, Justice, Freedom, the Will of the People, and Unalienable Rights. High-minded catch-phrases precede and spur all revolutions, whether American, French ("Liberty, equality, fraternity!") or Russian ("Workers of the world, unite." "The dictatorship of the proletariat." "From each according....").

In the American case, principled naïfs like Tom Jefferson and George Mason saw democracy, or said they saw it, as the road of the future and an instrument of morality. It would make things better. It would end tyranny, the preferred form of government in Europe at the time.

It did, pretty much. Or did if you were not an Indian, a miner in West Virginia, an indentured servant, a black slave, or a kid of ten being sweated in New York's garment industry. In Europe, tyranny was imposed by the central government, usually an inbred royal family that bled when touched. In America it was under local control, spread over tenant farms and cotton fields. The political right pretends this didn't happen, and the political left pretends that nothing else happened.

The United States, as it became, progressed less because of political democracy than because of economic freedom. Then as now, most of the electorate knew little of the issues. Votes, depending on the period, were delivered by machines in cities at the command of political bosses. Newspapers, the closest thing to television until television, were as manipulated and manipulative as the media are today. Then, as now, pols understood that it profited more to gull fifty rubes than to try to persuade one of the informed. It was democracy of a sort, though not the sort trumpeted in texts.

Part of the conventional hooha is the notion that people want democracy, and will defend it to the death. To believe this is to misunderstand the very foundation of politics. Most people wanted, and want, only to be comfortable—i.e., fed, warm, dry, secure, amused, and sexually satisfied.

Tyranny has existed chiefly because it has been the only way for tyrants to live in what passed in their times for luxury. Until recently, the productivity of societies was so dismally low that the only way to be rich was to concentrate the exiguous wealth of the poor, which meant almost everybody. The way to do this was to get a sword and some henchmen and systematically rob everyone else. You needed the sword because, when a peasant didn't have enough to eat in the first place, he didn't want you to take half of it to have banquets in your castle. He would be likely to object fatally if he could figure out how.

Democracy appealed to him because he thought it meant he could keep his crops. It was the only reason it appealed. If he had enough to eat, he didn't care what went on in Paris. He still doesn't.

But today the factories are so immoderately fecund that almost everyone can live at a high standard. (A double-wide with a satellite dish, Internet connectivity, a pick-up truck and a beer supply is in fact a pretty high standard of living. Ask a thirteenth-century peasant.) Consequently oppression isn't needed: The impulse to revolt is nonexistent. Prosperity is the opiate of the masses.

And of tyrants. Those who in another century would have inclined to tyranny don't have to bother. They can get filthy rich by jiggering the stock market, doing leveraged buy-outs, or engaging promiscuously in real estate. Swords have become unnecessary. A Donald Trump can sack New York without putting anyone to death. Such is our national wealth that, after he has done it, no one notices.

The other incentive to tyranny was power. However, the flood of goods that pours from factories permits those who crave power to get it without riling the peasants (you and me). These, after all, are happy with their SUVs and home theater. Putting it succinctly, sufficient ambient money severs rapacity from oppressiveness. Men who would have butchered countries no longer have to. They can instead sell aircraft companies, elect governors, and otherwise enjoy, more or less harmlessly, the psychic emoluments of potency.

Which may not be a bad deal.

In any event, the principle that comfort trumps democracy underlies society today. We have the trappings of elections, the theater of close counts, the excitement of watching the polls—that is, the emotions associated with a tight football season. But what real influence do we have? Can we divert the remotely chosen path of our children's education, alter or even speak against the flow of immigrants across our borders, question racial preferences? No. These things are decided for us. We can lose our jobs for speaking of them. The more things matter, the less we can say about them.

Freedom? We have economic freedom, yes. We can start a computer company if we are smart enough, work hard enough, and find the capital. This keeps the ambitious from becoming radical.

We can exercise any freedom that doesn't endanger the status quo. We can live where we want, change jobs, watch pornography, read seditious books and even write them (provided we don't seek wide circulation), and buy endless things we don't need or much want. But we can't speak our minds.

Two things allow the appearance of democracy without the substance. The unanimity of the media permits the inculcation of appropriate values, while not providing lateral communication between individuals. The Internet changes this, but apparently in no practical sense. The other is the satisfaction of the drives for food, comfort, sex, and entertainment. Satiety breeds indifference.

Things could be worse. If you want to read the classics, or teach them to your children, you can. You just can't get the schools to teach them. Any book you want, any music, any vacation, any sport from golf to hang gliding, you can easily find. Existence is as secure as it is likely to get. Software gets better. Cable sometimes offers five hundred channels, I hear, or will soon. Life is good.

It is only the important things that are decided quietly, far away, by the political classes who know where the country should go, who know what is right and will, gradually, without any jackboots at all, make us what they think we should be.

Getting What We Wanted, Wanting What We Got

Maybe the world has become too comfortable, too easy. For long thousands of years, many of them lost to memory, the race has sought to tame the earth, reduce it to order, make it secure. It has worked. We are warm, fed, safe, but...have we lost something?

Of old the world was wild, forbidding, perilous, a looming unknown stalked by hunting animals, swallowed by drifting fog, wracked by storms of uncomprehended provenance, roofed by stars and planets sharper than those of today that had not yet been reduced to the dry equations of celestial mechanics. Men were few, the land large. We were strangers in that world, not yet its masters. Men defended, by violence and shedding of blood, pockets of warmth and safety for their wives and children. A fire in a Norse winter in 735 AD meant something that fire doesn't now.

That world was another place because we did not control it, or believe we understood it. The imagination had room to stretch. In the black forests of medieval Europe, in murky blue shadows closing around cultivated fields by twilight, in the vast soughing deserts of Roman North Africa—monsters lurked, or men thought they did, which was as satisfying. Horizons lay closer. Men often didn't know what was fifty miles away, much less on another continent. China, India, Cipango were lands of fabulous rumor, where men with three heads dwelt and one might fall off the edge of the earth on the way. There was magic, the pull of the unknown, a sense of things yet undone and places yet unseen.

Today little remains of that world of portent and possibility. The ensemble has collapsed, possibilities become knowns, become certainties ordered and catalogued in books and available on the Internet. There is little mystery, little to explore, little of that odd stew of danger and uncertainty that once spiced life. The explorers and swordsmen of other times are now clerks, speaking of gigabytes and megahertz.

We have succeeded perhaps too well.

Think. In 1800 a band of men setting forth into Africa did not know what they might find—mountains never before seen, great rivers, curious animals and savages of strange custom. Today, every inch of every land has been mapped, photographed, explored, trampled upon, and packaged for the Discovery Channel. Blue-haired grandparents in Toyota Land Cruisers make safari through Kenya—a Kenya as mild and ordered as Disneyland, and anyway they've seen it all many times on the babbling box. Travel has become not exploration but confirmation. Yes, the Taj Mahal looks exactly as it did on television. The Indians got it right, we think. It looks like television.

We know everything, have seen everything. Children of ten have watched the inner workings of nests of termites in the African veldt, have seen the surface of the Moon and of Mars, the mating of implausible worms in the black night of geothermal vents, and the social customs of gibbons. What is left?

In a world so very tame, in which all is controlled and watched and manicured, in which we keep as parks a few vestigial traces of the former wildness to visit like a movie theater—what is there for us in our more hell-for-leather moods, if we still have them? Where is the risk, the danger that once made life seem worth living? Where are the wolves, the dragons, the bears we feared? Bears? Once we ran from them. Then we built houses proof against them, then we hunted them, and now we put them in zoos.

Am I alone in thinking that we have circumscribed our world to death, made it vaguely pointless and without savor? In thinking that we might, some of us, be happier with less comfort and more to find?

Those who feel the pull of the distant, of the yet mysterious and the still hazardous, may even today find satiety, though it will be encrusted with artificiality. The hardy sky dive, ride motorcycles, swim 100 feet below the surface of the night seas. A few may still join the Pathan tribesmen and live as in the thirteenth century. Thirty years ago we hitchhiked and hopped freights. Some still do.

And yet...and yet there is a growing sense of fraud in the search for peril, for adventure, for a sense of not being in control—in the search for something left to do. So we have bungee jumping, paintball, and wilderness racing. One may walk the Appalachian Trail, tame as a topiary garden with the distant roar of the jets overhead. We know what we want. We try.

But we're pretending.

Ever the world becomes snugger, more secure, more enswaddling in its concern for our safety. I don't say that it is wrong precisely, only that it is—constricting. Motorcyclists must wear helmets, not an evil notion (one saved my life once), but too civilized. Now children must wear helmets on bicycles, and modern parents would never, ever, let their boys of fourteen take the .22 and go to shoot rats, or set forth up a river in a canoe. They would need life jackets and supervision and, no doubt, inoculations. And should the rash-but-alive decide to Kon Tiki their way across whatever ocean that may remain somewhat untraveled, they will have cell phones and air support and hourly coverage on television.

We have built our trap well.

Yes, always there have been people, the majority no doubt, who wanted only a roof in rain, fire in winter, enough to eat, and not too much work. Throw in a pub, a game of darts or, now, the idiot box, and they are content on their passage through whatever it is that we are passing through. But for some, for those who once set out on matchbox ships to cross the Pacific, it is stifling. And perhaps the tedious security robs the race of something important though not easily explained, certainly not to the wan little clerks who manage our fear of radon.

What of the young of today, who know nothing but the controlled and modulated? They sit in the meat bars night after night to hook up, not really happy with it, wondering what else there might be, and then go back to the office with its controlled temperature and fluorescents that never fail. Do we want this? One succeeds too well sometimes, and then one must live with what one has done. And so we have, and so we must.

Attack Of The Alpha Frump

Saturday evening on the Loot Loop, as Washington's beltway is called by those who understand the city. Traffic was light. Night stretched away before us, as dark as a cannibal's intentions. The trunk was full of guns. My friend Rob and I had been shooting out in Virginia, because it was a Patriarchal Phallocentric thing to do, with overtones of Oppression. At least we hoped it was. We were trying hard to be brutal hierarchical males. We would have slaughtered some people of color, except the only ones we knew were either mathematicians or really good-looking waitresses at the Asian restaurant down the street from me.

Maybe this isn't making sense. I can't promise it will get much better. Rob lives in a hunting shack way out in Virginia. In Washington, as a sort of hobby (in real life he works for a defense contractor), he tells women they ought to carry guns for self-defense. This sets radical feminists off like bottle-rockets. They want women to think they're victims, because that way they can scam Uncle Sucker for grants. It's how Washington works.

Anyway, as Rob tells it, he was at lunch near the Pentagon, innocently trying to make gun molls out of some women he'd met. He looked up and saw what he took to be a boxcar with fangs bearing down on him. (OK, Rob does ornament his stories sometimes.) It was a feminist contractor, who looked like Paul Bunyan's ugly sister. She was, Rob said, such an awful diesel dyke that she practically had valve clatter.

These gals are scary. You can get PTSD from them. It's a medical fact.

She squalled about how Rob was sowing the seeds of death. He says he didn't throw her down an elevator shaft. (It isn't easy to pry the doors open.) But he was shaken. He called me and said he needed a day of remedial patriarchy. Guns. Somebody to oppress. Beer. Normal women, with a sense of humor. Anything but Washington's virile law-yeresses and lemon-sucking shrews in shoulder pads.

We'd gone for football to a local dirt bar, dim and raunchy with a stuffed plastic fish on the wall and a huge American flag and pool tables and actual friendly waitresses like you have in North Carolina. It also had a projection TV screen the size of a tennis court. You don't really know a quarterback till you've seen his head eight feet high, with pores big enough for birds to nest in.

Our friend Gina works there. A year ago we'd found her on her first day of work. She's pretty so we'd flirted with her. Then Rob went to make a sacrifice to the porcelain god. Trying to stab him in the back, I told her seriously, "I think you should know. I'm his parole officer."

"Oh?" she said. "He told me he was your psychiatrist."

I can't trust my own friends.

She came over to the booth, it being a slow day. Gina's wonderful. For starters, she isn't an androgyne lesbo Death Star. She doesn't take Rob and me too seriously. (I can't understand why.) But she's good people. It's an alien concept in this city.

This isn't getting any better organized. Keep reading, though. I may put dirty pictures at the end.

Anyway, Rob was waving his arms and hollering about the horror of his experience. Vodka and grapefruit bring out a certain nuanced lyri-cism in him. "She was like a professional wrestler trapped in a space alien's body," he yelled. "It was like...have you ever stood in line behind a rhinoceros? Bring me another of these, would you? Do you have any opium?"

Gina's used to it.

We left about ten. Rob was recovering. We had done just about everything male except engage in linear thinking, or get Harley hogs and run over the homeless. These days, bums are too alert. Besides, only rich proctologists can afford Hogs.

We stopped at Blockbuster to document the decline of civilization. Behind the counter was a gasping adenoidal kid breathing through his mouth. He had thick glasses like base plates for a mortar.

"You got anything with lots of gratuitous violence?" we asked.

He didn't blink.

"That's pretty much the store. You want cowboys? Spacemen? Cops? Robots?"

It was true: Row after row of absolutely talent-free movies about guys blowing things up: cars, buildings, planets, each other. Gorgeous babes watched admiringly. They had perfect hair after being chased through the jungle for three days by mutant crocodiles.

I wanted this movie I saw once in a theater about space aliens that looked like bugs with eyeballs and a beak, and they lived inside you until they exploded your chest and popped out, spoing!, like a jack-in-the-box. The girls in the audience all shrieked, "*Ewwwwwwwwwwwwww-wwwwwww!*" and the boys said, "Oh, wow!" It's a sex difference.

Is this making sense yet? I don't think so.

Rob's cabin looks like a landfill gone to disorder. A real male's house has a thirty-thirty on the kitchen table, a set of large-bore pistons in the sink, girly magazines by the bed, and clothes strewn everywhere so he can keep an eye on them. Women don't understand this. They want to put things in hiding places, like drawers, so that life becomes an unending Easter-egg hunt.

My girlfriend used to ask me why my scuba gear was in the middle of the living room floor. Because that way I could find it, I told her. How hard, she asked, was it to find a large pile of scuba gear anywhere in a small apartment? Women get logical at all the wrong times. I didn't know, I said, but I figured it didn't pay to experiment casually with the unknown.

We had gotten a really terrible movie about spaceships. See, these Life Forms turned people into cocoons and stuffed them into caves on some planet. The good guys had to look for them. It was like trying to find your scuba gear after your girlfriend cleans up. Weird things that looked like badly designed termites scuttled after them in the dark and grabbed them one by one, to make more cocoons. I guess they didn't have enough.

It's another sex difference. A woman would have wanted a chick flick about two people in love, and how they overcame his brain tumor and worked out something about relationships, and lived happily ever after. No giant termites. No explosions. I don't get it.

This isn't making more sense as time goes by. I was afraid of that. Maybe I'll quit while I'm ahead.

Tales From The Lejeune Woods

Marine Corps training. Boot camp. Yawning gateway to military life, an adventure outrageously funny and frightening, source of a lifetime of lies, growing worse with each bull session. No one forgets boot. Get two GIs together over a bottle of gin, talking about old times, and sooner or later the talk will turn to tales of boot, A few of them will even be true.

Not many, though. It is all right for most stories to be based on fact, but the better recollections of boot have only a nodding acquaintance with truth. Facts inhibit flexibility. They stultify.

But boot is more than tall tales. For years it was part of American life. We talk of being a peaceful nation, but usually we have a couple of million men and women under arms and often a war going. A high percentage of Americans have spent time in the military. They shaped it, and it shaped them.

A particular aspect of the national character appears in the organized anarchy of military life. Literature finds the military a feast—Catch 22, M*A*S*H, A Farewell To Arms, Dispatches, and all the rest.

Boot is a gateway. Here's to basic, as I remember it, as everyone remembers it, as I saw it in going back this year. A boy's first great taste of life.

Next to finding a shark in the bathtub, the worst thing that could happen to a kid of 20 in 1968 was getting to Parris Island at a grainy-eyed two in the morning, flat exhausted, and meeting a drill instructor. Everyone's heard the tales. DIs will pull your fingernails off one by one, make you run until your knees corrode, bury you to the neck in sand and leave you for the mosquitoes.

When the bus pulls into the swampy lowlands of South Carolina and Parris Island signs appear, it all becomes plausible. And there's *no…way…out.*

I arrived on a chartered Greyhound crowded with Richmond boys who suddenly suspected that they weren't a Few Good Men. It was a raw deal all around—cottony taste in the mouth, somebody else sure to get the girl back home, bus reeking of stale sweat and beginning fear, no thought yet about dying in Asia, just a sort of *uh-oh* feeling.

The driver had picked up a sergeant at the gate to give him a ride. "You wanna get off before the stampede?" the driver asked.

Stampede? It sounded ominous.

On that loneliest morning I'll ever see, my introduction to the Marines—the Green Team, the Crotch, Uncle Sam's Misguided Children—was a little man 32 feet wide and about as high as my chin. He had killed Smokey the Bear and stolen his hat. He had a voice like Krakatoa in full eruption, and his name was Staff Sergeant Bull Walrus. At least I think it was.

He exploded into the headlights like one of hell's more vicious demons, trembling with fury.

"GiddawfadatgawdambusNOW!" he bellowed, blowing several windows out of the bus—I swear it, three windows fell out—by which we understood his desire that we disembark. We did so in sheer terror, trampling one another and no longer worried about our girls. To hell with our girls. Bull Walrus was clearly about to tear out throats out with his bare teeth, that was the important thing.

There we were, The Few, The Proud, standing in deep shock with our feet in these silly golden footsteps painted on the pavement. Move one inch, Walrus screams, and he will do unspeakable things, after which our girls will no longer want us. I figured they kept Walrus in a dungeon by day and just let him out to torture recruits by night.

We are groggy with fatigue, minds buzzing with adrenaline, and Walrus is inspecting our suitcases to take away glass objects. So we won't commit suicide with them, see.

I imagine myself tearing out my carotids with an Arid bottle. Suddenly he is in front of me. I lied. He's not 32 feet wide. He is 40 feet wide. He's got arms like anacondas and his head is held on by a bolt.

He also is confiscating porn books, to protect our morals and read later. He reaches for a book in my suitcase and glares at me with eyes of tin and death. I realize, with calm that still surprises me, that he is going to murder me. The book is *Medieval Architecture.*

A recruit, a drill instructor told me much later, after I had been reincarnated as a journalist, "is the funniest goddam animal alive. He's gotta be. You get these kids, some of them are street kids from the city, some of them farm kids, and these suburban kids who just don't know nothing—every kind of kid.

"And dumb? Jeez they're dumb. And they've got about two months to adjust to a complicated life they've got no experience with. They've got to learn how to think Marine Corps. Military thinking isn't like civilian thinking.

"Half of 'em don't even know how rifle sights work. Like this friend of mine is teaching a class about the M-60 machine gun, and he's telling them its rate of fire, it's gas-operated, and this skinny recruit says, 'But where's the gas tank?'"

"Jeez, they're dumb."

Sergeant Sly is a man with a sense of humor. He's black, strac, and cocky—the DI cockiness that says there's nothing on God's green earth better than the Green Team, and I'm the coolest thing in the Corps, and, Prive, you gotta sweat to be as good as me. All DIs are like that, all the good ones anyway. Sly is a good one.

Sly runs recruits along the hot, dusty weapons ranges of Camp Lejeune—hot and dusty in summer, anyway. He tries to keep his recruits from getting hurt.

"All right," he tells a platoon, who listen in sweat-soaked utilities. Nothing looks quite as dispirited as recruits in a hot sun. "While you're in the field, you gotta take certain precautions against the wildlife. I don't have to tell you about some of it. Don't feed the snakes, or try to pick'em up 'cause they're pretty.

"I'm talking about the *other* wildlife. Most of it's harmless, but one kind is bad news—what people down here call the Wampus cat. It's related to the bobcat and it's not too big, 'bout like a cocker spaniel, but you don't want to make one think he's cornered."

Another afternoon at Lejeune. The recruits listen, barely.

A few scenes are so close to boot camp that they deserve inclusion here, embodying as they do terrors near to those of boot.

On a massive grinder at Camp Pendleton, California. A private, fresh out of training and spending a week on maintenance duty before his school begins, has been sent to pick up toilet paper for the barracks. Battalion issue has no box in which to carry it. He ponders, has an idea, sticks a dozen rolls on a mop handle, puts it over his shoulder like a rifle.

A bird colonel rounds the corner. The Marine is new enough to the real military that officers terrify him. Panic strikes. He hesitates and, driven by reflex or some buried death wish, gives a snappy rifle salute. The colonel's jaw drops. His hat slowly rises on a column of steam.

You learn. It just takes a while.

Boot camp is a very quick education in the ways of the world—of many worlds. For a weird collection of people, the average training platoon beats midnight in a New York City bus station.

In my platoon we had a Mexican kid named Rodriguez who couldn't speak English, a black kid who said he was Bill Cosby's nephew, three college students—one of them a physical chemistry major, one a tiny blond guy who couldn't have been more than 11 years old—and a bunch of judicial draftees. ("I'm gonna give you a choice, son," says the judge. "Four in the slammer or two in the Marines." It's supposed to be illegal. So are a lot of things.)

Many of these judicial draftees were burglars from Tennessee. Free enterprise seems to be broadly interpreted in those parts and usually begins after midnight. One of them was named Mulvaney. He had been caught in a second floor bedroom collecting someone else's silver-ware. He preferred the Marines to the slammer, not necessarily a wise choice in those days—I later heard he got killed outside of Danang.

Anyway, Mulvaney was built like one of those Martian robots on the late show, with logs for arms and the legs of an offensive lineman, and he had gray eyes and a long, slow smile that meant he was about to break your legs in 20 places. He didn't get mad easily, but it was spec-tacular when he did.

For a college kid accustomed to settling disputes by reason, Mulv-aney was a revelation. He didn't care about right and wrong. Either he liked you, or he tried to kill you.

One night Mulvaney was standing fire watch in the latrine—the Marine Corps thinks they are flammable—and he somehow got into a fight with Rodriguez. A Mexican kid from Brownsville is not the best choice to throw hands with. We could hear it all down the squad bay—terrific thumps with a splattering sound like a sack full of hog kidneys hitting a tile wall, and not a word. Neither wanted to waste energy talking. It was one of those extended fights engaged in by men who simply like fighting.

Next morning it was hair, teeth and eyeballs all over the deck, and enough gore that you'd have thought they'd been slaughtering hogs. Both combatants looked like they had lost a discussion with a cement truck. Mulvaney's left eye looked like an egg fried in blood and Rod-riguez's nose wasn't quite where I remembered it.

"What you pukes been doing?" snarled the drill instructor. Pukes was the nicest thing they ever called us. He really wasn't mad. Fighting was a sin, but not as bad as falling out on a run.

"Walked into the door, sir," says Mulvaney, deadly serious.

"Wha' sir?" says Rodriguez, looking puzzled. His English deterio-rated when he was asked inconvenient questions.

For hours, Mulvaney and Rodriguez pounded round the grinder in full packs, holding hands and yelling, "I love Mulvaney more than poking my girlfriend." When they finished, I bet they did. It was justice of a sort.

If there is any possible way to do something wrong, a recruit will find it.

There was the ambidextrous kid at the grenade range at Lejeune. The idea was to stand between two walls of sandbags and throw the grenade over a high parapet. He pulled the pin and rared back to throw. Then he stopped. You could see the puzzlement in his face. No, that hand didn't feel right. He casually tossed the thing in the air, caught it in the other hand, and threw it. By the time it exploded, the instructor was in the next county and accelerating.

I remember lying in lovely cold muck behind a log at Lejeune, firing at enemy oil barrels a few hundred yards away. It was one of those implausible situations that occur regularly in the military.

Cold rain drizzling down my helmet and running neatly down my spine, my helmet slipping down over my eyes, and I'm in a firefight with a bunch of extremely dangerous barrels. The rifle is a worn out M-1 probably left over from the Napoleonic Wars, in use only because the government has several hundred billion rounds of ammunition for it.

The trigger mechanism is broken. Every time I fire it, the damned thing falls out and hangs down like a wounded clock. I slap it back. Bang, slap, bang, slap. Every fourth round, the clip pops out of the top of the rifle—spoing—and lands on my helmet.

Bang, slap, spoing, clunk, adjust the helmet. Bang, slap. I begin to see that it could be a long war.

A recruit was standing on a roof at Parris Island in the burning sun at parade rest. His DI had put him there to work on the roof and somehow had forgotten him. A passing sergeant noticed, stared curiously for a second, and bellowed, "Git down from there, prive."

The private didn't move.

"Goddamit, git down here," bawled the instructor, unused to being ignored.

Nothing. The private looked deeply unhappy, but didn't so much as twitch.

Another DI came along and yelled, but nothing moved the recruit. He gazed desperately ahead, either deaf or crazed by the sun. A group formed on the sidewalk, including a warrant officer, a lieutenant, and, finally, a passing light colonel.

The colonel snapped his crispest order. The private stared ahead. The crowd conferred, decided they had a mental case on their hands and prepared to send for a struggle buggy and some big corpsmen. Then the private's DI returned.

"*Jaworski*, Ten-*hut*! Git your butt down from there."

Down came Jaworski. From parade rest, you see, the only acceptable order is "attention." The manual of arms says so.

"Thing is," a drill instructor explained to me, "a recruit's in a place he doesn't understand at all, and nothing ever works for him. Back home, he knows the rules. Maybe he's a big dude on the block, got it made. Not here. Everybody's yelling at him and he can't ever do anything right.

"So he figures he'll do exactly what he's told. It's his way of protecting himself. If something goes wrong, he thinks at least it's not his fault. This is what a drill instructor's got to learn—nothing's too crazy for a recruit to do if he thinks it's what you told him. And you really got to think about it. Otherwise you can get him hurt.

"One time in winter a friend of mine, Sergeant Grunderling, had evening duty at some building and he wanted to go take a leak. So he tells this recruit who's with him, 'I'm going out for a minute. Don't let anyone in who doesn't know the password. You got that?'

"The recruit says, 'Yes, sir,' so Grunderling relieves himself and realizes he can't remember the password. So he hollers, 'Minter, open the door.'

"What's the password?"

"I forget. Open the door."

"I can't do that, sir. You told me not to let anybody in who doesn't give the password, sir."

"Goddamit Minter, now I'm telling you to open the door."

"'No sir, I can't do that."

"Minter, it's cold out here."

"No, sir, I can't do that."

"By now Grunderling's mostly frozen and so mad he can't see straight, but he sees threats ain't going to help him.

"Please, Minter, let me in. I ain't gonna yell at you. I won't do anything to you."

"Aww, you're trying to trick me."

"No, Minter, honest, I ain't trying to trick you. Open the door.'

"You're gonna yell at me, aren't you sir?"

"No, Minter, I promise."

"Finally, old Minter opens the door and Grunderling nearly kills him. But he should have expected it. A recruit does exactly what you tell him."

"You probably won't see a Wampus cat," Sergeant Sly continues, "but if you do, remember he's fast. A cat isn't built for endurance like a dog is, but he's lightning in a dash. Don't think you're gonna tease a Wampus and run away when it starts spittin' and howlin'.

"They're not that fast—I mean, a Wampus cat can't keep up with a cheetah or anything, but they've been clocked at 50. It takes a damn good shot to hit anything at that speed."

A September day in a clearing at Camp Lejeune. Our company of trainees sits in weathered bleachers, scratching and, after three months of training, feeling as salty as three bosun's mates.

A massive black sergeant with a velvet Georgia accent is teaching us the care and feeding of a white phosphorus grenade, otherwise known as Willy Peter (and several other things unfit for a family magazine). Willy Peter is an unpleasant weapon that throws white phosphorous around, a nasty substance that sticks to you and burns.

The sergeant holds the lethal cylinder in his hand, tells us what horrible things it can do to Luke the Gook, who was then the hated enemy, and announces that he will trot into the field and demonstrate.

That is fine with us, as long as we can sit in the sun and relax. We watch with interest as he lopes into the grass.

For days we've been watching weapons specialists trot into Lejeune's clearings, and something spectacular always happens. Something blows up or goes bang or makes colored smoke.

So the sergeant gets out there next to this little steel hut he's supposed to hide in while Willy Peter does his stuff. He chucks the incredibly vicious grenade downfield and ducks into the steel hut.

Two seconds later he streaks out at roughly Mach Four. He has the unmistakable gait of a man who is flat terrified. About that time Willy Peter goes *whoomp!* and the air around the sergeant is filled with long smoky trails of flaming phosphorous. He streaks on as if he took showers in the stuff, ignoring it, a mountain on the move in blind fright.

Somehow all that smoking agony misses him and he reaches us panting hugely.

"Goddam wasps."

Training has changed. Ten years ago, reveille at Parris Island meant a GI-can lid sailing down the squad bay at oh-dark-30. The lights would come on suddenly and 10 seconds later a hundred recruits would be standing at attention in their underwear, half-conscious and miserable.

Now the GI-can lid is gone. So is much of the stress of training.

"What happened, some kid's mother heard about it and wrote her congressman. He came down and said, Oh dear, ain't this awful, what if they hit somebody with that lid. So they made us stop that.

"And one time a recruit died of heat stroke carrying his first issue to the barracks, so everybody's mother started writing her congressman. Now we gotta carry recruits around in cattle cars.

"Hell, you can't put thousands of people through military training without somebody getting hurt. It just ain't possible. If they don't train hard, they get killed in combat. They ought to shoot the doctor that let that kid in here in the first place. Congress doesn't give a damn about training.

"And you know what? The recruits want training to be rough. That's why they joined—to do something hard."

Parris Island can make a Marine out of almost anything with a detectable heartbeat. What a kid wants most at Parris Island is out, and the quickest way out is to behave. Most kids have a well-developed sense of self-preservation and see the wisdom of obedience. A few are hopeless.

I remember a tall black kid named Gurdy from the Chicago slums who was terrified of the water. He had a tiny cue ball of a head and held it to one side, like a rattlesnake. There was a mean, cautious defiance to him, the look of a trapped animal. Gurdy had lived so much on the outside of society that he didn't realize you ever had do anything.

We were lined up at the pool for the swim test, if you could call it that. I think you had to swim about as far as most of us could broad jump. Gurdy stood there wild-eyed and strange, leaning his head one way and rolling his eyes the other. He didn't say anything.

The rest of us were going through boot camp, but Gurdy didn't know what he was going through. I guess he thought we were going to make him walk the plank. He was out of some remote tenement world of Chicago, and beyond even the military's ability to handle.

We could see him getting crazier and crazier as the line got shorter. Tension was building up in him like a head of steam. Finally he broke and ran like a jack rabbit, just shot out the door and kept going.

God knows where he thought he could run to on Parris Island, where it's hard for a fugitive in a bathing suit to hide. I don't think he much knew himself, probably figured it was like ducking a cop in the city. It was the last we saw of him.

I had thought it was baloney from some book like *Battle Cry*, but it happens: Private Mulligan walking down the squad bay at Parris

Island, chanting, "This is my rifle, this is my gun…," firmly holding onto both.

The worst hazard for a recruit is not shrapnel or even dismemberment by Sergeant Bull Walrus. It is tattoo parlors. These garish dens abound near big bases and prey on recent recruits longing for any evidence of manhood. New soldiers spend fifteen minutes getting that impressive eagle, and then they spend 20 years pricing plastic surgeons to get their boyhood back.

Some recruits go stark nuts over tattoos—Wasloski, for example, a red-headed Polish kid from Chicago I met in the drab barracks of Pendleton.

Wasloski was crazy. He had an angular, pugnacious face with half the world's strategic reserve of freckles, and claimed he had graduated from the University of Pennsylvania, which for obscure reasons he called UPI, and had less judgment than a volunteer for kamikaze school.

God help him, Wasloski discovered tattoo parlors. It had to happen. He showed up at the barracks one night with a half-naked Vietnamese girl tattooed on his forearm. It was conspicuous to say the least. I mean, it had colors like a Day-Glo detergent box and probably had batteries.

Before it had healed the poor maniac had another on the other arm, and then on an upper arm. I don't know where it ended, if it did. He's probably got naked bar girls running up his spine.

Nothing is quite so military as a tattoo, and he wanted to be military. He just didn't know that guys with tattoos spend the rest of their lives trying to get rid of them. If Wasloski ever has a girlfriend, which is barely possible, he'll have to have his arms amputated. And maybe his back.

Junior enlisted men have a limitless capacity for avoiding work. Among the better recruits, this talent verges on religious inspiration. Trainees learn it quickly.

My first experience with this useful ability was watching a platoon that was walking in line across a sandy field to police up cigarette butts. Instead of picking up the offending butts, each man carefully pushed sand over them with this boots. They hadn't planned it or seen anyone else do it. The idea simply came to them as the obvious response to the situation.

They left a spotless field. Thirty minutes later, wind blew the sand away and the place looked like a public dump. I suppose those butts had been accumulating for 30 years, buried repeatedly by generations of recruits.

Then there was Jean LaPierre, a Louisianan assigned to water the grass at a chow hall on a blazing California day. There wasn't a puff of wind. The heat would have baked a camel's brains. Asphalt was turning to a sticky ooze. LaPierre was supposed to walk back and forth across the lawn, spraying each patch until it was thoroughly wet. A Russian would have done it, but the American trooper thinks for himself.

LaPierre found the opening for a storm sewer in the ground in the shade beneath a tree. For three hours he stood in the shade and watered that grate. The grass never got wet, so he always seemed to be watering a dry patch. A hundred yards below, the gutter flooded.

"Now the Wampus cat isn't any damn killer bogeyman, no matter what the locals say. All that stuff on TV about how it killed seven Boy Scouts in a swamp is so much crap. At least in my opinion. But it can get real savage, like any cat, and we do lose three or four recruits every year to it. It's mostly their own damn fault because they don't take the right precautions.

"When you put your tent up, just make sure you're at least four feet from the tree line. Four feet, got it? And the Wampus cat tends to hunt on a north-south line, so I want those tents facing east and west. That's all it takes, and the colonel won't be chewing my ass because the Wampus cat killed one of my recruits."

The beach at Lejeune, a chill gray day with fog wafting over greasy Atlantic rollers. A platoon of infantry trainees stands shivering beside the looming bulk of an amtrac—the old LVT P-5, the beach assault of the Marines in those days.

It's shaped like a steel loaf of bread with tracks. It runs up on the beach and drops its ramp, whereupon the grunts run out and get machine-gunned.

At least, that's what the crewmen tell the grunts. The grunts are trainees. They'll believe anything.

The corporal in command yells and the trainees scramble aboard—37 of them. A trac is like a steel coffin, dark and cold inside, with only two small windows on the side.

Sometimes they become coffins for real. Once, a hatch was left open and a big roller came aboard, dragging the trac down in 150 feet of cold water. Nobody has heard from the occupants and, as this was some years ago, they are presumed dead.

The crew tell the grunts about it as the ramp closes.

The engine revs up to a deafening roar, hollow and sepulchral, for the dash into the breakers. The beast crashes into the surf and sinks to within a foot of its top, which is what it is supposed to do. Green water comes over the windows and shoots in streams through the minor leaks a trac always has.

The recruits don't know this. They are very, very uneasy in this death trap, imagining the terrified scramble should it sink. There would be no hope of avoiding a wet grave.

A hundred yards from shore, the crewman stands under the machine-gun periscope and looks out like a U-boat commander.

He eyes the rollers, which break over the top, and says laconically, "It's too rough up there, Charlie. Let's take her down to 50 feet and hope the bulkheads hold."

Three recruits faint. Trainees will believe anything.

"I had this guy Handley, couldn't do anything right," one DI told me. "I mean, he was the kind of guy who tries hard, but everything he touches turns to crap. Big doofus guy outa Miami. You can't persecute that kind of guy, because he genuinely is trying his best.

"One day Handley is sitting in this 10-holer latrine we had, along with about six other guys, all with their trousers around their ankles. Well, the colonel comes in to take a whizz, and Handley stands to attention and yells, '*Ten-hut!*'"

Oh-dark-thirty, a frigid morning at Lejeune. Our last day of training. We line up single file to go into the dark administration shack and collect our boot pay. We are harder and heavier than we were three months ago, cocky, confident, aware of new muscles. Inside the shack we have to stand to attention and do some silly boot rigmarole: "Sir! Private Smith reportingforpaycall—serial number twothirtytwotwentyfivefiftyone Sir!" all in one breath.

We also have to stop just outside the door and count the crisp new bills. One of the squad leaders—Bergland, a beefy kid from Alabama—has been ordered to be sure we do.

He is feeling full of himself on the dark sidewalk and well he might. For the first time in his life, he is in charge of others.

A figure comes from the shack, like twenty before him, but counts nothing.

"Marine, count them bills!"

The figure doesn't stop, so Bergland grabs him around the waist and pulls him back, unaware that he has grabbed the meanest gunny sergeant in Camp Geiger.

"*Gityourbuttback...here...oh...my...gawd....*"

"Sir, what's a Wampus cat look like?" a recruit asks Sergeant Sly.

"I wish I could tell you. You see, a Wampus is unusual in one way: It only runs backwards. It's one of the mysteries of science. A lot of people have seen the back end of a Wampus, but nobody's seen the front. That's why you gotta run your tents from east to west, so the Wampus cat doesn't back into it. And let me tell you, if you ever see the butt end of a Wampus cat coming in, you better kiss your ass goodbye, 'cause it's all over."

Noon in the Lejeune woods, chilly with autumn and the slowing drizzle, goopy red mud making sucking noises under our boots. Rain-laden pine branches brush across faces like cold hands. "S" Company is coming off the flame-thrower range for chow. Why the scene sticks in my memory I don't know, but it is my most vivid impression of training: a company of sodden recruits, shivering.

There were inexplicable moments when it all came together and we were proud to be in the service, the real world, not pumping gas or pulling frogs apart in some tedious laboratory. A fair number of us would be dead in six months, but we didn't believe it yet.

Steam rose from the field kitchen, the only warm thing in the entire world, and we held out mess kits for the cooks to fill with savory glop. At nineteen you're too dumb to know when you're uncomfortable. We were used to 3 1/2 hours sleep, at ease with rifles and seven-eighty-two gear, beginning to feel like Marines.

One blond kid with huge, round, blue eyes has lost his mess kit. He takes chow in his canteen cup—stew, spinach, bread, canned peaches dumped on top, string beans. It all goes to the same place, he says. When you've been up and running since 4:30, you don't care what it looks like.

Sergeants bark at us, but act like we're human, which may or may not show good judgment. I line up with the rest of these olive-drab warriors at chest-high log tables. We eat standing up in the soupy clay, gray clouds rolling and twisting overhead. Someone passes a rumor that we have declared war on Red China. Some believe it. Some always do.

There is no such thing as a recruit with enough to eat. Chow isn't, not like at the chow hall where, when the cook scooped up the powdered eggs with an ice cream scoop, green water filled the hole.

Along the log tables are jars of peanut butter and jelly for making Geiger-burgers: two-pound sandwiches that keep you going through the training ranges of Lejeune's Camp Geiger. Huge wasps and yellow jackets crawl around in the jelly jars.

The man next to me eyes a hornet the size of a heavy bomber in his jar. The beast is obviously dangerous. On the other hand, the Marine wants a sandwich.

It doesn't pay to stand between a recruit and food. With a quick twist of his knife, he forces the hornet deep below the surface of the jelly and makes his sandwich with the top layers.

Others before him had done the same thing. I counted seven buried wasps, some still twitching. You do what you gotta do.

The Times Magazine of Army Times

Diaper Rash And The Politics Of Academia

The next boom market may be in cosmetic accouterments for faculty lounges at universities. I have in mind training bras for the men and, for the women, maybe penis gourds—big ugly ones, such as denizens of New Guinea's rain forests wear. The idea isn't as strange as it seems. A penis sheath might double as a Walkman antenna, and you could fly a Cuban flag from one.

But their real purpose would be much like that of a child's throwing creamed spinach from a high chair: To make Mommy mad. That now seems to be the purpose of universities, whose faculties appear less mature than the college students of, say, 1964. The professoriate is holding its breath and turning blue.

What brought this on, you may be wondering. I'll tell you.

I'm reading *Comedy and Tragedy 2000-2001*, a book of adolescent psychology published by Young America's Foundation. Actually that may not be quite what YAF intended it to be. Then again, it may be exactly what they intended. Anyway, the booklet is a listing of peculiar courses taught in American universities.

By now nothing can surprise anybody. Still, a few examples from among hundreds:

Harvard: "Women's Studies 133: The Queer Novel: Narrative and Sexuality." Or, at the former University of Pennsylvania: "Women's Studies 226: Vampires—The Undead." The title may or may not describe the students. Then at UC Santa Barbara you have "English 129: Queer Textuality," and "Black Studies 136: Black Feminist Thought." If any.

241

I like this one, from Bowdoin College: "Women's Studies 248c, Music and Gender—Is Beethoven's ninth symphony a marvel of abstract architecture culminating in a gender-free paean to human solidarity, or does it model the processes of rape?" Or did someone forget to take her medication?

Finally at Princeton you have "English 404: Huey, Dewey, and Louie: The Capitalist Tragedy of Emasculated Ducks With No Pants." (OK. I made that one up.)

Comedy and Tragedy is good reading just for snippets in the introduction. I particularly like:

"Last year Oberlin College offered a course called "Queer Acts," and the description stated that "Drag will be encouraged, but not required." If I went to a class called Queer Acts, I'd wear an armored bathysphere.

"In 1997, an arts instructor at the University of Southern California permitted a porn star turned student, Annabel Chong, to perform sex with two other women in front of the class for her term project."

But it gets better. The pseudo-scholar's frantic desire for attention actually leads to support for pedophilia. Says YAF,

"*The Gay and Lesbian Studies Reader*, the first and most widely used anthology on the subject, demonstrates what faculty activists want their students to tolerate. One of the authors, Gayle Rubin, writes, "Like communists and homosexuals in the 1950s, boy lovers [i.e., pedophiles] are so stigmatized that it is difficult to find defenders for their civil liberties, let alone their erotic orientation.'"

I guess we're kind of having to stretch for oppressed groups.

Now, if you didn't know better, you might be outraged, but that of course is exactly the desired response. One senses in all of this an overweening juvenility, a preening callowness. These folk want to stick their tongues out at adults. It is the puerile righteousness of the newly pubescent: "Mo-mmmy! People are starving in India. Why can't I give them my college fund?"

But what is normal in an early adolescent is pitiable in faculties of what once were institutions of learning. Pitiable and, to some extent, inexplicable. The usual course of events is that people grow up. In the past, professors grew up. Why not now?

Do they expect us to believe that they are serious? What would Gayle Rubin do if she found a middle-aged man sodomizing her brother of eleven years? Would she coo, "Oh, Mike-ey! You've found a progressive ungendered non-ageist relationship"? Or would she call the police? Does she really want to see a heartwarming pervert diddling Mikey? Does she really want it to happen to the children of others?

Or is she throwing an extended adolescent fit?

In the atmosphere of arrested development that enshrouds the schools, consistency gets short shrift. It would be easy to point out that the same uncomprehendingly angry people who pretend to want to promote pedophilia, also will demonstrate against the incest that they pretend to believe that fathers regularly commit. It's silly, and so are they.

Here I think is the explanation for the enormous hostility on campus to expression of ideas other than their own: They know they're absurd, and they know people would say so.

Why would any professoress, even an imposter, let some escapee from a skin bar wrestle with a couple of lesbians in class? To instruct? Hardly. We all know how sex is done. I suggest she does it for the same reason a teenage girl wants to wear black lipstick and blue hair, or her brother puts a chromed bolt through his tongue and spends his afternoons trying to astonish people.

Part of the explanation is insecurity. Professors in some fields—mathematics, physics—are necessarily at least reasonably intelligent. They know their subjects, which are real subjects. But professors of Black Studies, Women's Studies, and Chicana Queer Theory often are neither very bright nor very well educated. Nor do they work in legitimate fields. They aren't quite professors, really. And, at bottom, they know it. The defensive aggressiveness of the self-aware inadequate is boundless, all the more so for fear of exposure.

Read the academic journals of these pseudo-subjects and you will quickly realize that many of the authors can't write English well enough to get a job at a newspaper. Ask one what a subjunctive is. Do you really think a professor of "Black Lesbian Orphan Oppression in Chicano Queer Literature" could tell you within a century when Chaucer wrote, or what he wrote?

They're pretending to be professors, as children pretend to be Zorro. They have to erupt in pathetic foolishness so that no one will notice that they have nothing else to offer. For this you're paying $10,000 a semester.

Penis gourds are the best answer, perhaps in designer colors. We could issue them to instructors of nonsubjects, so that they could shock us, and then we could go back to having universities. I think fluorescent strawberry would be nice.

Them Terrorists Got Their Towels Too Tight

The whole curious affair began when Fatima Ali Rezah, a citizen of Algeria, refused to unveil for a driver's license photo in Florida. The clerk, who didn't follow society carefully, thought she was joking. She wasn't. Her religion, she said, prohibited baring her face. The laws of the United States were irrelevant.

The clerk stared at her, puzzled. She was covered head to toe in black cloth and looked, he later told friends, like a large raisin. He was what is nowadays called a good ol' boy, meaning someone with a Southern accent and common sense—that is, starkly unqualified for diplomacy.

He refused her request. A photo was supposed to identify, he said. This one wouldn't. One black bag was like another. No, he said. And that was that. Or should have been.

With encouragement from the ACLU Fatima sued, and won on grounds of religious freedom. To insist on a photo would be discrimination, said the justices without noticeable rationality. DMV argued for separation of church and at least the state of Florida, but was told it applied only to conservative Christians.

Things snowballed. About seven thousand Mohammedans lived in Florida, most of them studying crop-dusting. Skeptics pointed out that they came from countries that didn't have crops. The Moslems said this was because their crops hadn't been dusted. The State Department accepted this explanation, saying it showed initiative and would result in self-sufficiency in vegetables in the Sahara.

Anyway, the Muslims all demanded photos of textiles on their licenses. The hooded look was in. One of the crop-dusting students, who was studying pesticide chemistry in night school, said *he* wanted a bagged photo too. Not to allow it would be sexual discrimination, he said. The courts agreed. Florida, they said, would not countenance special privilege.

Soon dark blobs were everywhere behind steering wheels. The police, notoriously insensitive, began referring to them as BBJs, for "Black Bag Jobs." This led to agitation by the civil-rights apparatus. "Black" might offend African-Americans, "Bag" would damage the self-esteem of the digestively incontinent, and "Job" would cause intense distress, perhaps panic, among the welfare population. Besides, it was the name of a book of the Bible, and banned from public discourse.

But this was minor compared to what was coming.

Unexpectedly the black Muslims in the penitentiary at Calhoun filed suit, saying *they* wanted to wear bags too. The real reason was that they were engaged in ongoing warfare with the Aryan Brotherhood, a white supremacist organization noted for its shankwork. Wearing masks, thought the incarcerated Muslims, would be a tactical advantage.

But they weren't women, objected the warden, who didn't read the papers and wasn't aware of the unisex decision. "Man, you discriminate because we be guys, just like because we be black. Can't nobody git no justice no how. *Damn.*"

This made no obvious sense and thus qualified for judicial review.

It got worse, or at least stranger. Months later the jailed faithful, no dummies, discovered that their beliefs required the wearing of gloves during fingerprinting. It was, they said, a tenet of their religion that had never been written down. Western civilization lacked respect for Oral Tradition, they said. This too began working its way through the courts.

Unaware of the searching revision of jurisprudence begun by her case, Fatima Ali Reza returned to Fort Myers, where she lived with her husband Abdul and three teenage daughters. They were in most respects a normal American family, except that they spoke English. Abdul was a branch manager at a local bank and gardened as a hobby. In the interest of economy, he had bought two tons of ammonium-nitrate fertilizer and kept it in the garage. The girls, good students, served as crossing guards at their school (where they became known as the Safety Rezahs.) Every morning Fatima made breakfast, made sure that Abdul had a clean towel, and got the girls off to school.

More trouble ensued. There were, as it turned out, implications for airport security. One Saturday at Miami International, the personnel at a security gate were strip-searching a 93-year-old woman in a wheel chair. Next in line, ignored by security, was a bearded Arab wearing a turban and carrying a briefcase marked "Bomb."

A woman in line behind him repeatedly tried to get the attention of the security people. It took a while because the woman in the wheel-chair was struggling, which distracted the searchers. Finally her gesticulation roused the suspicion of a supervisor.

"Don't you *see*? He's got a bomb. Do something. Search him."

"Ma'am, we can't profile. It's illegal. We search at random."

"Yes, but it says *Bomb*, for God's sake. Look."

The guard made a mental note to search the woman, who had an Alabama accent and was therefore probably bigoted against Moslems. He explained to her that the man had a First-Amendment right to write anything he chose on his luggage. To suspect a Moslem male with a bomb of bad intentions was stereotyping, he said, bordered on racism, and could lead to prosecution for Hate Thought.

The woman was so infuriated that she stormed off, muttering that she was going to move back to the United States, if she could find it. Her luggage was never found among the debris.

National attention grew. *Newsweek* picked up the story, running a cover, "Mass Murderers: Victims or Martyrs?" Dr. Saxa Prolimet-Mantequilla, who taught Lesbianism and Tantric Symbology at Yale, argued that Muslims had a history of oppression in the West. Challenged, she made the peculiar assertion that Anglophone peoples had used Moslems in ritual sacrifices and even in cannibalism; why, she said, nursery rhymes proved it.

Anyone but a reporter would have had the sense to let this one pass. A reporter didn't.

Quoth Prolimet-Mantequilla, "Little Miss Muffet sat on a tuffet, eating her Kurds in Hue. That's cannibalism. Note that she says *her* Kurds. Indisputable evidence of slavery."

The idea was silly enough that several campus organizations began campaigning for reparations for enslaved Kurds, correctly thinking that it would annoy their parents. The *Atlantic* solemnly picked up the story. Hillary Clinton was then running surreptitiously for president, hoping to finish off the country. She flew to Gainesville and said that she favored reparations for mistreated female Kurds of color. These came to be called Reparations H. Her approval rating rose to 76% among the functionally illiterate, which pundits said assured her the Democratic nomination.

Fatima Ali Rezah was blissfully unaware of all of this. She made supper for her husband, who was downtown renting a truck, and got the Safety Rezahs ready for bed. America, after all, was built on immigration.

Pilots In Pantyhose

A*viation Week* for February 18 says that a Great Debate—"furious, behind-the-scenes"—rages over whether pilots of airliners should carry weapons. Granted, debate in Washington has the intellectual legitimacy of professional wrestling, but without the dignity. Still:

Did we not just lose four aircraft, several thousand people, two and a quarter buildings, and get ourselves into an open-ended string of wars, and begin to turn ourselves into an officious security state, at a cost of many, many billions of dollars—because pilots did *not* have guns?

Key point: A pistol is an overmatch for a small knife. You can probably keep guns off aircraft. You cannot keep sharp objects off. There exist, for example, hard, sharp plastic knives intended as weapons. I've seen them.

OK: Mahmud in economy whips out his box cutter, a stewardess shouts a warning and, as Mahmud rushes to the cockpit, the copilot opens the door and shoots him five times with a .45 semi-automatic. Mahmud ceases to be an international terrorist. He is now a carpet stain.

In fact, had the pilots been armed, do you suppose Mahmud would even have tried?

Yet here in the City of Living Tapioca, people argue that we should do anything but arm the pilots. Why? Because among the political overclass the ideological aversion to guns, and particularly to people who own guns, outweighs concern for lives.

What, pray, do we expect unarmed pilots to do? Idiotic suggestions abound. My favorite is that they should throw the terrorist off his feet by maneuvering violently, always a good idea in a 747. Let's imagine it:

Ahmet arises, whereupon the pilot maneuvers hard. Unsecured babies fly from their mothers' arms and smash against things. So do the stewardesses. (Exactly what one wants to do in an emergency: cripple the only people trained to handle it.) Heavy metal sandwich carts thunder about, crushing people. Passengers in the lavatories have their necks broken. Chaos, panic, wreckage prevail.

The terrorists, who knew this would happen, are least likely to be hurt because they will have been expecting it.

But...now what? The problem has not been solved. The terrorists are still there. People unbuckle, wanting to help the hurt. A mother will not sit insouciantly in her seat while her injured baby bleeds out of her reach. The pilot again violently maneuvers an aircraft not designed for it. Crash, thump, scream, maneuver wildly, crash, thump, scream....

Practical.

But we mustn't *shoot* the sonsofbitches.

It gets sillier. Says *AvWeek*, "Critics have warned that armed pilots would be more of a hazard to passengers than the remote threat of terrorist hijackings." Oh. We trust the pilots to take off in a huge aircraft, fly it and us at an altitude of seven miles across a cold, deep, and wet ocean, and land the brute in marginal weather at Heathrow—but we don't trust them with sidearms. What *could* be more reasonable?

Nice, frightened naifs say we should use non-lethal weapons. Good. Water cannon, perhaps. Rubber bullets? Tear gas? Foam? Flash-bangs? The salient characteristic of non-lethals is that they work poorly, especially in confined spaces (where, incidentally, they tend to be lethal).

Besides, I don't want non-lethal weapons. I want lethal ones. I don't like people who want to fly me into a large building. Killing them would suit me fine.

Sheer unfamiliarity with guns plays a large part here. I found myself talking some time ago with a pilot for American, one of apparently few who fear guns. The terrorists would take the guns away from the pilots, he worried, and kill them. The solution, he averred, was stronger cockpit doors.

Solution for whom? The passengers remain with the terrorists.

Having better doors to delay forced entry is a good idea. It isn't a guarantee. There are ways of opening locked doors quickly. I have seen adhesive-backed charges of plastic explosive that can be slapped against a hinge. They stick. The impact starts the ignition train, and five seconds later the hinge blows apart. They can be made with no metallic parts. SWAT teams and commandos have, or know how to make, such devices.

This guy didn't know that either. He knew how to fly an aircraft. He didn't know squat about protecting one. And he didn't know he didn't know.

But assume that the doors hold. The terrorists appear and begin cutting throats. First they kill the flight attendants. The pilots drive on, cowering behind the door that is their only protection. The terrorists say they will kill passengers until the pilots open the door. The pilots, now flying an abattoir, drive on—because, being unarmed, they have little choice. Should the terrorists figure out how to open the door, which is definitely doable, the pilots will be helpless. Splendid.

But we mustn't shoot the sonsofbitches.

The fear of depressurizing the aircraft is exaggerated. Cabins are pressurized to something like 8,000 feet, well below 14.7 psi. Even if the aircraft were in orbit, it would be only a dozen or so psi over ambient. A bullet hole would make a hissing sound. It would not, a la Hollywood, suck people out. Aside from which there are frangible bullets, hard enough to kill a man but that shatter into powder on hitting metal.

But I doubt that the American guy knew about bullets either.

Now, *AvWeek's* polls find that 73% of aircrew want arms on the flight deck. Most of the public agrees. The Overclass do not agree. Why?

On a guess, because they come from the coddled suburbs and pampered universities where it is always safe, where the police defend them from the human cockroaches a mile away, where everyone is against violence and sings Kum Ba Yah and dabbles in Ethical Culture. As we become more effeminate, more a nation of mall children, the cosseted just don't know that, occasionally, it really is kill or be killed. They've probably never held a firearm.

And there is the curiously American disjuncture from reality, our penchant for insisting that the world is as it isn't, and then living as if it were. We begin a military campaign against the world's terrorists, people who avowedly want to kill us, who want to drive aircraft into nuclear plants to poison us with radiation, who want to destroy our cities—but we pretend we don't need to arm ourselves. We know the terrorists are Moslem males, but act as if we didn't. We wage war on terrorists, but eject little boys from school if they draw pictures of soldiers.

And *AvWeek*'s ominous phrase—"behind the scenes"—means that we are likely to get what the Overclass wants, not what we want.

(In fact the government did decide that pilots could not have guns.)

The Hulk Was Green, Wasn't He?

I'm going to feed them to hyenas. The prissy passive-aggressive do-gooderesses in the schools, I mean: The ones who think dodge ball is violence, and get their undies in a bunch over plastic ray guns. I figure to coat them with Spam to make them more appetizing to the hyenas, who might otherwise prefer a week-old dead zebra.

In the Wilmington (N.C.) *Morning Star** a headline appeared a few months back: "Tempest in a toy chest: State rater deducts points for preschool's 'violent plastic soldiers.'"

I'm going to get big nasty hyenas—retarded ones, just to be sure. They'll eat anything.

It seems there's a preschool in Wilmington called Kids Gym Schoolhouse, and it was getting evaluated by the state. Now, this makes reasonable sense. You want to make sure the school wasn't built around an open mine shaft, and that the owner isn't a maniac who locks the kids in a basement and feeds them poisoned turnips, and that the building isn't a fire trap, or full of hornets. OK. That works. Got it.

As it turned out, Kids Gym School was just fine, nothing wrong with it, except—one of the inspecting do-gooderesses, ever alert, noticed that the little boys were playing with green plastic soldiers.

Yes. Green ones. The horror.

"If stereotyping or violence is shown with regard to any group, then credit cannot be given," wrote evaluator Katie Haseldon. "It was observed that nine 'army men' were present in the block play area. These figures reflect stereotyping and violence, therefore credit can not be given."

253

I understand her concern. You know how kids are: First it's toy soldiers, then it's human sacrifice. Studies show that kids who start with G.I. Joe, especially if he's green, move on to vivisection of unpopular classmates, particularly orphans.

The labored English of the indictment puzzles. What has stereotyping to do with it? A stereotype is the aggregate observation of many people over time, which is why stereotypes are almost always accurate. Stereotyping means recognizing the obvious. In an academic context, or in the public schools, it means noticing that the wrong groups are better at things. This we must never, ever do.

But...what was Kids Gym Schoolhouse stereotyping? Green men?

Anyway, do-gooders. Methinks that people who Do Good to people who don't want it done to them are actually up to something else entirely. They're playing "Gotcha!" Remember the class tattletale in third grade? Peggy would tell the teacher "Ricky's got candy in his desk!" and watch with smug hostility as Ricky caught it. Little boys didn't do this, not because some of them weren't wormy enough, but because they knew they would eventually have to leave the schoolyard. For girls there was no accountability. There still isn't.

The point is that Peggy wasn't energized by an abstract concern for the rule of law, or solicitude for the future health of Ricky's dentition. She was angry, she didn't know at what, and had discovered that she could use the system to punish others in the name of virtue.

Gotcha.

A similar vague anger underlies today's widespread animosity, ostensibly toward violence—little boys ejected from school for pointing a chicken finger and saying "Bang!" or for drawing a picture of a soldier. Are we to believe that the commissars of niceness really believe that drawing a GI is a punishable offense, or a sign of budding psychopath (who will be cured by a three-day suspension)? Of course not. They are not so stupid, nor are they quite crazy. They are hostile. They want the satisfaction of making others knuckle under. And they have learned to use the system to do it.

Mostly they are women. Why? Part of the obsession with imaginary violence may derive from the female drive for security, security, security. But the constant assault on little boys is, I think, an extension of The Chip, the snappish, distempered animosity toward all things male that characterizes American women. This ferret-like bad humor drives the feminization of the United States. In the schools it manifests itself in the opposition to rough boys games (violence), to competition of any kind (self-esteem might suffer), to grades (some grades are better than others). Performance has always been a male focus, niceness a female one.

Women are said to be more psychologically astute than men. I don't think so. They know how to manipulate men—flash a leg, cry, look helpless, withhold sex, withhold the children. They seldom have the dimmest idea how men think, why they do what they do, or why they might want to. They don't understand why males want to go faster, take things apart, fiddle with computers, see what would happen if.

They aren't happy in a male world, and so work furiously to feminize it. And, being angry at they-aren't-sure-what, they have decided that men are responsible for, well, whatever it is. Thus, among many other things, the desire to turn little boys into little girls.

Malignant feminization has consequences. After Ahmet and Mahmud got the World Trade Center, America took up hobbyist patriotism. Yuppies everywhere became willing to send someone else to fight wars. Yet at the same time, the schools punish children for playing soldier, for drawing soldiers, for playing with plastic soldiers, and for chickenstickery. How sensible: As the military desperately seeks recruits, the government of North Carolina, and apparently the public schools in general, teach little boys that being a soldier is Bad, Bad, Bad.

Note that it *is* the state of North Carolina. The owner of the preschool said, correctly, that the position of the raters was absurd. "But Anna Carter, supervisor of the N.C. Division of Child Development's Policy and Program Unit, said authors of the Environmental Rating

System consider toy soldiers inappropriate because they represent a violent theme." It wasn't just one distressed do-gooderess. North Carolina, by governmental policy, is hostile to the American armed forces.

In the military itself, the same feminization, powered by The Chip, has brought a focus on feelings and self-esteem, a drastic lowering of physical standards, the usual obsession with sexual harassment, and the conversion of the armed services into homes for unwed mothers. In none of this is there any comprehension of what militaries are for. Nor is there sympathy for the competitiveness of the military male, for the urge to push limits, for charging hard and taking chances, for the rough camaraderie of barracks and encampment. Instead, blank incomprehension.

Tell you what. Virulent niceness is going to turn us all into angry, confused semi-male women and repressed male milquetoasts living in fear of the vengefully good. Salvation, I say, lies in hyenas.

*By Victoria Rouch, The *Wilmington Morning Star*, November 15, 2001.

Immigration: I'd Prefer Small Pox

Ｗhat if we are wrong? What if different kinds of people just plain don't want to live together? What if federal bullying, stamping our feet, and holding our breath and turning blue won't change things?

A powerful current in today's compulsory thought is that hostility between groups is anomalous and remediable, an exception to natural law—that it results from poor socialization, defective character, or conservative politics. If only we understood each other we would then love one another. Such is the theory.

But we don't love each other.

When the desired affections fail to develop, which is the usual outcome, we try compulsion. People *must* love each other, under penalty of law. Any expression of displeasure with another group is punished. We brainwash our children with an almost North Korean intensity to persuade them that groups should cuddle and value one another.

And still it doesn't work. Might it not be just a bad idea?

If one looked around the world, one might reasonably conclude that different groups should be separated, not coerced into proximity. Note that most of the internal violence that afflicts nations occurs between ethnic, racial, and religious groups—not between rich and poor, between those who bowl and those who golf, or between the left-handed and the right-handed. Would it not make sense, when possible, to separate disparate populations?

In the United States, serious violence—riots, burning of cities, not to mention a heavy (and carefully disguised) element of racial targeting by criminals—takes place along the black/white/Latino fault lines, with occasional black/Jewish fighting in New York. Again, race, religion, ethnicity. Different kinds of people don't get along. Why do we not recognize this?

The pattern is universal. In France, horrified fluttering recently arose when Jean-Marie Le Pen, a very anti-immigration sort of fellow, got 17% of the vote in presidential elections. How surprised should we be? France has some five million North African Mohammedans. Antagonism is predictable. When the French were in North Africa, the North Africans didn't like it. Now that the North Africans are in France, the French don't like it. Is there a pattern here?

Tension is high in Germany between Germans and Turks. In India, Mussulmans and Hindus riot bloodily. In Ceylon, Tamils and Sinhalese; in Iraq, Kurds and Iraqis; in Ireland, Protestants and Catholics, in Yugoslavia…in Burundi…. Canadians and Quebecois are not killing each other, but they think about it.

Given that the mixing of dissimilar peoples leads with remarkable consistency to trouble, and that the price of the trouble can be high, might it not be reasonable to take this into account when making policy? Might it not be wiser to permit, or even to encourage, people to live with their own? In particular, might it not be desirable to discourage immigration from anywhere to anywhere instead of encouraging it in the name of fuzz-headed adolescent enthusiasm, thus preparing the way for conflagration?

For some it is too late. The United States has lost control of its borders and lacks the political will to do…well, anything. We amount to a dead whale decaying on the beach of civilization. Other countries may yet have time.

We are, of course, unendingly told that to favor separation is to be racist, hateful, and reactionary. It is always easier to call one's questioners names than to answer their questions. But need one be a racist to favor a comfortable distancing? Or is to do so just cultural good manners and wise politics?

Originally, racism meant a belief that one race was inferior to another, usually one's own. The street definition is a dislike of another because of his race.

I do not regard myself as racially superior to, say, the Japanese. I certainly don't dislike them for neglecting to be white. I've spent time in the Japanese hinterland, crawled the mountains, eaten in remote noodle stands. I like the culture and the people. Passing through Tokyo last week, I reflected (as always) at their superior efficiency and civility. I have no racist notions, by either definition, of the Japanese.

But do I think we should encourage heavy immigration of Japanese (assuming they wanted to come), or they of Americans? No. A very bad idea. Antagonism would result. The differences are too great.

It works this way. Suppose that you are a considerate traveler, American, and go to a foreign town—pick your country—unaccustomed to outsiders. The likelihood is that you will be treated with courtesy and some degree of curiosity. Should you attempt to learn the language and take an apartment, the people will be flattered by the former and unconcerned by the latter.

Should other Americans come (or Germans, or Chinese), the locals will be unconcerned—at first. The early arrivals will per force adapt to the local culture. However, as the numbers reach a certain point, visitors will begin to be seen as invaders. They will cluster together, come to constitute an alien enclave and then, without intending it, begin to impose themselves on the natives. The ways of the immigrants will inevitably conflict with the ways of the natives.

As an example, American are noisier than most Orientals, prefer informal camaraderie to formal courtesy, and have different notions of proper manners in public. Behavior that is informal and friendly in one society is oafish in another. It isn't a question of right or wrong, but of expectations.

Soon interests will diverge, hostility appear, incidents occur, and retaliation follow. Us-agin-them thinking comes natural to people.

Note that in the United States, when blacks move into white neighborhoods, nothing happens—at first. When the proportion of blacks reaches a certain point—thirty percent is a figure I've often seen—the remaining whites flee. The same happens in reverse. When white gentrifiers move into the black city, they clump together. When they become conspicuous by their plenitude, resentment arises among the black population.

By contrast, when groups have their own territory and do not too much come into contact, feelings improve. Neither side feels in danger of being dominated by the other. Thus homogeneous countries tend to be happier countries.

All of this is obvious. And yet we follow policies sure to cause unending trouble, certainly cultural suicide, perhaps catastrophe, because of bullheaded insistence that things are as we wish, not as they in fact are. The spirit of Marxism is much in evidence here—the view that people are amorphous, anonymous, barely sentient putty to be shaped by soulless theoreticians. (Can there be a more contemptuous word for humanity than "the masses"?) For all of this, I think, we will pay a price.

Terror, Terror, Everywhere. And Not A Drop To Drink.

Because bin Laden or someone else has done us irreparable harm, people, or some people anyway, spend much air in calling him, or them, cowards, criminals, and mere terrorists. No doubt this is satisfying. Yet it also serves to diminish a very dangerous enemy. In times of national enthusiasm it is hazardous to go against the prevailing winds. Let's do it anyway.

A few thoughts:

1. Our enemies are not mere anything. They have demonstrated that with a $2 box-cutter and an airliner full of fuel ($250 from any travel discounter: good price for a 757) you can do damage hitherto possible only with sustained attacks by heavy bombers. They've mangled the stock market, humiliated the United States, seem to be putting airlines out of business, cost hotels billions, grounded our crop-dusters, caused massive lay-offs, and seem to be, because of the stock market, about to keep a lot of kids from going to college. They have also frightened the country permanently. They may well turn us into a semi-police state, and have certainly caused us to go into a war of indeterminable outcome.

    All this for, presumably, under a thousand dollars. It is probably the best return on investment in military history.

2. Their crucial realization was that a vehicle is not a target, but a weapon. The effect is to increase the possible damage from an attack to levels that a nation cannot ignore. Previous efforts by terrorists, such as blowing up an airliner, in national terms consti-

261

tuted no more than annoyances. Modifying a skyline and killing several thousand people cannot be brushed off.

Vehicles are formidable weapons. How many ships would have to ram the supports of the Golden Gate at high speed to bring it down? What clever things might be done with a tanker? Big ones today amount to positively enormous bladders of aimable petroleum. Many sail under foreign flags.

The rub is that we cannot do without vehicles. This means, for example, that when Congress is being addressed by the president, enormously powerful weapons will be flying into Dulles in large numbers. It only takes one.

3. The damage possible with ships and aircraft changes the problem of security qualitatively, not quantitatively. In the past, security could be treated statistically: If an airliner were lost every three or four years, it wasn't good, but it was good enough. Civil society continued. The economy didn't collapse. Life went on. Preventing most hijackings was adequate.

    Today, if we discourage 19 attempts, and the twentieth takes out the Capitol, we will have lost.

4. We don't know how to attack a small group of terrorists not clearly attached to a specific country. This too is crucial. If Libya had destroyed the Trade Center, we would have had the answer, and Libya knows it. So it didn't. But if one Guatemalan, an Irishman, a disaffected American, and a Russian blow up the Capitol—do we nuke Ireland, Guatemala, ourselves, and Russia?

    The key to defeating a more powerful enemy is to force him to fight in a manner that prevents use of his strengths. This the terrorists are doing.

5. Increased electronic surveillance by the spook agencies probably isn't an answer. The plotting needed to take over a freighter and

run it into a bridge can be done by three guys on a park bench. No? Terrorists with the intelligence of grapes know that cell phones can be intercepted, that the Internet can be watched, encryption recognized and possibly cracked. So, I presume, they just won't use them.

6. In the coming war, how will we know when we have won? Killing bin Laden, it seems to me, would merely make a martyr of him. The assassinations of JFK, Martin Luther King, and Che Guevara served chiefly to raise their stature. A trial would be a platform. He would become, if he isn't already, the Elvis of terrorists.

7. I do not think Bush and Powell are stupid, don't know what they have planned, certainly hope that it works, and don't have a better idea. This is in itself an important point: It is tactically astute to leave your enemy with no good answers. That's where we seem to be.

Afghanistan is far away, supply lines long, airpower of limited use against a primitive lightly populated society, the number of our deployable troops small, our coalition fragile, the terrain awful, the Afghans ferocious. They'll skin you this week and leave you to die the next, and regularly did. In two decades of covering the military, I have met several of their leaders. They were very, very hard men. Ask the Russians.

It limits our options. Colin Powell knows this. A lot of people seem not to.

8. Maybe the surge of national unity will hold for a while. Maybe it won't. I have recently heard polls saying that 69% of the public is willing to prosecute the war even if it means taking casualties, and that 65% are afraid to fly in airliners. The conjunction of statistics is fascinating. Presumably the people afraid to fly in airliners are willing that other people should take casualties.

Few are fiercer than the recently patriotic, but for how long? Already I see signs on telephone poles saying, "Retaliate with World Peace." Sure, kids are probably doing it, and this is Washington. But it's a good bet that the bad guys will try to turn whatever we do into a long, slow grind with dead people coming home, the theory being that we would then quit. Can they? I don't know.

9. If we attack Afghanistan, and something similar to New York happens in response, then what? Bin Laden and I don't hang out together at the sports bar, so I don't know what he has in mind. But if he can pull off something spectacular in return, he will be seen as single-handedly defeating the United States. Then what? How much would we take? For how long? And what would we do about it?

10. This could get lots uglier. I'm not an Islamicist. I have friends who are. They point out that Pakistan is unstable. If it falls into chaos, they say, as the stress of helping us will encourage, and some of its nukes disappear with their arming codes or whatever, one might show up in New York, bang. This is no longer morbid fantasy. These guys would do it. At that point the United States would likely say the hell with it and eliminate countries.

Not good. Not good at all. But why is it not possible?

All done with simple box-cutters. Remarkable.

How We Were: War In The Storm Sewers

Today we will speak of war.

I will tell you of my days as a tunnel rat.

It was, I think, 1954, not a decade removed from V-E Day. We lived in Arlington, Virginia, where my father was a mathematician designing warships for the Navy Department. It was a time of intense tranquility. After the war, people wanted prosperity, washing machines and, above all, to be left the hell alone.

The post-war economic boom was in full flood. Fathers worked, mothers stayed home, kids read Hardy Boys books by thousands and played with fifty-bottle Gilbert chemistry sets. Prosperity came in standard units. Houses were identical, comfortable, and laid out in a griddle, like those square iron warts on a waffle iron. People watched Ozzie and Harriet. Consult your paleontologist.

I was nine, a virtually instant product of my father's return from the Pacific. He had spent four years trapped on a destroyer, the USS Franks, with men who, he said, became exponentially uglier by the month. Seen in those terms, the Baby Boom wasn't surprising.

I digress. War. We were three: Mincemeat, Dukesy, and I. Mince (his parents believed him to be John Kaminsky) was a crew-cut blond who could outspit anyone. Spitting was an art. You did it sideways, casually, as if you were really thinking about something else, such as 12,000 suicidal Japs storming ashore at Wake. Spitting suggested ironic defiance as you fused your last artillery rounds. Dukesy—Michele Duquez—was a darkly handsome kid of Frog extraction. Later he joined the Foreign Legion and terrorized the Silent Quarter of Arabia.

Well, maybe he didn't, but he should have.

We played baseball, endless baseball, on the sloping plains of North Jefferson Street. Home plate was a manhole cover, first and third the bumpers of cars. On the day of The Great Discovery, the ball was an old and ratty one, coming unstitched. Flaps of horsehide hung from it like a spaniel's ears. It wasn't much of a ball. It was, however, the only ball.

Dukesy smacked a long liner that rolled into the storm sewer at the bottom of the hill.

"*Geez, lookit!*" we all hollered, because that was what you hollered in times of stress or wonder. We ran down and peered into the opening. We could see nothing.

There, in the eternal sunlight of 1954, we pondered. The ball was in the storm drain. We absolutely weren't supposed to go into storm drains. On the other hand, nobody was watching. We were boys. If you are wondering what happened, you need to get out more.

Once inside, we realized that we had to pull the manhole cover back over the hole, or else we would be caught, perhaps by someone falling on top of us. We buttoned up, and found ourselves in that most splendid of boy things—a Fort. There was a concrete platform to sit on, and the opening at gutter level to peer out of unseen, and, below, a forbidding concrete pipe, half the height of a kid, leading into pitch dark nowhere.

And nobody else knew about it. A private world.

The entrance to that pipe was dark and yawning. It echoed. It was musty, forbidding, and probably dangerous. Rain might come, and trap us. Scary things with teeth probably lived inside. Cave-ins were a near certainty. It would be foolish to go inside. Obviously the thing to do was get candles and explore. We did.

Above ground, mothers baked, grass grew, the sun shone. Below, in the entrails of Arlington, trickling with water, we crept through flickering darkness. A boy of ten can bend in ways that would cause early arthritis in a garter snake. We crouched into more-or-less the shape of paperclips and spraddled through the sewers, splonk, splonk, splonk. That *splonk*, the rubbery slap of sodden Keds on concrete, is known perhaps to only three people. And one of them was crushed by a falling camel in the Silent Quarter.

Probably, anyway.

Ayer's Five and Dime, the ten-cent store in the shopping center at Westover, may have wondered about the surge in sales of candles. We crawled and duck-walked and splashed our way through a widening network, finding a storm drain opening onto Washington Boulevard. We staged sandwiches there, and pea-shooters, the kind with the little bowl on top to hold lots of peas. You can't have too many peas, not when cars are whizzing by two feet away with hubcaps to shoot at. Around the Fourth of July we sent bottle-rockets slithering and ricocheting into the murky distance. We had to stop the space aliens who were attacking from the center of the earth.

If you were to look on Washington Boulevard for that storm drain, which exists to this day, you would find on the roof, written in candle smoke, the initials of our gang, "SSI." I can't tell you what they stood for, because we pledged not to. But they're there.

I was going to tell you about war.

We discovered an outflow that was beyond our supra-terranean territory, so we didn't really know where it was. A larger pipe, perhaps three feet in diameter, debouched into a grassy trench with high walls. Thereabouts older kids, perhaps fourteen, played. We snuck out, showered them with rocks, and yelled, "*Nyaa nyaa nyaa, your mother's a queer!*" We weren't sure what we meant, but it was universally held to be an insult. Then we dove into the tunnels.

The leviathans were too large to follow us. And we knew it. No drug can equal the excitement of fear devoid of danger. "Nyaa-nyaa-nyaaa! Come get us. Dare you!" *Splonksplonksplonk.*

Ah, but the Rat with Red Eyes that we found under Westover. The world may not be ready for this. We discovered a place where the round pipes gave way to a huge square drain, where we could stand up, and the water became ominously deep. Light filtered in from somewhere. There was a curious smell, like earwax. We got half-inflated inner tubes, squashed them through the smaller pipes, and floated on them a short distance to a sort of subterranean beach. It was the exit, now buried by development, to Westover.

There, crouching on the shore, was a vast Rat with red eyes. As I remember it, the beast was about the size of a St. Bernard, and probably radioactive. It whiffled its whiskers and eyed us with, we thought, carnivorous portent.

Sewer rats don't have red eyes. We agreed that this one did. We didn't go back. There are limits. Even the Foreign Legion will tell you so.

Sex, Equality, And Kidding Ourselves

Men of today's older generation grew up in the chivalric miasma of their time, which held that women were morally superior to men, and that civilized men protected women against any available vicissitude. A corollary was that women needed protecting. So common has this understanding been throughout history that one may suspect it of being based in ancient instinct: In a less hospitable world, if men didn't protect women, something disagreeable would eat them, and then there would be no more people. So men did. And do.

Instincts have consequences, particularly when the circumstances requiring them cease to exist.

Because women were until recently subordinate, and in large part played the role of gentility assigned to them, men didn't recognize that they could be dangerous, selfish, or sometimes outright vipers. They were no worse than men, but neither were they better. Men believed, as did women, that women were tender creatures, caring, kind, and suited to be mothers. Males deferred to women in many things, which didn't matter because the things women wanted were not important.

When women came into a degree of power, it turned out that they were as immoral, or amoral, as men, probably more self-centered, and out for what they could get. Not all were, of course, as neither were all men, but suddenly this became the central current. This too followed lines of instinctual plausibility. Women took care of children and themselves, and men took care of women. It made sense that they should be self-centered.

These newly empowered women knew, as women have always known, how to wield charm, and they quickly learned to enjoy power. The men of the old school didn't notice in time. They deferred, and they were blind-sided. They gave gentlemanly agreement to one-sided laws hostile to men.

Political deference became a pattern. It remains a pattern. It probably springs in part from the male's instinctive recognition that, by giving women what they want, he gets laid. Between individuals this worked tolerably well, but less so when applied to abstract groups.

When women said they wanted protection against dead-beat dads, the old school fell for it. They were attuned to saving maidens and the sheltering from life's storms of white Christian motherhood. "Dead-beat dads" was of course that sure-fire political winner—an alliterative slogan of few words that embodied a conclusion but no analysis. So sure were men that women were the kinder gentler sex that they never bothered to look at the statistics on abuse of children, or the track records of the sexes in raising children.

The romantic elderly male believed, and believes, that women were the natural proprietors of the young. This led to laws virtually denying a divorced father's interest in his children, though not the requirement that he pay for their upkeep. The pattern holds today. Male judges in family law defer to women, almost any women no matter how unfit, and female judges side with their own. The demonstrable fact that women can and do abuse and neglect children, that a female executive clawing her way up the hierarchy may have the maternal instincts of a rattlesnake, that children need their fathers—all of this has been forgotten.

The reflexive deference continued. Feminists wanted congress to pass a vast program of funding for every left-wing cause that incited enthusiasm in the sterile nests of NOW. They called it the Violence Against Women Act, and men deferentially gave it to them. Of course to vote against it, no matter what it actually said (and almost no one knew) would have been to seem to favor violence against women. A law to exterminate orphans, if called the Domestic Violence Prevention Act, would pass without demur.

There followed yet more male deference to female desires. When women wanted to go into the military to have babies, or a Soldier Experience, men couldn't bring themselves to say no.

When the women couldn't perform as soldiers, men graciously lowered standards so they could appear to. It was the equivalent of helping a woman over a log in the park, the legal and institutional parallel of murmuring, "Don't worry your pretty little head about a thing."

On and on it went. The aggregate effect has been that women have gained real power, while (or by) managing in large part to continue to exact deference and, crucially, to avoid the accountability that should come with power. A minor example is women who want the preferential treatment that women now enjoy, and yet expect men to pay for their dates. In today's circumstances, this is simple parasitism.

Today men are accountable for their behavior. Women are not. The lack of accountability, seldom clearly recognized, is the bedrock of much of today's feminist misbehavior, influence, and politics. Its pervasiveness is worth pondering.

A man who sires children and leaves is called a dead-beat dad, and persecuted. A woman who has seven children out of wedlock and no capacity to raise them is not called a criminal, but a victim. He is accountable for his misbehavior, but she is not for hers. It is often thus.

Consider the female Marine officer who complained that morning runs were demeaning to women. A man who thus sniveled would be disciplined, ridiculed, and perhaps thumped. Yet the military fell over itself to apologize and investigate. Again, men are held accountable for their indiscipline, but women are not. Men expect to adapt themselves to the Army, but women expect the Army to adapt to them. And it does. The male instinct is to keep women happy.

Note that a woman who brings charges of sexual harassment against a man suffers no, or minor, consequences if the charges are found to be

unfounded—i.e., made up. A man who lied about a woman's misbehavior would be sacked. He is accountable. She isn't.

Yes, large numbers of women are responsible, competent, and agreeable. Few engage in the worst abuses, as for example the fabrication of
sexual harassment. Yet they *can* do these things. A man cannot throw a
fit and get his way. A woman can. Only a few need misbehave to poison the air and set society on edge. And the many profit by the misbehavior of the few.

People will do what they can get away with. Men assuredly will, and
so are restrained by law. Women are not. Here is the root of much evil,
for society, children, men and, yes, women.

Ammunition Comes To The Faith Market

The tall scrawny freak with the red hair converted in the spring of 1972, several months before Jerry wandered, roaring, onto the scene. I had recently graduated from both Vietnam and college and, not knowing what else to do, was living with a collection of hippies at Stafford Court House, Virginia. The other freaks were the usual unemployed prophets, fruit-juice drinkers, tarot-card readers and desert patriarchs in from communes in New Mexico. Most were sane without being extreme about it. A few were psychic train-wrecks trying to reassemble themselves, and mind-burnt druggies who had learned to package brain damage as mystical insight.

The Sixties were waning fast. The freak years had been fun for those who could handle them, but by now everybody sensed that the ride was over. Kids looked sourly at the future, judged that the market for aged hippies was limited, and wanted out. They weren't sure how to get there.

Seeking the escape hatch, the crowd at Stafford started changing religions the way other people changed their socks. For a while the preferred faith was acid. Everybody stared for hours at patterns in the upholstery, garnering wisdom. Buddhism held a corner on truth for a week, but faded. Hinduism had its brief moment. A bearded seer form somewhere out West once peered into my eyes with bovine serenity and said, "Hinduism. You know it's true, man." His cow-like assurance was like a current of water, carrying me along so that I thought, "Yeah, hadn't thought of it, it is true, isn't it?"

Finally the skinny red-head thumbed to Washington with his girl-friend, who had been a Moslem the week before, and returned full of confused faith in someone called Sun Moon. At first we assumed that anyone named Sun Moon must be an itinerant witch doctor from one of the desert tribes, perhaps a protégé of Carlos Castaneda. We soon heard that Moon was a Korean guru with holdings in an ammunition factory.

"I think I really believe it," the red-head told me regarding the epiphany of the weekend. "It's really, like, you know, true. I know it is."

"What's true?"

"I'm not sure yet."

He wanted to believe that something was true. He didn't much care what, and anyway he could find out later. Within two weeks several others from Stafford had joined Moon's church. They were formally committed to the worship of a Korean arms manufacturer.

The idea was curious, even for the times. The Sixties were treasure years for the connoisseur of oddities: bikers, SDSers, hopheads, hallucinating paranoiacs, anything you wanted. Moon's church, however, seemed a genuinely new kink in the social rope. For the next several months the lunar faithful (I tried desperately not to call them Loonies) was a hobby, sideshow, and source of free meals. Seen from the inside, from the level of the sidewalks of a giddy age, they didn't bear much resemblance to later accounts in the newspapers. They didn't bear much resemblance to anything.

Soon the Stafford believers thumbed up to Washington, to the Moonie hives at 1611 Upshur Street, NW. I went along, wondering what to expect. The Moonies were not the only new product on the faith market. There was the New American Church, which worshipped the better grades of dope, and the Hare Krishnas, who seemed to worship attention and Georgetown, and something called Maharaj Ji, such a tender golden-brown butter ball that one's instinct was to baste him.

The Moonies were the first faith to crack the defense sector however. A faith based on ammunition was categorically worth seeing.

The Moonies had rented several adjacent row houses on Upshur and, as I soon learned, held picnics to attract proselytes, of which there seemed to be a bumper crop. We arrived looking like refried death and discovered a swarm of kids in suits, ties, stockings, pretty dresses, and a state of unearthly cleanliness. An attractive girl in an up-market blue dress hailed us with a bright smile. She was pretty, deliberately pretty, which was startling in an age of funk.

"Hi! I'm Linda Marchant. I'm so glad you could come. Won't you join us?"

I thought to myself, "Soap." Even today people think "soap" when they meet Moonies. But the outgoing friendliness was undeniably nice, very nice. They could turn it on and off like water, but it was nice. It appealed powerfully to the lonely and confused who, however they talked of Thoreauvian independence, were getting older and suspected they had missed an important boat. This assertive gregariousness, grown devious and systematized, later become known in Moon-talk as "love-bombing."

Under spreading trees in the back yard, girls rushed about with bowls of salad. They all looked like Heidi. The guys looked like stock-brokers. Several other freaks stood around, kind of embarrassed but kind of...you know...digging it.

We all sat. After a brief prayer to a god as yet unspecified, whose chief quality seemed to be syllabic extension ("*Faa-aa-a-a-ther....*") there were a few words about the sacred mission of the United States. Characteristically the Moonies told us very little about themselves. They preferred that a recruit find out what he was committed to only after he was committed to it, an idea acceptable to a surprising number of people. The peculiar gift of the Moonies was to pursue sincerity, frankness, and a revival of ethical values by means of deception, manipulation, and a disregard of ethics.

A heavily freckled kid next to me, explaining that he was in real life in the Coast Guard, said, "We ought to put naval mortars on the roofs. For protection."

Good idea. "Protection from whom?"

"Communists. They want to break up the church. These people need military advice."

He kept looking up at the eaves.

Shortly thereafter, in hopes of working the fertile recruiting grounds of the University of Maryland, the Moonies established a splinter cell in Hyattsville in a decaying frame house that is now a parking lot. Like most political cells, it should have been padded. They began rehabilitating the house furiously in shifts. About that time I was angling for a job as a part-time special-education-and-computer-science teacher at Suitland Senior High, and hoped that maybe some of the Stafford converts might arrange to let me stay at the new hive for a week while I found an apartment. They couldn't unless I converted, which was too much rent. For a week I lived in the back of my 1957 Chevy, the Blue Bomb, which had a mattress running from the back seat into the trunk. By day I helped the Moonies rebuild their house The stability of the set-up was uncertain. Instead of killing the termites, I noticed, the Moonies caulked up their holes.

At a Moonie recruiting session one night in an apartment in College Park Towers, I met Jerry, a short club-footed Nazi who liked blacks and Jews. Actually he wasn't a Nazi, but said he was, which is stranger than being one. The Moonies were hawking the Divine Principle, as they called their theology, to a gaggle of freshmen. These latter were all agog, what with being at a real college for the first time, and hearing about a genuine exotic oriental religion and all. They had never heard of anything so advanced, not even in Wheeling.

At the time Principle involved something called the Base of Four Positions, which looked on the blackboard like a baseball diamond with God on second, Adam and Eve on first and third, and humanity at home plate. The idea was that Satan, currently in the guise of communism, had long ago gained control of the earth, and God kept send-ing people to try to redeem it. Abraham, Moses, and Jesus had all tried and failed. ("Oh Lord, whyfore hast thou forsaken me?" was consid-ered corroborative.) Moon by implication was the next redemptive Marine to storm ashore on the cosmic beach.

People drifted and munched on potato chips. I was bored to the point of twitching but didn't want to go back to the Chevy. The door opened and a deep bass voice growled, possibly not intending to be audible, "Hello. I'm looking for a bunch of maniacs...wait. I think I'm here."

Jerry was about five feet six inches tall and nearly as wide, with bushy black hair, a tangled beard, and a big orthopedic shoe. A fierce angry energy radiated from him. We shook hands—he had the delicate fingers of a pianist—and he growled, sotto voce, "You don't look like one of these. Are you?"

"God no."

"Let's go somewhere and talk."

We escaped to the balcony. Jerry then spoke roughly as follows, always in staccato bursts. "Yeah, I'm getting a Ph.D. in political sci-ence...God, it's nonsense...quantification of political behavior. I can make it work but who cares? These crazies, ain't they something? It's the decline of Rome all over, the Weimar Republic gone bad...four thousand years of progress for nothing...everything is downhill, *heehee*. This little Nazi is sick of it...If there any hope, it lies with the proles."

Jerry called himself a Nazi, but purely as a rhetorical device. He lacked the ideology, the mean streak, any obsession with race, in fact any of the traits necessary to Nazism, and had in most respects the pol-itics of an angry Democratic populist. He said he had been a real ros-trum-pounding right-winger in school up north, but reality had grown on him.

"Right wing politics is nonsense. So's left-wing politics. The center doesn't have politics...Took me a long time to see that...God, it's awful." He was mad at everything in general, perhaps because of a difficult life and a crippled leg, or perhaps because of excessive observation. He was too rational to be mad at anything in particular.

Anyway, Jerry was drawn to the Moonies by their psychiatric interest, by his lack of anywhere else to live, and by Caroline Libertini of the Hyattsville nest. Lib was a basic broad-hipped Italian earth-mother with bronzed skin and high cheekbones that looked almost Indian. She radiated the Italian womanly virtues, genuine in her case, like an antenna: Warmth, security, friendliness, concern, and a funny sense that you were part of her family. The lonely and shell-shocked fell in love with her, absolutely inaccessible though she was, whereupon the Moonies tried to convert them. I don't think it was conscious tactics, but it worked.

Soon Jerry was following her around like a growling congenial puppy. Then he moved into the Moonies' tiny unfinished basement on the tacit understanding that he might convert any day now, which he had not the slightest intention of doing. It was strange to see him stomping around the kitchen making spaghetti or acting as a towel rack for Lib, a troll among Snow White's dwarves. Beneath the fuming, he was sociable, and they were pleasant by ideology.

The Moonies didn't know what to make of Jerry. They themselves were given to indirection, manipulation, diplomacy, and a certain understatement of the truth. Jerry had the finesse of the Wehrmacht. Upon listening to a circuitously phrased obliquity intended to get him to do something, Jerry would amiably say, "Dumbest goddam idea I ever heard. What idiot thought of *that*?"

"Hey, Reed, gimme a hand moving my hate. Gotta lot of hate to move," Jerry said to me one day.

By this he meant a large collection of screwy far-right books. He also referred to mail as hate: "Gotta go check my hate-box." Soon we were laboring up and down the stairs to his bare cubby hole with some of the strangest literature known to man: Six-volume sets about the communist influence behind the fluoridation of water, and disintegrating works by obscure syndicalists. I felt trapped in a comic book: In the basement of a weird Christian cult somewhere in the nation's capital, a right-wing troll and his accomplice, a crazed hippie anthropologist, discuss the destruction of America's brains by toothpaste...." Jerry banged away with hammer and scrap wood. He didn't believe in his books any longer, but he collected them as a connoisseur.

"Need some more hate shelves."

"Jerry, this stuff is nuts."

"Yeah, bonkers. Real loony-tune stuff. Let me show you something really wild...."

We became friends, in part because of a common fascination with the curiosities inhabiting the ground floor. We discussed them endlessly in the beer dens of the University. Jerry would sit bristling with horror and foretell the collapse of society.

"It's all over. You see, don't you? Cults are the sign of collapse. The Orphic mysteries all over. Except they're sexless. Like monks. I'm going to go to Canada and live. Tell them I went to Mexico, will you?"

Sexless they were. Despite all the mass gimme-eight-hundred-volunteers weddings, mostly in the future then, they were as hostile to sensuality as the early Christians. The few married couples had pledged four years of abstinence to *Fa-a-a-ther*. I forget why they thought he wanted it. Dating outside the church was discouraged. So was dating inside the church.

"Oh, twaddle," I said, "It's just...well, auto-therapy."

"It's brainwashing. Just like a North Korean POW camp. You see how much sleep they get? None. They don't sleep. It's destroying their biochemistry."

"Moon doesn't make them crazy, Jerry. He just collects them. I think."

Actually I had to admit that Jerry might be right. No sleep, constant frantic activity, the unvarying presence of the group, rigorous discipline, lots of ritual. Maybe it did gum up the old metabolism.

The Moonies were a peculiar phenomenon: Extremists of the center, militant middle-wingers. Yet theirs was a cultural, not a political, centrism. They were kids who had grown up in the optimistic brick-box suburbs of 1953 when the economy was booming and it really seemed possible that all of humanity, after thousands of generations of struggle and evolution, might finally get a washing machine. On countless Saturday mornings the Moonies had watched Superman jump out of the window in a howl of wind while the announcer intoned approvingly of "Truth, Justice, and the American Way," which were then thought to be synonymous. Two Buicks and glossy teeth were ingrained in their psyches.

Then somehow they had fallen into the fetor and anomie of the Six-ties. For them the age was not a time of thumbing through glowing green mountains and having adventures. They were the casualties. They had waked in too many sour crashpads, engaged in too much thoughtless sex, done too many drugs. Moon's church was the way back. It was the faith of clean shirts and fanatical normalcy. Thus they managed to be those strangest of creatures, zealots of moderation.

I was still living in the Blue Bomb when Jerry saw his first prayer session. The Moonies knelt in the living room as the spirit moved them, put their foreheads on the floor, and gasped, "Fa-a-a-a-a-a-a-a-a...ther!" with a little explosion on the last syllable. Then a tumult of prayer would burst from the penitent, mostly apologizing to Fa-a-a-ther for the pain caused by errant humanity. Then they looked at Jerry and me to see whether inspiration might have taken hold of us. Invari-ably it hadn't. The first time Jerry looked at me in candid dismay.

"This isn't happening, is it?" he whispered.

"Why?"

"It can't be happening. That's obvious."

"Oh."

"It's the end of civilization."

Later, Jerry learned to grin an aw-shucks-fellers, maybe-next-time grin. The Moonies waited, figuring he had to crack sooner or later.

Washington had now discovered the Moonies and contemplated them with a pleasant sense of alarm. The war in Vietnam had grown boring. Here was a new lunacy to titillate the jaded palate of the Potomac Byzantium. With luck, the Moonies might do something horrid and interesting.

Liberals, easily puzzled by unfamiliar categories, decided the Moonies were fascists. Almost everyone assumed that they had some hidden agenda, the reason being that they had no obvious agenda. Generally ignored was another possibility, that they had no agenda at all, a suspicion supported by the eerie pointlessness of everything they did. All zealots are narcissistic tragedians, wrestling with destiny beneath their inner Klieg lights, and not especially interested in practical results. This is a truth that few in Washington could afford to concede so they figured the Moonies had to be up to something.

Actually they seemed to be engaged in the passionate, urgent, frantic pursuit of nothing in particular. Nothing they ever did had an effect. Their propaganda persuaded no one, and wasn't well calculated to persuade. If Moonery was a conspiracy, it was a conspiracy without a purpose.

One day in late fall they came running into the house from a local shopping mall, faces red with cold, an ecstasy of self-sacrifice lighting them like bulbs.

"We've been having a Rally for God! It was great!"

"Yeah! People were spitting on us!"

They constantly invented new religious tics. For a while they made a fetish of standing for a second of silent prayer before entering any door. Then there was Holy Salt which they sprinkled around at times of solemnity. I've seen sumo wrestlers do the same thing.

One evening in winter I dropped by to see Jerry in his cubby hole and found the whole cell bundling up.

"Hi! We're going to Holy Ground. Want to come?"

Holy Ground, it seemed, was a patch of earth on the Mall which Moon, for mysterious reasons, had declared sacred. Stranger things have happened, though probably not much stranger.

"Sure, why not?"

Off we went down Michigan Avenue. They were bubbling and happy, infused with the usual sense of warmth and illusory direction. They knew Father was with them, pulling them through life like a rope, and they left a broad wake of enthusiasm. At the Monument they piled out, well-groomed and middle-class and home at last from the alien ideologies of scag and Lenin. They rushed to a spot apparently located by triangulation, stood in a circle, and looked reverently at the sod.

It had grass on it.

The church was starting to get a bad name, not so much because of anything it really did as because it stole children—or so the parents preferred to put it. With few exceptions the Moonies were so warped by a wretched home life that they became susceptible to Moon—but this was not the wisest thing to tell parents whose kids were buzzing and clicking.

And there was the practice of Divine Deception, which is exactly what it sounds like. Some of it was airport technique ("Hi! I'm taking a survey....") but through the years a lot of kids would go to what they thought were summer camps, only to find out later that they were at the robot factory. Angry apostates told tales of psychological ruthlessness that wobbly proto-Moonie egos couldn't take. The Moonies responded that anyone who wanted to could leave. Unfortunately many of those sufficiently off balance to be Moonies in the first place were not good at independent action.

The Moonies earned their worst reputation among those groups who produced the most Moonies. Jews seemed especially hard hit, perhaps because they were especially vulnerable. The Jewish Moonies, all from secular families, had the usual Moonie problems of unloving homes. They also had the additional burden of not being Jewish enough to feel rooted in it, but too Jewish to be entirely at home in the surrounding society, and not about to convert to Christianity to

assuage their spiritual yearnings. So they ducked the question by joining Moon.

Kids from military families also showed in up numbers. Having
authoritarian fathers possessed of a certain combative simple-minded-
ness and not much affection, and having gone through the terrible
insecurity of moving and losing their friends every two years, they
needed something warm and fuzzy to hold onto. A fair number of
Catholics showed up, feeling at home in a heavily ritualized faith. So
did kids from Protestant families in which a great show is made of
Christianity for the purpose of browbeating the child and out-holying
the neighbors. The parents were furious, twenty years too late.

For a while Jerry resisted my view that the Moonies were dynamic
idlers, but the evidence kept coming in. For example, they held what
everyone called a Nuremberg rally on the Monument grounds. It was
wonderful. Scaffolding went up. Technicians in white jump-suits scur-
ried about, assembling great banks of phenomenally large loudspeakers
and a big platform for dignitaries. An enormous speaker's platform
went up. The reverend Moon's face in cyanotic blue began to peer
from posters on every fence in the city.

Sound buses drove crazily through the streets. Suddenly in front of
Woodies would come an unintelligible blare of loudspeakers. A bus
would turn the corner, plastered with blue Moons. As it drove past bellowing nothing understandable, which echoed from buildings (*"Arble-
wargmonumentwunhwarbworworworld"*), scrubbed faces peered out
with the characteristic crazed expression, hands waving mechanically.
"Join us, join us!" The impression was of a mechanical asylum worked
by a spring.

On the day of the rally the big speakers roared, perfectly intelligible
from anywhere on the grounds. The technicians had not been ama-
teurs. The grounds began to fill as an efficient Moonie organization
bussed people, mostly puzzled blacks, in from Philadelphia. A hootenanny outfit began singing to pull in more audience. The chestnut
smell of dope wafted about in clouds.

284 Nekkid In Austin

The scale, the volume of sound, were Orwellian. The moment demanded a howling demagogue to bay hatred at the cosmos. This was it, everybody figured with a little *frisson*. The Moonies were going to demand that Nixon be made Reichsckanzler. Instead, the political speech was brief, a hiccup in the hootenanny, and said America was a great country and the world depended on us, and now have a nice day and back to the music. That...was...all. I walked through the crowd, mostly hippies and inner-city blacks, and asked what the rally was for.

"Hey, man, I don't know, wanna toke?"

I didn't know either. Neither, I think, did the Moonies.

One night Jerry and I were sitting in my largely bare apartment, drinking beer and trying to figure out Moon's Barbie Dolls. He started talking about himself, and I suddenly realized why he knew so much about nickel-and-dime politics. He was a celebrity of sorts. A few years back on the strength of his then-impeccable conservative credentials, Jerry had gotten a job with Liberty Lobby, which exists in the airy region where the right wing runs out of feathers and empty space begins. Discovering a lot of passionate anti-Semitism in the Lobby's files, he had decided that Liberty Lobby was nuts, stolen the files, and given them to Drew Pearson.* There was a certain brutal directness in Jerry's approach to things.

The resulting *expose* had somewhat tarnished his reputation in the circles of the loon right, and left him unsympathetic to cults, political or otherwise.

Who did he like, I asked? Well, just sort of folk, he said. Especially the under-folk, such as blacks, and those who had otherwise suffered discrimination-you know, Italians, Jews, Poles, Indians, and so on.

God, I thought. I'm living with a liberal Nazi.

The ferment rose again at Upshur Street. The Moonies were gearing up to smash world communism. The trouble was that, being mostly kids, they identified communism with the student left, the only left they knew. Consequently they attached great importance to the

Trotskyite left-deviatonist schismatics of the International Bracero Labor Party's Maoist-revanchist wing, consisting of two half-literate sociology majors who were about to graduate and become management interns. The central hive on Upshur Street seethed with excitement. They began having workshops on the techniques of political action. Jerry and I showed up for one of these.

We got a chilly welcome. Friendliness to the Moonies was a political technique only, their real interest being their spiritual scar tissue. They got real cold real fast.

"Are you expected?" asked a prim girl who reminded me of a motel manager. All Moonies reminded me of motel managers. I'm not sure what brought on the freeze, but I think too many hippies had learned that you could, as at the Salvation Army, get a free meal if you listened to the prayers.

"We're from Hyattsville," I said, thinking it would be adequate explanation.

"Who do you wish to see?"

"Barry Cohen," I told her, Barry being head of the Hyattsville cell.

"One moment. I'll check with Mr. Cohen."

Mister Cohen? Another administrative lunge. First names were too informal for a movement that saw itself as a spiritual IBM. The frost princess finally let us in. The basement was full of folding chairs. A fellow with a flip-chart was lecturing approximately as follows:

"To be effective we have to know the enemy and how to counter his techniques. The communists and their allies use street theater, for example, a powerful technique. What do you do when you see three SDSers dressed as Vietnamese peasants with American soldiers beating them? We have to learn to speak effectively, how to handle hecklers. And remember, it won't be easy or pleasant. We will be abused, even beaten up. Possibly some of us will even lose our lives...."

Hard and lonely work, I thought, but somebody's gotta do it.

"Martyrs looking for a stake," growled Jerry. "It's the end, I tell you. This stuff is spreading." Jerry's problem was that he took the collapse of civilization personally.

To demonstrate counterhecklerism, the instructor appointed some Moonies to simulate the SDS and launched into a speech on American values, a big Moonie theme.

"And save...."

"*Fascist pig! Fascist pig!*" shouted the heckler-appointees, warming to the role. The speaker, demonstrating correct countermeasures, waited in lofty silence and continued with heightened feeling.

Jerry was chortling with delight. "Aw *right*! *Belt* out that hate! Let's hear some good hate!" The Moonies weren't sure what to make of this, not understanding that his was the technical appraisal of a student of maniacs.

"Hate! Hate! Hate!" shouted Jerry encouragingly.

"Stop giggling, dammit," I said, "or they'll turn on us."

The Moonies thought they were combating communism, but really they were just scraping up fill dirt for the inner emptiness. None of it mattered at all.

Nothing lasts, not even the end of civilization. One day Jerry got seriously fed up with political science and decided to go to Florida and live by tuning cars. Exposure to a political-science department will make any sensible person want to work with engines. My teaching job ran out. For that matter, the Hyattsville hive was showing sings of falling apart: Only the hardy can stay with a cult for long.

One last time Jerry and I sat in the apartment with a case of beer, trying to understand Moon's giddy sideshow, lobbing the empty bottles across the room into a cardboard box.

"Its the age of the cult, amigo," he said. "They're starting the slide into the mist. The whole show's gone bonkers...If there's any hope, it lies with the proles."

The next day he disappeared southward. I never heard from him again. I packed the Blue Bomb for a drive to California, planning to go on to Taiwan and learn Chinese.

For several years I heard nothing from the Moonies. Then in maybe 1979 I bumped into Diane Something-or-other in Dupont Circle, a nice kid from the Upshur Nest. She wore a turban and spoke of her devotion, to Islam, which had given meaning to her life. Her eyes were unhappy and she was looking a bit old for that sort of thing. Moonies? Oh, she had passed that stage. We said we should have lunch soon and, by tacit agreement, didn't.

*Drew Pearson was a noted political columnist.

Unpublished. Written in the early Seventies.

Thinking About The Black Underclass

The recent race war in Cincinnati—which is what it was—might reasonably lead one to ponder the black underclass, its nature, behavior, crimes, and intentions toward whites. Permit me a few unpleasant observations, inescapable after years on the police beat:

Crime by the underclass is racial, predatory, and very much targeted against whites. The motive is hatred more often than economic gain. The media carefully, systematically, by deliberate policy, hide these truths.

The foregoing can be independently verified by anyone. The data are there, on the Internet.

During the Cincinnati riots, I heard through police back-channels of blacks pulling white women from cars and beating them. I didn't write about it. If I had quoted my sources, they would have been fired for talking. Without sources, I'd have been dismissed as engaging in racist fantasy.

But then, on April 23, the columnist John Leo of *US News and World Report* broke journalistic ranks. He wrote of one white woman (probably the one I'd heard about) who was attacked and beaten. More chillingly, he reported that "Another driver assaulted by the mob was Roslyn Jones, an albino black woman, hit by a hail of bricks, one of which struck her in the head. *The attack stopped when someone shouted, 'She's black!'*" (My italics.)

It's racial, people.

Rioting blacks regularly beat whites. We know about Reginald Denny, kicked into brain damage by gangs of blacks in LA. Similar instances have occurred from Los Angeles to Dade County to Cincinnati. All were quickly buried by the media. On the streets of Washington I have myself seen whites swarmed and beaten bloody on two occasions—two young Australian tourists walking in Georgetown, for example.

The viciousness merits attention. Whites kids riot, yes, usually about politics. They run excitedly about, get arrested and gassed, wave signs, and assuage their hormones. They do not stomp people. White college kids do not grab an official of the IMF, kick him until he hemorrhages to death, and laugh.

The underclass does. When urban blacks surround a car, pull out a terrified woman they believe to be white, and hit her in the head with bricks, they're not playing. They want to hurt, cripple, kill. That's what bricks do.

The underclass is what we have in the cities. One day it will come out. We won't like it. They are not the nice black family down the street with the two polite kids and a Toyota. They are something very different.

In the recent Mardi Gras riots in Seattle, gangs of blacks again attacked whites. So many people saw it, and got it on videotape, that the media couldn't quite hide it. For example, blacks attacked a white woman, after which a young white guy tried to help her. They stomped him to death. Press was minimal. Can you imagine the furor if whites had attacked a black woman, and murdered a black rescuer?

The media, again, are consciously lying about race. It is lying by crafted omission, by artful editing, but it is lying. If the police stop too many blacks on the highway, coverage is national and unending. If the underclass stomps a white to death, a hush follows.

Examples abound. In Wichita this year two black men captured five young whites at gunpoint, forced them to perform various sexual acts on them and each other, of course raped the women, and then killed them all, execution style, except for one woman. Bleeding and naked, she walked through the snow for help.

Two things: First, the motive was hatred. You can rob people without harming them. The attackers intended to humiliate and kill. Second, note the near perfect suppression of the story. If you heard about it at all, it was probably on the Internet.

The hatred of the underclass for whites is not new. Neither is the targeting of white women. In the Sixties the rapist and Black Panther Eldridge Cleaver wrote at length in *Soul On Ice* (chapter one), of the underclass black's desire to attack white women. Don't believe me. Read it.

The foregoing anecdotes are just that—anecdotes. The Department of Justice, however, collects data on crime—the Uniform Crime Reports, the National Crime Victimization Survey, and so on. The author Jared Taylor analyzed these figures and found that a black is 55 times as likely to attack a white than vice versa, 103 times as likely to rob, 40 times as likely to rape a white woman than a white man is to rape a black woman, and 237 times as likely to gang up on whites to rob them.

This will be unbelievable to many. But check the numbers for yourself.

Now, I will be accused of racism for saying these things. All right. I hereby make a proposal to the NAACP: Let's hire a first-line accounting firm to make a study of the figures, and publish both its results and its methods. If I'm wrong, I'm wrong, and will say so. Do I have any takers?

Unless this stops, we face disaster. One day things will explode.

Nothing suggests that it will stop. I see no signs that the black underclass is shrinking, and many signs—the huge number of children—that it is growing. These people simply cannot be integrated into a techno-industrial European society. They bear no resemblance to middle-class blacks one sees in offices. They are parasitic, uneducable, criminally predatory—and they hate whites.

As blacks grow in numbers, they take over city after city. While these governments are not of the underclass, and don't want riots, they will of political necessity support the underclass. And, I suspect, no blacks at all really like whites. The danger is that whites may weary of it. If they ever push back, the potential for irremediable, ghastly, self-sustaining conflict will be high. I'll guess the country couldn't recover.

It had better not happen, but it could. Any spark could light it. One day the underclass, rioting, may go into white neighborhoods to stomp and burn. They won't expect resistance, because they have never met it. I don't think Al and Jesse quite know how many deer guns, how many Weatherbys and .223s sit quietly in closets out here. If a mob comes toward a man's home, where his wife and children are, the results will be astonishing. The police will immediately polarize, black versus white. So will everybody else. Government will be irrelevant. And the whole country just might blow up.

If that happens, God help us.

Sex As Tennis

I'm trying to figure out sex, and why people get in an uproar about it, and run around waving their arms and hollering, and everybody's mad at everybody else.

I guess it's because men can't tell sex from tennis. We can't help it. It's a character defect built into us, like tail fins on a fifty-seven T-Bird.

Yep. That's it. I've just solved the question of the ages. Right here. Contributions welcome.

Best I can tell, ninety-eight percent of women are mad because all men want is sex. (Actually we want other things too, like big-block engines, dogs, and really bad movies with lots of gratuitous violence.) On the other hand, men are ready to become monks because they can't talk to a woman for five minutes on a bus before she wants commitment. To a woman commitment seems so obviously good that she can't see why he'd rather have pellagra. Which is what men think about sex. So the two glare at each other like two possums with only one garbage can.

It's too bad. A lot of people end up being unhappy because of it.

The problem, it says here, is that to men sex is a primal drive that doesn't have much emotional content. It's just sex. It's like when you have athlete's foot, you scratch it, but you don't have an emotional bond to it. Sure, a guy can commit to a woman, as evidenced by innumerable marriages that happen despite experience and common sense. Sex can have emotional importance to him with a woman he wants to keep. But he doesn't have a hard-wired connection between sex and commitment. To him they're separate things, like jackhammers and Vienna sausages. You can have both at the same time, but you don't have to.

By contrast, for women, sex seems epoxied to a lot of emotional freight. A woman sees sex as a step toward commitment, as fifty years ago a man saw commitment as a step toward sex. When the man doesn't see the connection, she thinks he's just plain wrong-headed, and mean spirited, and a riverboat son of a bitch.

Which brings us to tennis. (Bet you didn't see that coming.)

Men think of sex the way they think of tennis. Suppose I want to work off some energy. I call my buddy Ralph, and we meet at the courts, and have a good time for a few sets—sweat and grunt, twist our ankles, fall down and break things, and end up in a mild coma.

When we're through, he doesn't want me to marry him. When in fact I don't, he doesn't feel exploited. In fact, he feels deeply relieved.

That's how men look at sex. A man genuinely doesn't understand why he can't say to the young lady in the next cubicle, "Hey, Jane, what say we go to my place at lunch for a roll in the hay?" ("Fred—you've got *hay* at your place?") He may like Jane, think she's bright and fun, have no desire to exploit, use, or degrade her. They may have been friends for years. But if he made what would seem to him a perfectly reasonable suggestion, she would explode and file at least a dozen lawsuits.

Yet he knows that she isn't opposed to sex, and isn't opposed to him. If he took her to three movies, so that the whiff of commitment hung in the air, like methane over a swamp, she'd be worried if he *didn't* make the suggestion. So why not...?

He doesn't get it.

The woman's lack of the tennis instinct, or the man's possession of it, complicates life for everyone. It ain't her fault. It ain't his fault. It's how we are.

To aggravate things, we're timed all wrong, like streetlights in New Jersey. After a certain age, somewhere around thirty, a woman's interest in commitment rises, while a man's declines—just as a man's sex drive declines as hers rises. (Actually, sex may be a vast practical joke. If there's a better explanation, I haven't heard it.) Guys who are single in their mid-thirties are frequently comfortable with bachelorhood or, having been raped in the divorce courts, attached to it as tenaciously as panicked barnacles. And so guys, not looking for marriage, go into relationships knowing that things are going to end miserably. Three months later, the Marriage Monster raises its fanged head. It's as predictable as morning.

Somehow having a mate seems much more crucial to women than to men. A guy with a girlfriend may figure she's peaches, better than a competition yo-yo with extra strings. He may be proud of her and proud of himself for having her. If the Red Army attacked her, he'd leap in front of her like a spring-wound damned fool and die a pointless but gaudy death. (That too is built in.) But she will still be only a part of his world, along with motorcycles, the job, great software, rock climbing, or drinking beer and talking dirty with other guys.

Maybe this is why men are happier than women with intermediate degrees of commitment. If Willie Bob starts dating Maggie Lou, and she's fun, he'll just naturally keep on doing it. Left to himself, two years later or twenty, he would still be dating her, and be perfectly happy. His attitude is that if it works, why meddle with it? He doesn't see dating as having to Go Somewhere as if it were an evicted tenant. Depending on how much company he really wants, he may figure seeing her three times a week, and being left alone the rest of the time, is just right. He isn't exploiting her. He's just happy as things are.

She won't see it this way, or at least not for long. It's not because there's anything wrong with her, or with women, or for that matter with men. We've just got different operating systems. What she sees as God's intended result of dating, so clearly right as not to be examined, he sees as at best an unnecessary complication, at worst as giving up title to his house. He asks the, to him, reasonable questions: "Gee, Maggie, what would be better if we got married? Would sex be better? Food? What's your point?" He's genuinely puzzled. She thinks he's being exploitative, that she has been had again, another five years wasted, men, the bastards.

There's got to be a better way. I just don't know what it is.

The War On Boys

I note without surprise that we wage war not just on Islamic terrorists, but on little boys who play cops-and-robbers. Yes. Listen:*

"From California to New Jersey, public schools are banning the children's game of 'cops and robbers' and threatening students with expulsion. For example, at Lewis Elementary School in Fort Irwin, California, one father removed his nine-year-old son from class after the school principal threatened to expel the boy if he didn't stop playing cops and robbers on the playground."

With idiots blooming everywhere, you would think spring had come early. But there is more.

"[We have] suspended play when they're using imaginary weapons until the guidelines can be developed to help the staff differentiate between dangerous and imaginary play." This pearl of lucent sanity from Gary Thomas, the District Superintendent, who doesn't know the difference between "imaginary" and "imaginative."

The rigid, hostile, puritanical control of little boys is now national policy. Very, very bad, cops and robbers. It could be worse, though. Little boys might play Cowboys and Injuns. (They certainly couldn't call it that. Perhaps "Genderless Animal Care Technicians and Preternaturally Noble At-One-With-Nature Role Models" would do.)

One laughs, having no recourse, but it isn't funny. There is at work here something somber and ugly. It isn't just the schools. The country is eating itself, as if it had an autoimmune disease, as if it were undergoing cultural apoptosis. The political classes, using the minorities as bludgeons, and appeals to virtue as pretexts, seek to eliminate boyhood, the pursuit of excellence, the rewards of achievement, sexual identity, the family, religion, standards of honesty and civility, and per-

297

sonal responsibility. Half-educated teachers practicing playground Stalinism are just a part of it, one front in a larger war.

What do we think we are doing?

It isn't politics as usual. Nor is it liberalism. In my lifetime, liberals have wanted to end apartheid, allow women to become chemists if they chose, ensure equal opportunity, permit the Pill, guarantee decent treatment of farm labor, and tone down a sometimes puritanical morality. None of this is evil. European nations have embodied most of these ideas without ill effects. Practice has fallen short of theory, as happens in politics. Measures have perhaps been taken too far or not far enough. Civilized politics consists largely in fine-tuning the reasonable. Yet it hasn't been evil.

This is.

Current policy has become a twisted caricature of reasonable impulse. Affirmative action, an understandable if ill-advised idea, has led to the sclerotic hierarchies of a permanent caste system. Welfare has produced an eternal underclass. To ensure that things be decided without regard to race, creed, color, sex, or national origin, we insist that nothing be decided except according to race, creed, color....

To raise blacks, we lower academic standards for whites. Being against violence, we let Hollywood bathe children endlessly in moist-brains-on-the-ceiling violence, treated with loving sadism. Then with an almost prurient squeamishness, we expel kids for playing "violent" boy games—meanwhile encouraging girls to go into combat.

The nation has become a milkshake of confusion, hostility, and sexual antagonism, always disguised as something else. Note that while the schools punish little boys for playing soldier, adventure movies now routinely show women slugging men, kicking them in the crotch, or becoming naval commandoes. The opposition isn't to violence, but to masculinity.

We become a nation of unmen and half-women. A man who publicly worries because a child says "bang," and then calls the police, must have painful problems of sexual identity. A normal adult who sees a boy doing something he shouldn't, which does not include playing cops and robbers, says, "Bobby, stop it." A male who can't do this, who has to have police support and sends the child for psychiatric treatment, has something wrong with him. So does a society that permits it.

The Soviet Union placed dissidents in mental institutions and drugged them into conformity. We do it to our children. The difference is...?

In the campaign of cultural self-mutilation, stated motives are seldom real motives. The news media lavish attention on child-molesting by Catholic clergy, while simultaneously advocating acceptance of homosexuality in Scoutmasters. A contradiction? No. They aren't against homosexual clergy because they oppose pederasty, but because they dislike Catholicism. They do not want homosexual Scoutmasters because they favor pederasty, but because they don't like the Boy Scouts.

If memory serves, the Scouts when I was one long ago said that a Scout should be: Trustworthy, loyal, helpful, friendly, courteous, kind, obedient, cheerful, thrifty, brave, clean, and reverent. Does that not have a sun-lit, Fifties-ish, Normanrockwellian sanity that is a total reproach to our ghetto zeitgeist? A retro wholesomeness that makes the political classes cringe?

The desire to treat homosexuals decently was perhaps a manifestation of liberalism. To force the children of people you don't like into intimate association with homosexuals is a manifestation of hostility. Or are homosexual Scoutmasters thought to have a restraint that we deny in Catholic clergy?

On and on it goes. Have we gone nuts? (Yes.)

All of this is of course done in the name of this or that moral imperative—justice, equality, fairness, what have you. The country reels under the onslaught of malignant goodness. But do the metaclasses seek to put women in combat because they think women want to be in combat, or because they detest the military, hate its conservatism and (once) unapologetic masculinity, and want to humiliate it?

The unspoken agenda, to bring down the former United States as a cultural entity, sluices through metagovernmental policy. Do they truly like blacks, or merely want to shove them down the throats of the hated white Europeans? To judge by their policy rather than their protestation, the political class holds blacks in contempt. Note that racial policy invariably assumes that blacks are helpless, shiftless, require hand-feeding, and cannot be expected to achieve. Our managers simply use them as a weapon for destroying the society.

All of this ties into the diffuse anger that eats away at the country. We are not a happy people. Racial animosity runs deep. Blacks don't like whites don't like Latinos. The hostility of women toward men corrodes society. The breakup of the family leaves children angry at they aren't sure what. It adds up. Over years one sees the public mood change. Road rage is rage expressed on the road, not caused by traffic. More and more I see people walking against street lights, deliberately forcing cars to stop. Manners deteriorate.

I think we're on the way out.

* CNSNews.com, March 20

When New York Bubbles Merrily

I n pondering the relentlessly invoked War on Terrorism, it seems to me we need to hold in the forefront of our minds a question: What would be the consequences of a nuclear explosion in an American city?

First, though: Is such an explosion really possible?

In the extremes of political discourse, particularly where the right wing runs out of feathers and giddy space begins, one finds a sort of ardent romantic paranoia, which seems to serve its partisans as a substitute for bowling. Those imbued with it argue that that the Russians plot a nuclear first-strike on the United States. Never mind that the Russians probably couldn't coordinate sock hops in neighboring high schools, aren't crazy, and have no reason to start a nuclear war. Alternatively, argue the chronically apocalyptic, the Chinese will nuke us. With a population of a billion-three, they say almost happily, China wouldn't mind losing 200 million people in a nuclear exchange. (This suggests a very peculiar understanding of the Chinese.) We therefore must become a frightened military state and build armed space stations or whatever.

A reasonable response, certainly my response, to these enthusiasts of global pan-frying is, "There, there, take your medication. Try on this nice white jacket with the *lo-o-n-n-g* sleeves. Yes, we're taking you to dinner. Everything will be all right."

Do you really worry that the Russians will nuke us? Me either.

Now ask yourself: If Moslem terrorists had a nuclear bomb and knew how to set it off, do you think they would hesitate to do so in an

American city? Do you trust Iraq not to supply such a weapon if it had one?

Exactly.

Now, what would be the consequences of a nuclear burst in Manhattan? (Or Cleveland, which is probably less well guarded.) In physical terms it's hard to say. The damage would depend on the bomb, and bombs come in all sizes from small backpack models to great big huge ones. The destruction might be less than some would expect. American cities are made of concrete reinforced with steel, whereas Japanese cities in 1945 were of paper and wood. On the other hand, a ground burst, which it necessarily would be, would presumably be very dirty, producing large amounts of radioactive fallout.

These are details. They wouldn't matter.

Remember that after the towers went down, two things happened. First, the nation became engulfed in couch-potato blood-lust and ready to send somebody else to fight terrorists. Second, the airlines saw bookings drop precipitously. People were afraid to fly.

Now, if a nuclear explosion destroyed even a few blocks of New York, would anyone ever go back to work in the city?

There might, after all, be another bomb waiting. There would certainly be radiation. The public would not think arithmetically in terms of rads and roentgens and allowable dosages. New York would be crippled. It happens to be the economic hub of the nation.

And of course we couldn't know whether there really was another bomb in New York, or in another city. In a sense it wouldn't matter. The possibility would be enough. What would Cincinnati do if, a week after New York went high-order, an Arabic accent called to say that the city was next?

I've seen Washington nearly shut down because somebody left jello somewhere marked "Antrax." (Spelling is a lost art, even among terrorists.) Imagine the panic if a city were told it was going to melt in two hours. The traffic jam would be monumental. People would be crushed to death. And the next day another city would panic.

In short, it seems to me that one small nuke would bring the country to a devastating halt, force it to become a police state, and leave us to live forever scared.

It may be that Moslems do not quite grasp what they are playing with. Some do, no doubt. Some don't care, yet, or else believe that nothing can happen to them. Terrorism aimed at the US relies on the principle that if we cannot attach an attack to a particular nation, with assurance bordering on beyond-reasonable-doubt, we can't, or won't, do anything nuclear.

But the United States can't allow nuclear terrorism and continue as a polity worthy of habitation. Further, if pushed hard enough, America could end Islamic civilization in a day. And might. The Moslem world would do well to bear this in mind. There are lines one doesn't cross, things that cannot be permitted no matter the cost of preventing them. Further, a nation can become impulsive after losing 150,000 people and its principal city. Every country suspected of complicity could be bubbling slag before the sun went down, and probably would.

If this sounds like crazed doomsday maundering, ask yourself what else we would do when the Twin Towers looked like a minor traffic accident by comparison and the whole nation began living in fear of the next one.

And after that, what? It strikes me as probable that Europe would recognize that the same could happen to it, and support the US. (Except for France, which keeps a surrender document on the Internet, with blanks you can fill in.) Japan also has terrorists and cities. I suspect that the civilized world in totality would decide that nuclear incendiarism was intolerable, since all would be vulnerable. The planet might decide that children, primitives, and zealots cannot be permitted to play with Bombs.

The result would be the virtual colonization of any Moslem country able or anywhere near able to produce nuclear weapons. The oil would be no barrier. As long as Russian didn't back the Arabs, Saudi Arabia could be occupied in about five minutes. By Papua-New Guinea, the Boy Scouts, or three Marines.

We should perhaps remember that large wars happen. Few wanted WWII or would have in 1932 thought it possible. Pearl Harbor, the 9/11 attacks, a nuclear bomb on American soil—all, before they happen, sound like the ravings of dementia.

The world would be better off if these particular things didn't happen. Frying several million people is not to be lightly undertaken. The results of major upheavals are not readily foreseen. How can a convulsion be prevented?

Answer: By taking any measures necessary, any measures at all, to prevent Iraq from building nuclear weapons. If it were not for the nuclear potential, one might argue about the President's policy toward Iraq. Or one might not. But Saddam Hussein cannot be permitted any possibility of having nuclear weapons. It's that simple. Whether we like it or not, we need to say "no," and we need to mean it. The potential consequences of not doing so leave no choice.

Hant Explains Policy. 'Bout Time Somebody Did.

Come morning, early, I walked up the holler to Uncle Hant's moonshine still. I wanted to ask him about American policy, because he knows everything.

You walk along the railroad, rusty now, past the old mine entrance that's been closed thirty years, and turn right along the creek bed for a ways. Birds were hollering and eating bugs. The sun poured through the mountains like it was going somewhere and the dew gleamed prettier than sunlight on chromed headers.

Hant was standing next to the cooker, pouring brake fluid into the mash.

"Hant, you gotta tell me about our national policy."

"Ain't any."

He kept pouring, like he was measuring in his head. He makes Authentic Shine for the yuppie trade out of Washington. Hant's tall and scrawny with a floppy hat he probably got from Nate Forrest. He doesn't really exist. He's a literary tool, like a hex wrench.

I said, "Why you putting brake fluid in that panther sweat?"

He pulled a stoneware jug from behind the still and sat on a stump. Hant's getting a few years on him. When he sits it's stiff and from the middle, like a pocketknife folding.

"Gives it a kick. Tried paint thinner, but it boiled off in the coils."

Hant's always innovating. Once he tried using wood alcohol, but the yuppies went blind and couldn't find their way back. He lost a lot of business. I asked again about American policy. Sometimes you have to kind of focus him.

"Radio said Hay-rabs are blowing up New York like they was dynamiting stumps. Said we shoulda, you know, been ready, or maybe thought about it. You reckon?"

He was quiet for a moment. He does that when he's about to say something solemn and dreadful.

"Son, it's just real hard for this country to be ready for anything. That's a natural fact. We mostly can't have a policy. Not long enough for the paint to dry on it, anyway. Democracies, like monkeys, can't remember anything they aren't actually eating."

"That last sentence ain't good rustic dialog, Hant. You're getting out of character."

"Aw shucks. Guess I was lunging for an apothegm. Like spearing a frog. I figure if we had a policy we'd forget it in a week."

"Oh." I puzzled a moment on it. "What if we wrote it down? Then we could look at in every morning. Everybody could have it on a little card maybe. Gimme that jug."

He did. It was a genuine stoneware jug from maybe 1900. They make'm in Taiwan and Hant gets them from a jobber in New Jersey. A yup won't buy shine unless it's in a genuine jug.

"Gimme that back," said Hant, sounding worried. He knows his priorities.

"Wouldn't work," he said, once the jug was safe. "We'd lose the card. Now I grant we can keep our minds on something that's right smack dab in front of us. Like when all them Russians used to point their deer guns at us all day. It got our attention. Soon's they went away, we went back to watching Lucy. Didn't we? We gotta see it or we figure it ain't there. It's how we are."

I wasn't sure I was learning much about national policy.

He said, "You think about it. Fifteen years ago we were helping the Afghanistans kill Russians. These days the Russians are helping us kill Afghanistans. I saw it on the television. I figure somebody just forgot what he was doing one morning, like when you accidentally go into the ladies' room. You don't mean anything by it. You're just thinking about something else.

"Now, I will allow it can happen to anybody. I remember I got drunk one night at Big Red's and drove away in the wrong pickup truck."

"I wouldn't think you could get that drunk."

"Judge didn't believe it either."

I took a big hit from the jug. It was Wild Turkey. Hant pours into a jug so it'll be authentic. He knows better than to drink that snake venom *he* makes. He may be imaginary, but he ain't crazy.

I said, "Well, it just seems like whenever anything bad happens, we ain't ready for it. Way I figure it, we could have a real simple foreign policy. Like Smack Hell Out Of Em. I reckon almost anybody could remember that, even folks up Colvin Holler."

They've been marrying mostly each other for a long time up Colvin Holler. Some of them got twelve toes and don't remember real good. A professor from some college up north came and said you couldn't find more recessive genes in one place anywhere else in the country. Everybody was real proud.

"Naw. Folks won't do anything that's ugly until they have to, and then it's worse. It's like not getting your teeth fixed." He passed the jug back.

"Smack'em" was my own foreign policy. Few years back, when I was dating this ol' gal named Jiffy Lube, we used to go to Abe's Pool and Beer. Her name was really Jennifer Imidazole Fergwiller. I guess she had some Eye-talian in her. Everybody called her Jiffy. Anyway she was cute and all these old boys wanted to hit on her and I'd smack'em. Sometimes I got beat up. They got tired of it and went away. You just got to make it more trouble to them than it's worth.

I told Hant, "Back in school that teacher lady we had told us about this president named Teddy Roosevelt. She said his policy was Speak Swahili and Carry A Big Stick. I bet he used to date Jiffy Lube's mother. That's why he'd need the stick, leastways if she was cute as Jiffy was. Anyway, I reckon people could remember that."

I felt pretty smart for remembering about Teddy Roosevelt. I always did like school more than the other kids, especially lunch.

Hant thought about it. "That might work, I calculate. I guess if I saw somebody talking Swahili with a big stick, I'd leave him alone. You can't tell what crazy people are gonna do. I used to know this ol' boy, he'd get drunk down in Bluefield and start thinking he was a poker game. He'd sit there and bet and raise himself and call. Nobody went near him."

He got up to check on the mash. I grabbed the jug. I could tell I wasn't going to learn much about foreign policy. On the other hand, I couldn't do anything about it even if I did learn. Might as well get a big jug, and sit on a good stump, and watch.

A Race Of Neutered Poodles

The two great social adventures undertaken by the United States in the last century have been first racial and, second, sexual integration. Racial integration hasn't worked well, because the races are simply too different. Blacks have progressed economically, but they remain deeply hostile to whites, and apparently incapable of assimilating.

One may wonder: Will sexual integration work better? Or are there intractable sexual differences, whose existence we refuse to admit, that will bollix things? Believing that something ought to work is not the same as establishing that it will.

The premise of the current adventure is that men and woman are fungible—that, perhaps after a bumpy start, and with the temporary encouragement of affirmative action, the sexes will work happily, and interchangeably, side by side. Any doubts regarding the probability of this sunny consummation are held to represent the most retrograde of social thought.

These were of course precisely the premises of racial integration.

To phrase it differently, can anyone who has been married believe that the countless incompatibililities, and ways of thought opaque to the other sex, will somehow vanish in public life?

For example, the sexes handle disagreement differently. Men keep conflict carefully impersonal. They know that conflict can quickly become physical. It's how men are. In the past, quarrels led to fighting and, perhaps, death. Today, even in the office, push a man too hard and he will revert to the instinctive: "What is your freaking problem?" The body language, unnoticed but decidedly read, will say, "Shut up or escalate."

Men don't like to do either. They keep disagreement abstract. It is safer.

Women by contrast prefer the personal and emotional. When a woman is angry, she becomes personally disagreeable in ways that would leave a man picking up his teeth. Men, wired to avoid the personal, to regard personal attack as serious, do not know what to do in the face of uncontrolled anger, tears, or emotionalism. In private life, they flee. At work, where women have real power, shrugging it off doesn't work.

By instinct men back down from angry women when, today, backing down isn't a good idea. This may be the determining idea of the coming century.

Further, men like hierarchy. In a sense it permits impersonality: You obey the rank, not the man. From a man's point of view, the effect is to promote efficiency, to allow a focus on the job at hand, while avoiding personal conflict.

Women neither like nor respect hierarchy, particularly male hierarchy, and their mere presence short-circuits it. Sexual tension is inescapable among humans. Sex generates equality. A male colonel regards a male private as a subordinate. Instinctively he regards a female private as a woman. Both feel the age-old contract, that women trade sex for anything they want, and men trade anything they have for sex. Most women in varying degrees will use the equation, while insisting otherwise. Men can't. The greater the degree of hierarchy, the greater the divisiveness.

The key word in all of this is instinct. We are wired to behave in these ways. When footsteps are heard downstairs at night, it is the man who grabs the pistol and goes to adjust the burglar. A man, with a little encouragement, will open doors for a woman, take her coat, hold her chair. Only with the aid of powerful drugs could one imagine a woman doing these things for a man.

For that matter, until recently men routinely paid for dates. Now women will often split the tab—but the woman never routinely pays.

A man with an adequate salary will usually, and without objection, support a woman who doesn't work, but the reverse is seldom true.

This isn't simple gold-digging. Rather, women seem by instinct to expect to be cared for by men, and men expect to do it. It no longer makes economic sense. The instinct remains.

The conflict between a woman's instinctive desire to be protected and maintained, and the political determination to have no part of it, plays a large part in sexual politics. Note the near-hysteria of the hostility to Deadbeat Dads—that is, men who don't meet the expectations of instinct.

We are dealing with inbuilt behavior, and telling ourselves it is politics. Note that women unendingly demand more funding for medical research into diseases peculiar to women. Yet it is common knowledge that men die some seven years earlier than women, suggesting starkly that men, not women, need more research. Never in fifty years on the planet have I heard any woman, ever, say, "My God, our men are dying. We must do something." Why not?

Either (a) women are grotesquely selfish or (b) they are wired to look after their own physical well-being, and that of the children, while letting men take care of themselves. Since women do not in general seem to be selfish, I'll take (b).

Finally, and crucially: The women's movement today is no longer a quest for equality. It was, but isn't. It has become instead a drive for revenge, for power, and for domination over and humiliation of men. It is never phrased this way, of course. For tactical reasons, feminists trade in the highly solvent currency of rights, justice, discrimination, and victimhood. Men say little. They cannot afford psychologically to admit the extent to which they are being walked on.

But think about what is actually happening. For example, the campaign to force Virginia Military Institute first to accept girls and second, to retain pregnant ones, was hardly founded on a pent-up desire among women to be in the infantry. The intent was to humiliate a profoundly male institution, and force men to swallow it. It worked.

The campaign of humiliation has succeeded all across the country, too wildly for easy explanation. Males in offices tremble in fear of charges of harassment. Powerful editors are afraid to be alone with a woman in their offices. A female officer in the military can complain that a morning run is demeaning, whereupon the Pentagon will obediently stop the runs.

Think carefully about this: The Joint Chiefs of Staff are afraid of a woman who doesn't feel like running. Something strange is happening.

The truth is that men are crawling like neutered poodles, and feminists are quietly laughing. They are instinctively contemptuous of men they can push around, which today means almost all of them. It's fascinating, twisted, almost kinky. One thinks of a dog rolling over to bare its throat to appease a bigger dog.

Whatever it is, wherever it is going, it is not as simple as we pretend. It is not even close.

Blacks, Basketball, and Electrical Engineering

Today I'm going to become a great moral leader, like Gandhi, but without the diaper. I'll win the eternal gratitude of all downtrodden people everywhere, and maybe a Nobel Prize.

Magazines, and those reprehensible lying TV shows like Twenty Minutes or whatever, are bleating like hung-over goats about how universities mulct black basketball players. Yeah. See, the players get used for the glory of the school. Then thrown on the street when their eligibility wears out, like cheap shoes with a hole in the sole. They probably end up uneducated and drained and bagging groceries for fat white ladies in Beverly Hills. At least that's what it sounds like. Every couple of years an uproar arises about it and nothing gets done. Black columnists holler and say it's exploitation and just no end bad and rotten.

Which of course would be true if the blacks had any interest in getting an education.

The predatory commercialism shouldn't surprise anybody. College athletics ain't a thing in the world but semi-pro ball, attached loosely to a presumed institution of higher learning. Schools will swindle labor like any other form of sweat shop.

It isn't really racial, of course. Give the universities credit for broader vistas of immorality. They would just as soon give basketball pseudo-scholarships to Polynesians, or paralytics, or giraffes, or construction cranes. They are indiscriminately unprincipled. It's just that black guys play better basketball.

What can the players do about it? I'm going to tell you. Right here. Copyright me. If black players want an education instead of being jerked around, they can get it. Easy.

If they want it. If they don't bother, then I will assume they don't really want an education.

Here's how. First, the captain of the team—probably named Ujaweem al Bundeswehr—at some major basketball factory, say UCLA, should get on the blower to the *Los Angeles Times* and all the networks. He should tell them, "Hey gang, next Thursday we're gonna have a big press conference and talk about how the brothers are getting tromped on and done evil by. You news weasels can distort it and blow it out of proportion and get Pulitzers. Is that a deal or what? Three o'clock."

They'll be there.

Next, Ujaweem should call the Maximum Leader of the university. Yeah, the Prez. The Big Guy.

Now, I have no idea who is currently the Reichskanzler of UCLA, or Field Marshall, or head mistress, or whoever universities have to give them form and direction. He may be anything, possible even a vertebrate. But let's assume that he's a typical neutered spineless frightened university president. He'll have a name like Dr. Erlenmeyer Flask and a wife named Florence who gives elegant tea parties. Ujaweem should advise Dr. Flask of the press conference, and suggest the advisability of his showing up. Three o'clock.

The Prez will show. Otherwise heaven knows what might happen, and he wouldn't be able to put the right spin on it.

OK. Picture it. A sunlit afternoon, with scruffy students wandering around like insouciant landfills. A sense of impending spectacle will hang in the air. Ten TV trucks will be there and seventy-five print types. Reporters flock to a racial story like dung beetles who have discovered an unusually meritorious camel dropping. Cameras will wave and point. Ditzy blondes with perfect hair will do stand-ups. Anchor persons will ask stupid questions.

And there will be Ujaweem and the whole UCLA basketball team, united, ominous, towering over journalists and most buildings.

Whereupon Ujaweem should speak to the Prez in this wise: "Now look here, Dr. What's-Your-Flask. We're getting just a little tired of this scam, see? We came here on scholarships, but all we do is play basketball for free, so this sorry school can make money and keep a bunch of rich alumni happy, and you can live in a big house and strut around like you amounted to something. Which you don't.

"That's fine for *you*. But we get outa here with some lame degree in Recreation, or Rhythmic Breathing—we got rhythm—or nothing at all and end up being gardeners and pruning the tops of short trees in Orange County. Ain't gonna happen, boss. That's over. Gone.

"You got ten minutes to get your scrawny white ass over to the academic dean, and sign us up for real degrees in whatever we want, and figure out a schedule so we got time to study. Otherwise we quit. Think about it. Now git."

At that point, Ujaweem will have him by the...yes. If any.

See, the Prez is going to think: "Headlines." Huge, grim, inescapable headlines. "UCLA Denies Blacks Education." "Racism Alive at UCLA." The *LA Times*. The *New York Times*. The *Washington Post*. None of them care about blacks, whom they regard as bushmen, but they love to eat the politically wounded. The Prez will know he's chow. He will also know it will be only a matter of time—about fifteen minutes—before one of the circling journalists comes up with, "The New Slavery: Black Life at UCLA."

A bit of technical advice, Ujaweem. I recommend that the players wear waders, like duck hunters do in swamps, or at least Gore-Tex socks. It's because ol' Prez will fall instantly on his face and start licking your feet like a puppy that's found a gravy stain. At least, he will if he's like those Ivy League presidents. Academic officials are cowards. It's their most useful quality. They're probably an example of parallel evolution. I mean, it's hard not to believe that Dan Rather evolved from a monkey, but university presidents seem to have started as jellyfish, and didn't get very far.

In an hour the entire team except the white guy could be enrolled in electrical engineering.

That's all it would take. The trick is knowing what the most important things are in academia: athletics, and political correctness. Schooling is a distant third. You guys control the first two, Ujaweem, so you can get the third. If you quit, the team would be three puzzled white benchwarmers, not very good, who would either have to play extremely fast break, or revert to law school, buy lousy suits, and become divorce attorneys. And the Dr. Flasks everywhere are scared to death of the race card. Use it. In this case it's justified.

Dead serious, guy. There's not a school in the country that would dare deny you a real education. Then you'd make out like a Democrat around other people's money. You'd be getting a fairish education in anything you wanted, for free, and playing basketball in front of the whole country and a bunch of scouts. Go for it.

If you want it. Do you?

Going Seriously Boom: Aboard
A Missile Submarine

We stood, the captain and I, high in the sail, the rounded steel dorsal fin that used to be called the conning tower. The sun rose red over the Cascade Mountains of the Pacific Northwest. A bitterly cold wind raced over the Hood Canal, leading to the open Pacific; the water was black and troubled. Below us, for 560 feet, stretched the USS Florida: a ballistic missile submarine, SSBN 728, third ship of the Ohio class, our newest and deadliest. From our position above, she looked ugly and industrial, the dull black of steel mills and railway cars—yet, in her odd way, lovely. Submarines are an acquired taste.

Should there be a next war, it is with such bleak ships that we will fight it, firing stumpy missiles that hide beneath the waves. The joy of battle has given way to the conventions of the board room, martial glory to the peculiar satisfactions of remote, anonymous, abstract death. The world has for years been moving away from a glamorous notion of war, first to the squat green ugliness of tanks and now toward computerized bombs that go it alone in their eerie search for targets. The Florida is the best and, just possibly, final artifact of the new anti-chivalry. If and when the call comes to kill the enemy, the crew of the Florida will never see them. This fits the clinical impersonality of our times.

American submarines, virtually all of them nuclear-powered, fall into two categories: missile boats, unambiguously called "boomers" in the Navy, and attack boats, which hunt other submarines. The United States now has ninety-six attack boats and thirty-six missile submarines, including eight of the Ohio class, which have twenty-four launching tubes for missiles. The boomers spend their days loitering quietly in launch zones that put them in range of their Soviet targets. Their job is to not be found, and they are indeed hard to find.

On the deck, if the rounded surface of a submarine can be called a deck, sailors readied the Florida to cast off from the dock at Bangor, Washington. A ship displacing 18,700 tons of water when submerged and costing a billion dollars does not take lightly to the sea.

"Single up all lines."

"All lines single, aye."

When the last lines were heaved ashore, sailors turned the cleats to which the ropes had been attached upside down and flipped them into the hull to present a smooth surface. Anything projecting from the hull causes flow noise. The crew of the Florida do not fear the Soviets, nor the terrible pressure of the depths, nor the acts of a hostile god. They fear noise.

Captain Robert Labrecque, a likable and thoughtful fellow in his early forties, father of two, chatted with me on the deck about torpedo technology and sonar while the mountain peaks turned molten pink and the wind whistled over the windshield. The windshield, along with radios and an antenna, detaches for diving. Looking down, I noticed how very little wake the Florida left. Wakes are turbulence, and turbulence is noise.

Sailors in bright orange weather suits, their faces masked against the wind, kept up a constant chatter with the control room. "Helm bridge left 10 degrees, steady course 270." "Bridge helm, steady 270, aye." Captain Labrecque took little part. American naval practice relies on training and the delegation of authority; enlisted men of twenty-five often bear major responsibility for the safety of the ship. The crew continued their steady patter of commands.

"Mr. Reed," the captain said, "it is time to go below. We are going to dive."

We climbed down one frigid metal ladder after another, through a narrow vertical pipe, and debouched into the brightness and warmth of the control room. The contrast was startling. Men in shirtsleeves sat at panel after panel of switches, dials, gauges, and a complex array of glowing indicators. From this small room the Florida is controlled, her speed, course, and depth determined; her twenty-four missiles, (carrying 192 nuclear warheads) launched on their 4,600 mile trajectories. Only by massive preventive maintenance can such ships be kept in running order. The maintenance is done. The ships work.

"Coffee, sir?" asked a sailor. I nodded, still chilled. The courtesy, the ordinariness of these men, was in the context somehow curious. There is nothing ordinary about the Florida. She is a doomsday machine.

The helmsman and planesman sat at their controls, rather like those of airliners; the diving officer sat behind them and quietly gave orders. The atmosphere was attentive but relaxed. For them, the day was like any other. There were taking a billion-dollar ship, easily the most powerful weapon the planet has ever seen, down to the frigid depths where light is dim and color flees. Nothing interesting was happening, but sailors nonetheless watched the gauges with care. There are many things one wants to know when submerging a submarine, as for example whether one has closed all the hatches. The point is not facetious: submarines have been lost because of open hatches. The deep sea is not a forgiving place.

Men passed through the control room on the way to other destinations. The Florida is roomy for a submarine, being forty-two feet wide, and she carries a lot of men, 165 normally. American naval philosophy discourages automation. The Navy believes that machines make more mistakes than people do. At depth, a mistake can occur quickly and cause a shattering implosion that will strew wreckage for miles. At thirty-four knots and a depth of 900 feet, typical figures for modern submarines, a faulty computer controlling the diving planes of an attack submarine could drive the ship below crush depth in seconds. The emphasis on safety pays off. The United States has lost only two nuclear subs, the Thresher in 1963 and the Scorpion in 1968.

"What do you think?" asked the executive officer, noticing a certain impassioned expression on my face. I am a certifiable technophile. Viewed as a machine, the Florida seemed to me the pinnacle of human achievement, and a very pretty pinnacle at that.

"I'm in love. I think I've got a First-Amendment right to own one of these things."

The officer smiled.

"All ahead two-thirds."

"All ahead, aye."

Hands went to switches, indicators changed color, and soon the ballast tanks began to fill. The tone was easy-going, congenial. In the confined quarters of a submarine, congeniality is essential. But on long cruises, edginess starts about two weeks out. First, some men get irritable and snappish, then they calm down and others take it up. The Florida is a comfortable iron pipe, but an iron pipe nonetheless.

Minutes later we were submerged, a fact making no appreciable difference except on the gauges. A submarine is a closed world, normally unaffected by outside conditions. My escort officer was Lieutenant Edward Wilson, a pleasant young man who never seemed to be out of arm's reach. We walked through long corridors, the temperature unchangingly cool and the lighting unchangingly pleasant. The cream-colored walls of a submarine are lined with cables and pipes, sprinkled with valves and gauges. The ship hummed—barely, by design—with air-conditioning and other very slight noises of machinery.

I am an amateur of submarine technology, and so I asked Lieutenant Wilson to show me the silencing measures. He did, but by prior agreement this article was submitted for security review, and much of what he said did not survive that review. The Navy was unfailing friendly throughout my trip, and indeed extended the invitation unasked. Yet there were many things the Navy would not let me write about, and others that it asked me not to write about. All were purely technical. There was no political editing.

Silencing is both an art and a science. Tiny accelerometers detect any vibration in rotating objects, whereupon the offending object is immediately replaced. Hydrophones on the outer hull listen to the ship itself to hear whether anything has begun to make noise. Lieutenant Wilson pointed out the omnipresent rubber washers, inches thick, separating everything from the hull. Most equipment rests on rubber, never touching the hull.

Noise to a submariner is not the simple matter it is to others. Flow noise, caused by the passage of water over the ship, is similar to the sound of wind over a moving car. It can be reduced by moving more slowly, by eliminating all protrusions and openings from the hull, and by using hydrodynamically streamlined shapes. Propeller noise can be reduced by careful design and precise machining (a chip in the propeller can produce a whizzing sound).

The worst propeller noise is caused by cavitation—the formation of bubbles or partial vacuums, which occurs when a high-speed propeller moves away from the contiguous water faster than the water can follow. The cavities immediately collapse with a thunderous racket. A partial solution is to use larger propellers, which turn more slowly. Another is to go more slowly, and another, to stay deep enough that water pressure prevents cavitation.

Machinery noise is another matter. A nuclear reactor produces steam, which turns turbines, just as wind turns the propeller on a child's beanie. Turbines produce a terrific whine. Reactors also produce heat, so cooling pumps—which make noise—are needed, at least at high speed. There are also air conditioners, compressors, footsteps, dropped tools. If these sounds reached the hull they would be transmitted into the ocean.

Near the end of our quick walk through the ship, Lieutenant Wilson led me through the missile bay, where huge red cylinders rose in neat ranks three feet apart. He stopped to show me a sailor's berth, nested between a pair of missile tubes, one of the earth's more esoteric bedrooms. He knocked first and asked permission to enter. The military believes that enlisted men have a right to privacy in their living quarters. Nobody was there. Inside, we found bunks with curtains, small lockers, and jacks for plugging headphones into the ship's entertainment system of several channels—usually rock, country and western, and a religious channel said to be widely listened to. The blankets were army-camouflage, which struck me as ridiculous.

"So the Soviets can't see you?"

He laughed. "No. We used to have wool, but the lint clogged the air filters. These don't make lint."

We traipsed through the sub and found a wealth of details that a civilian wouldn't think of. For example, how does one get rid of garbage at depth? There is the TDU—Trash Disposal Unit (anything military has to have an acronym to be taken seriously). The TDU, which resembles a vertical torpedo tube, ejects packets of garbage weighted to sink. Leaking hydraulic fluid can cause a visible slick, so the periscope uses a special water-soluble fluid. We stopped by the oxygen generators that produce oxygen by electrically hydrolyzing water. The result is gaseous hydrogen that is dumped overboard through a diffuser that breaks it into very small bubbles. Big bubbles might be visible on the surface.

The last stop on the tour was the crew's mess, a reasonably large room with a Coke machine, orange and cream walls, and checkered table-cloths. A Coke machine on a doomsday boat seemed incongruously human.

"What do you do for amusement?" I asked a lanky, dark sailor sitting alone at a table.

"Sleep," he said—the black humor of GIs.

"Sounds bleak. Why did you take this job?"

"I ask myself that."

"You going to get out?"

"No…no.

Such answers are common in the military, particularly in the undersea services: I hate it but I love it.

The Navy would say virtually nothing about the Florida's sonar. In particular, it would not say whether the Florida has a towed array, which is a long cable trailing far behind the ship and carrying hydrophones. All modern submarines that I have knowledge of use towed arrays because of their superior sonar performance. A photograph of an Ohio-class submarine published by the United States Naval Institute purports to show the stowage space for a towed array in the rear fins. The Navy will simply not confirm or deny anything about sonar. One might assume that the Florida, working in the same water as other submarines, uses the same technology. But I don't know.

In the sonar room a half-dozen men sat in near-darkness in front of screens. Luminous green sand drifted slowly down the screens, each grain representing a slight blip of sound. On submarines today one watches sound instead of listening to it. Small red and green lights glowed on indicator panels connected to powerful computers and to hydrophones outside the hull. Day in, day out, complex mathematical programs race through elaborate computer circuitry, adding this ghost of a whisper to that hint of a noise, analyzing, inferring, best-guessing to quantify almost no sound at all. Rows of switches control the equipment, but their labels would never pass security review. From this room the Florida gropes her way through the weird, deceptive hall of mirrors that is the acoustic ocean.

A submarine is blind, able only to listen, yet listening is not the simple thing it seems. Sea water is eerie stuff, rife with structure and peculiarities, less a substance that a place with semi-predictable corridors and ambiguous echoes. For example, warm water heated by the sun forms a "surface duct," its thickness varying with the time of year, in which sound is trapped as if in a pipe. Thermoclines—boundaries between warm and cold layers—reflect sound the way mirrors reflect light; a submarine below a thermocline usually can't be heard from above. At roughly 4,000 feet is the "deep sound channel," in which sound travels for incredible distances, sometimes halfway around the earth.

Strange things happen. Sound refracts—that is, bends—in the direction of lower velocity. It travels faster in warm water and faster in water under pressure. The curious result is that sound goes down into the deep sea, then comes back up, then goes back down as sinuously as a snake. The points of surfacing are called "convergence zones"; in the open ocean these are about thirty-five miles apart. Thus, a ship can be heard when it is 35, 70, 105, or 140 miles away, but not at 20 miles. All of these qualities vary with temperature, which is to say with the time of year, and with salinity. All can be measured and recorded. Navies do not have oceanographic vessels because of an interest in the ways of fish.

All of this matters to the crew, who are hunted every day of the year by their Soviet counterparts—who to the rest of us are chiefly budgetary justifications. The likelihood of survival is measured in decibels. "Three db down and I've got his ass," is a typical statement about an enemy's prospects. He who is heard first tends to be dead.

My escort and I went to the crew's lounge, a tiny space with a VCR, so I could talk to the enlisted men about submarine life. The Florida has a library, barely, but videotapes are the preferred off-duty amusement. Like most military men, these sailors were at first embarrassed by the here's-a-reporter-now-perform atmosphere, but they quickly adopted the reticence of used-car salesmen.

"Okay, you guys, give this gentleman straight answers," said my lieutenant.

"How do you like submarine life?" I asked a fellow from the reactor section.

"It sucks."

"Why?" I asked for the sake of journalistic propriety, having heard the answers a thousand times.

"I want my children to recognize me."

From the others came a chorus of "yeah" and "no shit." A cruise lasts roughly seventy days, followed by thirty days when the ship is in port. Each boomer has two alternating crews, Blue and Gold. This system results in sailors' spending about five months a year at sea. The strain on marriages is enormous, the effect on children, who cannot understand, worse. (The Navy's divorce rate is the highest in the military.) Young children desperately want their fathers to stay at home, and sometimes think that daddy's absence is their fault.

"My little boy—I can't figure how—decided that the reason I had to go away was because he wasn't potty-trained. When he finally got things under control, he was real happy because he figured Daddy would stay home now. It wasn't fun when he found out I was leaving again."

"My kid kept worrying because I must get wet and cold underwater, and how could I breathe? I had to bring her aboard to show her, and she got over it."

"It's like a divorce twice a year. This is my last cruise. A lotta guys are getting out."

During cruises the Navy wife becomes accustomed to independence, to making decisions, and taking care of business. Then the sailor comes home, and thinks that *he* is in charge. Just when they get it straightened out, off he goes. Not uncommonly it comes down to the Navy wife's ultimatum: "Look, sweetheart, you're married to me, or you're married to that goddammed ship. Which is it?" In a *menage a trois* with a pretty young wife, a submarine tends to be the weak link, and the civilian world gets a splendidly trained technician.

On the other hand, despite the grousing, which is as natural to GIs as breathing, they were aboard, and the Navy has no trouble filling submarine billets. I hate it, but I love it.

If I were a Soviet submarine captain ordered to hunt the Florida, I would pray fervently that I not find her: These ships are decidedly armed.

The Florida carries four torpedo tubes in the bow for Mark 48 torpedoes. These weapons, long bright cylinders, rest in racks in the center of a gleaming torpedo room. I have watched torpedoes loaded on attack boats, and it is an awesome thing. The crewman opens the tube door and that big fish slides smoothly in with deadly silence. A placard on one of the Florida's tubes warns, "Warshot Loaded." Live torpedo, ready to fire.

Modern torpedoes are usually guided most of the way to their targets by wires that trail behind them to the submarine. The range of a Mark 48 (the Navy says nothing, but published sources are available) is said to be thirty-eight miles Consequently the old World War II aim-by-eyeball is impossible. For reasons grounded in the laws of physics, a large receiver is needed to detect the very low frequencies that constitute much of a submarine's radiated noise, and also to get accurate bearings. The ship's sonar can guide the torpedo. When it nears its target, the torpedo pursues autonomously, using "pinging" sonar. One does not so much use modern weapons are merely supervise them, making, as it were, suggestions of a general nature.

Firing a missile requires several officers to have several keys to which no one else has access. Should Captain Labrecque develop a brain tumor and acquire Napoleonic aspirations concerning the Soviet Union, nothing would happen. Not only are several people required to agree to fire, but several different people must agree that an order to fire has been given. In the cryptography room, continuous contact is maintained with command posts on shore (radio waves of sufficiently long wavelength will penetrate sea water), and any message to fire missiles would appear in code. The order must be independently looked up, decoded, and verified by more than one person. The ship must then be brought to the proper depth for firing. Because firing missiles requires the concerted action of so many people, there is no way a few crazed crewmen could launch a missile. A boomer does not accidentally boom.

To my surprise, the captain let me watch a simulated launch. The drill begins in the control room, where Captain Labrecque stands behind what looks like a symphony conductor's podium. Labrecque chooses which tubes to fire, orders "Denote twelve," then "Fire twelve."

Down in the missile control room, other men sit at other banks of switches and indicators. The ship is so ridden with computers and sensors that it just misses being alive. The crucial switches, the ones that do spectacular and irrevocable things, are all locked. Again, the sequence is simple and quick; this part of the process is thoroughly automated. But the simplicity is deceptive. A few switches can cause a large number of things to happen in the ship's great banks of semi-sentient circuitry.

When a missile has been selected for firing, the computer must be given the target's location. The ship carries several extremely precise inertial navigation systems that give an accurate fix on position. Since the submarine is always moving, for maximum accuracy the information must be fed to the missile's own computers at the last moment before launch. The missile's guidance system is itself fearfully complex and precise.

The Trident I missiles aboard the Florida are easily accurate enough to hit cities. Before a missile can be fired, however, the gyros in the guidance system must be "spun up" and allowed to stabilize. This takes a good many minutes, although the missiles can be fired sooner with less accuracy.

The actual firing takes place at a fairly shallow depth. The first step is to pressurize the missile tube to a pressure equal to that of the surrounding water; otherwise, the missile hatch cannot be opened. The big circular hatch over each missile swings up, leaving the missile dry in its air-filled tube beneath a breakable plastic cover. A gas generator then produces sufficient pressure to drive the missile through both the plastic cover and the water to the surface, where its motors ignite and, no longer under human control, it flies off to kill a few hundred thousand people. Missiles can be fired quickly. All twenty-four can be dispatched in the time it takes to get a hamburger at McDonald's when lines are short.

Crewmen talk among themselves about the possibility of having to kill tens of millions of people they have never seen, in a country they have never visited and know next to nothing about, in order to defend the West against communism—something few of them can discuss intelligently. No one wants to do it, so perhaps it doesn't matter that these sailors have little notion who they would be killing. The psychological protection they employ is to believe they will never have to do it. They are almost certainly correct. A common saying is that if the Florida ever fires, she will have failed to do her job.

But of course there is no escaping the awful what-if. The missiles exist and work. In this world anything can happen. What would the crew do after firing, knowing that their families would very likely be dead, or knowing that there wouldn't really be any place left that would be worth going to? One imagines sitting in the unchanging cool and quiet, everything functioning as always, missiles tubes empty. The unseen world out there is ending, the submarine bases—as priority targets—destroyed. What now? There are plans, escape zones, all the rest, but...so what? No, the best thing is to say that it will never happen.

Personally, I have wondered how many of the subs would actually fire. If America has been obliterated, what purpose would be served by burning to death millions of bewildered Russians who have no more interest in war than do the crew of the Florida? These are difficult questions. I, too, stick with the thought that the ship is a deterrent, and therefore won't be used.

The Florida exists not to fight, but to remove doubt. Her deterrent strength lies in the utter inevitability of her retaliation. Half-mad men of limitless ambition will gamble on winning a war. If you were the Soviet Union, would you start a war in the perfect certainly that your empire would be vapor by nightfall? There would be no gamble.

The afternoon was edging toward dusk as we approached the pier at Bangor. Again I sat in the sail while the crew went through the delicate job of docking the ship. Countless small adjustments were needed. "All ahead two-thirds." "All stop." "Easy, easy." To my eye, none of these instructions changed the ship's motion, but the pilot could read nuances of wake hidden to me. The huge hulk crept into her berth.

Below, a hundred technicians, none of them wanting to hurt anybody, worked the machinery of continental incineration with the quiet efficiency of operating-room technicians. Somewhere out in the fathomless oceans, Soviet technicians did the same in their own launch centers and undersea board rooms. Behind us on the hump formed by the missile bay, the dark circles of the missile doors lay in outline. The wind was again turning brisk.

Harper's, September, 1988

Digital Surveillance. Oh Good.

A few years back I was chasing beans and bacon as a high-tech writer and ran across a company called Viisage, whose business it was, and is, to make computers that recognize faces.

Technologically, the idea was cute, though not original. A camera looked at your face. The computer then reduced your mug to a set of numbers and stored them. Next time you came by, it knew who you were. At the time, if memory serves, Viisage could not do it in real time. That is, the computation took long enough that it couldn't pick faces out of a moving crowd. Further, it didn't seem to work real well. But computers were getting faster.

I wrote a column somewhere saying that one day we'd have cameras everywhere, tracking us. People who didn't follow computers doubtless dismissed the idea as paranoia. Those who did, didn't (if that makes sense).

A few days ago, on the web site of The Register, a British site that covers developments in computers, I discovered the following story, also in many US papers:

"Super Bowl 2001 fans were secretly treated to a mass biometric scan in which video cameras tied to a temporary law-enforcement command center digitized their faces and compared them against photographic lists of known malefactors."

Bingo. Not good, not good at all.

The jury is still out on how well real-time recognition works, with many saying that it isn't ready for prime time. Perhaps. Yet if it isn't now, it one day will be. Technology advances apace.

But Fred, you might say, what a convenient way to catch bad guys.

It sure is.

Hidden cameras could be put in all manner of public places. If a wanted criminal, or missing child, or suspected terrorist walked past, an alarm would go off, and the gendarmes would appear. Note the words, "fans were secretly treated" in the Register's story. The public need not know—and apparently didn't in Tampa—that it was being watched. After a while, we would get used to it.

This is fundamentally different from the use of security cameras at Seven-Eleven. Unless the store is robbed, nobody has the time or interest to look at those tapes. There is no computer and no network. Nobody can track your movements with an ordinary catch'em-robbers camera.

But when a computer takes over, it becomes possible to keep a database of faces anywhere (say at the FBI building in Washington) and check huge numbers of people across the continent. The Internet makes it easy. Notice how fast Google does a search of an appalling number of Web sites. With perfect ease, the central server could record the time, the place, and a still of the video. Presto, you're being tracked. People wouldn't know whether they were on the watch list, and probably wouldn't notice the camera. The legitimate uses of face-recognition are compelling. Putting a camera at entrances to governmental buildings appeals: What better way to stop terrorists? Department stores would love to know when a convicted shoplifter entered. With a central repository of faces, a serial killer wanted in Massachusetts would be caught when he walked into a gas station in Texas.

Why would a gas station want this kind of equipment? Because it would instantly warn the proprietor that the customer was a robber, and flash the villain's identity to the police along with his tag number, and record pictures of him. All this for a few grand.

Why not cameras on street corners? In many jurisdictions they are already in use, without image-recognition, to catch runners of red lights. Add the right software and the police could automatically read the license of every passing vehicle to find stolen cars. Surely you want to recover stolen cars?

Now of course the cops would say that they just wanted to catch criminals. That's true. I know lots of cops. They don't favor Stalinism. Neither, however, do they usually think beyond their immediate mission.

For example, *USA Today* in its story quotes Major K. C. Newcomb of the Tampa police as saying, "I was fully comfortable that we were not infringing anybody's rights."

I have no doubt that he meant it. And he has a point. If a cop can legally stand at a ticket gate and look at people walking by, which he can, why can't a camera? The problem is that Major Newcomb clearly hasn't a clue as to the downstream ramifications of what he is doing. Therein lies the danger.

The paper also quotes Beverly Griffin, of a company that uses the technology in the casinos of Las Vegas, as saying, "It's the wave of the future. It's for your protection."

See? It's good for us. Actually it's good for the casinos. But it's going to be sold as good for all of us.

The likely progression of uses is obvious. First we will look for criminals. Then for wanted suspects who haven't been convicted. (What? Don't you want to catch the guy suspected of chopping up three co-eds before he does it again?) Then for known troublemakers. Don't you think hit men for the Mafia ought to be watched? Next will come people disliked by incumbent politicians. Finding one's political opponent going into a gay bar, or out with someone else's wife, would be just peaches.

Remember that government already has your photo. Check your driver's license. Some states already digitize them. Some already deal with Viisage.

The potential for intimidation is fantastic. If the technology becomes widespread, which it will, you will never know whether there is a camera, or what it is networked to. It won't matter, unless you do something that displeases those in power. Then it will matter.

A digital, networked world isn't like the world of twenty years ago. Previously, the sheer work involved in spying on people made it largely impractical. Sure, it could be done. With effort and a large likelihood of getting caught, the government could steam open mail, read it, and put it back together. Phones could be tapped. Cars could be tailed. But watching many people, much less everybody, just wasn't workable.

Digital is different. Cheap cameras, commodity computers, and ubiquitous networking make mass surveillance easy. Monitoring email, without anyone's knowing it, is technically a snap. Telephone conversations aren't safe: Shrink-wrapped software for voice-recognition is fairly good; you can bet the spook agencies do it a lot better. Now we have cameras that know who you are.

Do I think the government is out to get us? No. But the technology of mass surveillance that catches criminals is precisely the technology of a degree of social control America cannot imagine. It's creeping in, innocuous step by innocuous step.

Managing Us. We're So Easy.

T he crucial truths of the current age may be these: First, people will watch any television rather than no television. Second, sooner or later they will begin to imitate what they see on the screen. Third, while you can't fool all of the people all of the time, you can fool enough of them enough of the time, especially if you are a lot smarter than they are, and do it patiently, calculatedly, over time, like water eroding stone.

That is all it takes.

Finally, television is scalable: Swathing the earth in Baywatch is not much harder than covering a state.

It is easy to miss what is happening. Criticisms of the vast wasteland are hardly new. Denunciations of televised fare have become commonplace, conventional, have sunk into clichédom and ceased to be noticed. The gibbering box dulls the mind. You get used to it. You forget what it is doing, and how well it does it. Until you are away from it for a while.

Maybe two years ago, I got rid of cable, reasoning that while the world was full of idiots, I wasn't going to pay $40 a month to look at them. Recently I resubscribed because I wanted the Spanish channels. The experience was startling—though nothing had changed. I had just forgotten how appallingly propagandistic it was, how didactic, how gnawingly relentless in inculcating its messages.

The genius of television is that, to shape a people as you want, you don't need unrestrained governmental authority, nor do you need to tell people what you want of them. Indeed, if you told them what to do, they would be likely to refuse.

No. You merely have to show them, over and over, day after day, the behavior you wish to instill. Show them enough mothers of illegitimate children heartwarmingly portrayed. Endlessly broadcast storylines suggesting that excellence is elitist. Constantly air ghetto values and moiling back-alley mobs grunting and thrusting their faces at the camera—and slowly, unconsciously, people will come to accept and then to imitate them. Patience is everything. Mold the young and in thirty years you will have molded the society. Don't tell them anything. Just show them.

Television is magic: People can't not watch. No matter how bad the fare is, how much it offends against their most deeply held values, they will stare at it rather than be alone with their thoughts. Some of them will say, those who know they ought to know better, "There are *some* good things on TV. I like the History Channel."

Yet they watch, and not just the History Channel. They cannot read a book instead. In saying this I am not striking a literary pose or making a conservative argument for high culture. I'm stating what I believe to be a psychological fact: People will watch a screen.

The packaged urgings flow from here, from America. Television is profoundly American, yet respects no borders. Movies and TV from the United States permeate much of the world. The less civilized parts of the planet particularly depend on dubbed or translated programming from America, because they cannot produce their own. With satellite feeds, supplying these countries is easy. The message is remarkably homogeneous. How surprising.

Last summer I was in Manzanillo, Mexico, and sometimes saw CNN in Spanish. The silent voice-over was exactly that of the big American networks: The same instruction on race, feminism, homosexuality, the same subtle disdain for religion, the same attack on traditional morality and on independence from the hive. There was, for example, a favorable segment on a Mexican movie depicting druggery and casual sex among the young of Mexico City. The reviewer argued that the film was realistic and merely showing the world as it was. He pointed out that sex is natural. (So it is. So is tuberculosis.) The implication was that discouraging spontaneous coupling in adolescents was not properly progressive, and in any event would represent an intolerable rein on artistic expression.

The effect of the movie was of course to foster early sex and druggery. Exactly the American message.

To me, however, the arresting observation was how much of it was in opposition to Mexican culture. Whether for better or worse, television is grinding away at a whole society, imperceptibly turning it into a near-copy of ours. Few call this imperialism. It is, with a vengeance. New York is arguably the world's most influential government, remaking the United States and the world in its image.

CNN is not alone. The Spanish channels in the United States inculcate exactly the same doctrines. There is for example Christina, a talk show out of Miami that deals in soft porn and therapy. Same message: the heroism of single moms, the moral duty to tolerate anything at all, that idea that the degraded is of the people and therefore praiseworthy.

Cristina is syndicated through much of South America. All it takes is a satellite and the entire Latin world can be bathed in American values—or at any rate in the values of American television. Scalability. It's what made the Internet great.

I do not say, note, that the ongoing catechism is always objectionable, but simply that its pervasiveness will over time determine culture. I have no desire to persecute homosexuals, to keep women in chadors or out of school. I'm not sure what racial policy should be, so I'm not sure that I disagree with the compulsory sermon. What bothers me is that we can't escape, that the same instruction whispers and babbles from sets in bars in Casper and Guadalajara and Nairobi.

Some believe that the drone of right thinking springs from a conspiracy, from some cabal at the top of the journalistic pyramid. I don't know. Through some inadvertence I am not invited to meetings of the boards of the networks. But I find the same values in desk editors and lowly reporters throughout those parts of the media that I know. The old admonition against suspecting a conspiracy when stupidity, or insularity, is an adequate explanation may apply here. But it doesn't matter. Whether through plot or simple lemmingry, we have what we have.

The consequence is a ferocious centralization. Washington, New York, and Hollywood in large part determine what the world may see, what we may know and may not know, and how it will be explained to us. The effect can be overstated, but so can it be overlooked.

And while television makes it easy for New York to talk to the world, the world has no corresponding way to talk to New York, which wouldn't listen anyway. Nor do people have effective means of talking laterally to each other except in small groups.

The telescreen owns us. In the long run, we will do what it tells us to do.

Gather Ye Flowers. Don't Buy The Garden.

Were a young man to ask me, "To marry perchance, or remain forever single?" I would, given the hostile circumstances today of law and love, urge caution. "Marriage is a commitment of several years of your life, plus child support," I would say. "Do not make it rashly."

The question is simply, "Why marry?" As a young man full of dangerous steroids, your answer will probably be, "Ah, because her hair is like corn silk under a summer moon; her lips are as rubies and her teeth, pearls; and her smile would make a dead man cry." This amounts to, "I'm horny," with elaborations. It is as it ought to be. The race continues because maidens are glorious, and striplings both desperate and unwise.

Note, incidentally, that by the time October rolls around, corn silk is shriveled and brown.

Why marry, indeed? In times past, marriage occasionally made sense. Life on a farm required two people, a woman to work herself ragged in the cabin while the man carried heavy lumpish things and shot Indians. Later, come suburbia, the man did something tedious in an office and the woman did two hours housework and stayed bored for six. It worked, tolerably. In the Fifties, nobody expected much of life. It generally met their expectations.

And there was sex, though not enough of it—the scarcity being the propellant behind matrimony. Back then, before the miracle of feminism, women had not yet commoditized themselves. A lad had to pop the question before he got laid regular. Women controlled the carnal

339

economy and, in a world that was going to be boring anyway, that was probably a good thing. At least kids had parents.

Times change. Some advice to young fellows setting forth:

First, forget about how her lips are sweet as honeydew melon (though not, of course, green). It doesn't last. One of nature's more disagreeable tricks is that while men are far uglier than women, they age better. Remember this. It is useful to reflect in moments of unguided passion that, beneath the skin, we are all wet bags of unpleasant organs.

Soon you will be a balding sofa ornament and she will look like a fireplug with cellulite. Once the packaging deteriorates, there had better be something to get you through the next thirty years. Usually there isn't.

Prospects have improved for the single of both genders. Sex is nowadays always available. If you don't marry Moon Pie, which would be wise, you may get another chance when she comes back on the market with the first wave of divorcees. It's never now-or-never. Getting older doesn't diminish your opportunities. As you gain experience, you will recognize the tides, the eddies, the whirlpools of coupling—the urgency of the biological clock, the lunacy of menopause. Men by comparison embody a wonderful clod-like simplicity.

As you ponder snuggling forever with Moon Pie, compare the lives of your bachelor and your married friends. The bachelors come and go as the mood strikes them, order their apartments with squalid abandon, drive Miatas or Harleys if they choose, and live in such pleasant dissolution as is consonant with continued employment. The married guy lives in a vast echoing mortgage beyond his means, drives sensible cars he doesn't like, and loses his old friends because he isn't allowed to hang out with them.

Self-help books to the contrary, marriage does not rest on compromises, but on concessions. You will make all of them. Perhaps it doesn't have to be this way. But it is this way.

Moon Pie has only one reason for marriage: to get her legal hooks into you. She doesn't think of it in these terms, yet, and she has no evil intentions. She just wants a nice quiet home in the remote suburbs where she can live uneventfully, raise progeny, and keep her eye on you.

If you think surveillance isn't part of the contract, try going out late with your old buddies. Marriage is an institution founded on mistrust. If she thought you would stick around if not compelled, she wouldn't need marriage. She wants monogamy, at least for you and, with some frequency, for herself. She knows viscerally that you would prefer the amorous insouciance of an oversexed alley cat. You know it consciously. Marriage exists to control the male, until recently a good idea. Now, however, she can support herself, and doesn't need protection. She doesn't need you, or you, her.

She will, however, want to have children. Women do. At which point, God help you.

Given the schools, drugs, latch-keyism consequent to working parents and then to divorce, and the cultural pressure on children to be slatterns and dope-dealers, reproduction is a gamble. You may not even particularly like them, or they, you. Nobody talks about this, but how many people do you know who hardly talk to their grown children?

And you've just tied yourself into twenty years of raising them.

The moment Junior enters wherever it is that we are, Moon Pie will have you screwed to the wall. She won't think of it this way, yet. She'll be delighted with the cooing bundle of joy, his little fingers, his little toes, etc. But divorce usually comes. The chances are two to one that she will file: Women are more eager than men to enter marriage, and more eager to leave it—with the kids, the house, and the child support. It won't be amicable, not after seven years. You will be astonished at how ruthless she will be, how well she knows the law, and how utterly hostile to divorcing fathers the law is.

You don't understand how bad the divorce courts are. You probably don't know what "imputed income" is. You think that "joint custody" means "joint custody." Think again. Quite possibly you will have to support her while she moves with your kids to Fukuoka with an Air Force colonel she met in a meat bar.

In short, marriage often means turning twenty-five years of your life into smoking wreckage. Yes, happy marriages exist (I personally know of one) and there are the somnolent marriages of habitual contentment or, perhaps, of quiet resignation. But the odds aren't good.

Permit me an heretical thought. In an age when neither sex economically needs the other, in which women do not need protection from wild bears and marauding savages, not in the suburbs anyway, perhaps marriage doesn't make sense, at least for men. The divorce courts remove all doubt. A young fellow might do well to stay single, keep his DNA to himself, pick such flowers as he might find along the way, and live his life as he likes.

About the Author

Fred, a keyboard mercenary with a disorganized past, has worked on staff for *Army Times*, *The Washingtonian*, *Soldier of Fortune*, *Federal Computer Week*, and *The Washington Times*. He has been published in *Playboy*, *The Wall Street Journal*, *Harper's*, *National Review*, *Signal*, *Air&Space*, and suchlike. He has worked as a police writer, technology editor, military specialist, and authority on mercenary soldiers.

As he tells it, he was born in 1945 in Crumpler, West Virginia, a coal camp near Bluefield. His father was a mathematician then serving in the Pacific aboard the destroyer USS Franks, which he described as a wallowing antique serving more as a distraction than a menace to the Japanese.

His paternal grandfather was dean, and professor of mathematics and classical languages, at Hampden-Sydney College, a small and (then, and perhaps now) quite good liberal arts school in southwest Virginia. His maternal grandfather was a doctor in Crumpler. (When someone got sick on the other side of the mountain, the miners put Doctor Rivers in a coal car and took him under the mountain. His, says Fred, was a robust conception of a house call.) Fred says his family for many generations were among the most literate, the most productive, and the dullest people in the South. Presbyterians.

After the war he lived as a navy brat here and there: San Diego, Mississippi, the Virginia suburbs of Washington, Alabama, and briefly in Farmville, Virginia, while his father went on active duty for the Korean War as an artillery spotter. He describes himself as a voracious and undiscriminating reader and a terrible student. By age eleven he had an eye for elevation and windage with a BB gun that would have awed a missile engineer, and had become a mad scientist. He thinks he was ten when he discovered the formula for thermite in the Britannica at Athens College in Athens, Alabama, stole the ingredients from the college chemistry laboratory, and ignited a mound of perfectly adequate thermite in the prize frying pan of the mother of his friend Perry, whose father was the college president. The resulting six-inch hole in the frying pan was hard to explain.

He went to high school in King George County, Virginia, where he remembers being the kid other kids weren't supposed to play with. He spent his time in canoeing, shooting, drinking unwise but memorable amounts of beer with the local country boys, and attempting to be a French rake "with less success than I will admit to." He reports driving his 1953 Chevy "in a manner that, if you are a country boy, I don't have to describe, and if you aren't, you wouldn't believe."

As usual, he was a woeful student, asserting that if he and his friend Butch hadn't found the stencil for the senior Government exam in the school's Dempster Dumpster, he would still be in high school. He surprised himself and his teachers by being a National Merit Finalist, thus learning of the redemptive powers of standardized tests.

After two years at Hampden-Sydney, where he worked on a split major in chemistry and biology with an eye to oceanography, he was bored. After spending the summer thumbing across the continent and down into Mexico, hopping freight trains up and down the eastern seaboard, and generally confusing himself with Jack Kerouac, he enlisted in the Marines. He thought that it would be more interesting than stirring unpleasant glop in the laboratory and pulling apart innocent frogs. He reports that it was.

On returning from Vietnam with a lot of stories, as well as a Purple Heart and more shrapnel in his eyes than he really wanted, he graduated from Hampden-Sydney with lousy grades. He holds a bachelor of science degree with a major in history and a minor in computers. His GREs were in the 99th percentile.

The years from 1970 to 1973 he spent in disreputable pursuits, his favorite, wandering through Europe, Asia, and Mexico.

When the 1973 war broke out in the Mid-East, Fred says he decided he ought to do something respectable, thought that journalism was, and told the editor of his home-town paper, "Hi! I want to be a war correspondent." This, he says, was a sufficiently damn-fool thing to do that the paper let him try it, probably to see what would happen. "Writing," he discovered, "was the only thing I was good for. It's the moral equivalent of being a wino, but you don't have to carry a brown-paper bag."

He spent the last year of the Vietnam War between Phnom Penh and Saigon, living in "slums that would have horrified a New York alley cat," and left each city with the evacuation. After the fall of Saigon he returned to Asia and studied Chinese while waiting for the next war, which didn't come. For a year he worked in Boulder, Colorado, on the staff of *Soldier of Fortune* magazine, "half zoo and half asylum," with the intention of writing a book about it. Publishing houses said, yes, Fred, this is great stuff, but you are obviously making it up. He insists that he wasn't. *Playboy*, having undertaken the necessary verification, found itself surprised to agree that, no, he wasn't making it up. The magazine published it, making Fred extremely persona non grata at *Soldier of Fortune*.

Having gotten married somewhere along the way for reasons he says he can no longer remember, he is now the happily divorced father of the World's Finest Daughters, lives in Arlington, Virginia, and works as, among other things, a law-enforcement columnist for *The Washington Times*, technology writer, and a sometimes contributor to *Signal* magazine ("encryption and weird radar.") The income, he says, allows him to take trips abroad, ride around in police cars with the siren howling, and kick in the doors of drug dealers. His hobbies are wind surfing, scuba, listening to blues, swing-dancing in dirt bars, associating with the intelligently disreputable, and people of the other sex.

0-595-23713-4